THE ENDS OF GLOBALIZATION

THE ENDS OF GLOBALIZATION

mohammed a. bamyeh

University of Minnesota Press / Minneapolis   London

Published by the University of Minnesota Press
111 Third Avenue South, Suite 290
Minneapolis, MN 55401–2520
http://www.upress.umn.edu

Library of Congress Cataloging-in-Publication Data

Bamyeh, Mohammed A.
    The ends of globalization / Mohammed A. Bamyeh.
        p.   cm.
    Includes bibliographical references and index.
    ISBN 0-8166-3592-7 (HC : acid-free paper) — ISBN 0-8166-3593-5
(PB : acid-free paper)
    1. Globalization. 2. International relations—Philosophy. I. Title.
    JZ1318 .B36 2000
    327.1'7—dc21   00-008035

Printed in the United States of America on acid-free paper

The University of Minnesota is an equal-opportunity educator and employer.

11 10 09 08 07 06 05 04 03 02 01 00   10 9 8 7 6 5 4 3 2 1

To Randall Halle

Contents

Preface

The fact that a term so unwieldy as "globalization" has come to refer to a wide range of events, processes, transactions, and systems may just mean that its referent is scarcely joined together in any coherent way. Perhaps only when the dust settles on grand historical transformations will either more precise and elegant terms for them be found or the ad hoc terms begin to assume the lasting quality of bad habits.

The problem of ambiguity is less that of the term than of the world it seeks to describe. Systematic, totalistic clarities are in short supply these days, especially if one shies away from the customary clichés. The wheels of politics, culture, and economy, after all, are not obligated to spin together or at the same speed in response to the global siren song. As such, the world left to us by the advent of globalization is a world of *logical* disconnections.

This book is about these disconnections. A sense of disjunction could emerge only out of an experience of logical wholeness in which the world had been submerged since the inception of modernity. And that sense of wholeness, in turn, cannot be truly appreciated without a proper appraisal of its totalitarian features (although these were certainly not all that it was about). For the logic of modernity everywhere in the world has essentially referred to the effort to construct a new cosmos of complementarity between economy, politics, and culture. In liberal sociopolitical theories, the universal prototype for that complementarity was posited as the nation-state. The conflict between that prototype and alternative models seemed largely settled in its favor for almost seven decades, namely, from 1919 until about 1989. Liberal sociopolitical theories, which live on in some form or another today, saw in this universal prototype nothing less than the rational culmination of the logic of history. Following Hannah Arendt, such a line of thought likewise highlighted the ethical status of the nation-state, positing it as the unique agent for the dispensation of universal rights.

In this sense, in as much as liberal sociopolitical theory addressed the issue of rights and battled what it deemed to be totalitarian systems, it encouraged us to direct our gaze away from where totalitarianism was rooting itself most solidly, namely, wherever nationalism successfully competed against more diffuse cosmopolitan attachments and leanings. In an age of nation-states, everyone wanted to hear the good news that nationalism and totalitarianism could be disentangled from each other. Only a few had the bad manners to try to spoil the feast by pointing out the obvious, namely, that the preconditions of totalitarianism that Arendt, for example, singled out—the transformation of classes into masses, the elimination of all group solidarity, a pervasive sense of individual loneliness—are conducive just as well to *national* mobilization. In fact, they constitute the preconditions of modern *mass* democracies. The basic political features of global modernity consist precisely of such modes of mobilization and organization, which until today were held *across* various types of political and social systems.

The connection between the growth of modern world systems on the one hand and connective worldviews possessing totalitarian tendencies on the other is an important concern in this work. Today the concern is that the totalitarian features of modernity most likely to be left to the perusal of the transnational age pertain to salient expressions rather than to the bombastic expressions that were the focus of liberal theories. To that end, this work takes a more basic view of processes of globalization of modernity in the fields of politics and culture leading to the contemporary transformations. The global *similitudes* constructed in the spirit of modernity are more deeply rooted than the *differentiations* suggested by such procedural notions as "dictatorship" and "democracy." Across both ideal types of political systems, one discerns a basic assault on civil societies—one coercive, the other consumptive—whereby such societies either become appendages to the state or come to accept the state as the ultimate logical addressee of their actions and deliberations. Until this age of "globalization," the modern state came to embody vast cultural reservoirs and an entire gamut of economic jurisdictions, ranging from welfare guarantees to imperialist adventures articulated on behalf of "national" concerns.

This book traces the erosion of these totalities in our age; the politico-economic dissimulations are addressed in chapter 1, the cultural ones in chapter 3. There has been a plethora of negative descriptors summing up the outcome of these processes; "the end of the nation-state," "the end of politics," and even "the end of history" have all been proposed as outlines of some terminus shortly ahead. Yet one can argue that the pervasive anticipation of some sort of terminus expresses largely how the institutions of modernity experience the loss of their objective foundations. For instance, the removal of the economic pillar does not automatically lead to the end of the nation-state but merely to its loss of rational grounds to regulate the use of its historically acquired coercive muscle. Global capitalism, triumphant and without enemies, has far less use than in the past for political protection. This point, elaborated in the second chapter, concerns the way the political, encased in modernist institutions made for a bygone era, has little to do but does not disappear. The political either becomes self-referential or is compelled by an institutional survival instinct to invent a new purpose. In due time, either enough souls notice the anomaly and bury the corpse properly, or the conformist masses of mass democracies, long accustomed to passivity, delegation of authority, and taming of sensibilities, once again teach themselves to see beauty in a disfigured world.

I would like to clarify the grounds for my choice of certain points of emphasis over potential others in this volume. It has become customary to approach globalization by segmenting it into the three vectors of economy, politics, and culture. These differ in terms of their logic, but they also differ in terms of how humanity uses them as it faces the trials and tribulations of globalization. Today, few can be said to exist *outside* of the grid formed by global economies. On the other hand, it may not make much sense to describe people as existing inside or outside of transnational culture; it makes more sense, at least as a starting point, to observe that most people are compelled to somehow *respond* to it. And the individual distance from globalization appears greatest from transnational politics; most people can indeed be said to exist outside of political globalization, especially in the sense that they possess no direct capacity to act upon or even respond to it, much less influence it.

The focus of this book, therefore, is on those vectors from which most of humanity has been excluded, namely, politics and culture, rather than on what seem to be ineluctable processes of inclusion that are part and parcel of the logic of global capitalism, which is extensively discussed elsewhere in the field of transnational studies. In other words, what I am concerned with are the histories of modalities of response to those fields of transnational life toward which individuals, groups, and societies make a myriad of accommodations. That is, the focus on politics and culture, rather than economy, allows us to explore those elements of transnational life that are not determined exclusively in terms of *structures*. Rather, my concern is with aspects of our global experience that take the path of experimentation, offer ideological choices and room for subjective valuation, and introduce themselves in the context of struggle against alternative visions. The tale I seek to tell here is that of those vectors in transnational life that are most prone to transience and anarchy, even when they appear to be orderly and institutionally grounded.

These concerns inform my use of the term "rationality" throughout this volume, which I use in a different sense from that of such prominent exponents as Max Weber and Jürgen Habermas, or the Enlightenment tradition in general. I use "rationality" not as a venue of "reason" but, rather, as a namesake for an integrated vision of the world: A rational vision is for me one in which the logics of political, economic, and cultural life work harmoniously to reinforce each other. Thus, a rational vision is a total vision, which can only flow out of systematic coherence of the various spheres of social life. This approach means that the superiority or inferiority of one rational outlook to another can only be adjudicated in terms of its degree of wholeness and integration of the three spheres, and not in terms of how much it approximates "reason" and dispels superstition, magic, or conspiratorial thinking.

There are other advantages to using "rationality" in this way, especially in the context of globalization. "Rationality" as used in this volume does away with cumbersome and nonilluminating distinctions between "premodern," "modern," and "postmodern," making it possible for us to detect rationalities and irrationalities across various epochs. Ultimately, the advantage of this use of the term consists of its connection to *predictability:* Rationality does not necessarily introduce "enlightenment" to the world. Most importantly, rationality makes the world appear meaningful and predictable. Thus it bases calculations of conflict and coexistence more on coherent and multidimensional assessment of limits and possibilities and makes them less prone to accident and partiality. A rational outlook does, of course, change, but the change is orderly and slow, unlike an irrational outlook, which, as we witness at many levels today, changes in spasmodic, quantum, or erratic fashions.

This work is a substantial revision of an earlier monograph written in the form of a "trend report" and published as an issue of *Current Sociology*.[1] In this revised and expanded work I have pursued many discussions in more interdisciplinary directions. Chapter 1 examines the growth of governmentality on a global scale in modern times. The dimensions of "inside" and "facade" serve here as pointers to different games that, taken together, formed the parameters of the political on a world scale. Those parameters contributed to the growth of formalist similitudes. They were structured by the logic of comparative power but were ill-equipped to adjust with flexibility and vitality to changing historical circumstances. Chapter 2, an intermediate chapter, condenses conclusions about some of the major political aspects of future globalization and leads to remarks linking to the dynamics and use of such notions as "culture" and "civilization." Chapter 3 examines the general historical and contemporary formations of cultural globalization as a corollary to the political. The notion of "culture" in this sense is further specified along three dimensions; namely, those aspects contributing to a sense of social solidarity, those oriented toward lifestyle considerations, and those most involved in communicative practices. As a whole, this work aims to contribute to providing philosophical and historical bases for the discussion of the logical connections and disjunctions permeating contemporary transnational phenomena and processes.

I would like to especially thank John Michael and Randall Halle for providing extensive comments that helped me to clarify my own thoughts. For providing a supportive environment as well as many stimulating conversations in hallways, offices, and cafés, I would like to thank Angela Dillard, Barbara Cooper, Vasu Varadhan, Alexander Hicks, Stanley Aronowitz, and Laurin Raiken. Special thanks go to Kathy Delfosse, whose meticulous editing has certainly made this book far more readable.

Chapter 1

Governmentality and
the New Global "Order"

If the nation-state continues to survive and imagine a purpose for itself in an era of unprecedented globalization, then it is only because there is nothing more historically recurrent than institutional ossification. In every epoch, sociopolitical bodies modeled after the demands of a bygone era never fail to resist, misrecognize, discount, or misinterpret the creeping signs of their own impending irrelevance. Grand, self-assured bodies with borrowed glory, like the ancien régime or contemporary misfits, can leave the scene only in disgrace. More salient sociopolitical structures, like the guilds of medieval Europe (which, as Fernand Braudel observed, were not formally dissolved until several centuries after their energies had been spent), leave the scene through a long, inconspicuous process of depletion. Institutionalization, after all, stabilizes passing phenomena, but frequently at the price of shielding them from changing currents in such other spheres of social life as culture or economy. If there is a testament to the disjointed spheres of reason in today's world, it is precisely this extensive disjunction among politics, economy, and culture across a vast global scene. The ill-omened nature of such a disjunction is most pronounced, I will argue, in the political field, since it is there that catastrophic single-mindedness has become increasingly wedded to the imperatives of the exercise of power.

Political governance everywhere adapts to transnational encroachments through one of two methods: by *integrating* itself into larger systems or by constructing *similitudes* to the perceived essence of political entities in the world outside of its claimed borders. These two processes make it possible for us to identify a dual track in the logic of transnationalism, where notions of particularism and universalism seem to flow from congruent rather than contradictory logics,[1] as will become more apparent throughout this essay. In processes of integration, governing orders

1

surrender a certain degree of sovereignty to a higher instance in a way that involves surrendering part of their own self-definition as well. Today, such diverse regions as Western Europe, North America, Southeast Asia, the Commonwealth of Independent States, western and southern Africa, the Arab World, the Pacific Rim, and Latin America are attempting regional integration, with varying degrees of success and vision. A process of integration can be distinguished from a customs union or an alliance or a treaty between countries in that what is given up in the course of integration is the polity's self-understanding of its sovereign stature in the world. In a process of integration, contemporary and historical systems agglomerate, whether through conquest, incremental absorption, or consent, to form more regionally overarching domains of control.

Ironically, the surrender of sovereignty may in part be based on the belief that the country being absorbed into a larger system could keep some of its distinct features into perpetuity regardless. In this respect, Western Europe and the Arab world offer opposite recent examples. The success of the integration of countries housing national spirits that had been constantly at war with each other in Europe contrasts sharply to the failure of all integration schemes in the Arab world. This is all the more striking given that state-centered nationalism in the Arab world has historically been much weaker than and prone to challenge from pan-Arab nationalism or other articulations of solidarity transcending their borders. By contrast, individual European states were so confident of their bases in distinct national cultures that they never had to—and still do not—take pan-European cultural solidarity seriously. In some respect, the relative weakness of a unifying culture (based on common language, vision of common history, free-access passageways, and so on) in Europe compared to the Arab world may have actually helped the union, while stronger cultural commonality in the Arab world hurt it. One possible reason has to do with the fact that unlike Arab governments, European governments were less worried that the national identity they saw themselves as having historically guarded would be immediately diluted and ultimately dissolved once they embarked upon transnational integration. Thus, although no longer necessary, the cultural reservoir of power of individual European polities possessed (or was thought to possess) the capacity to remain operative within a transnational association. Arab polities, by contrast, were fearful that any move toward union would immediately take away from them the only power base they had—namely, the institution of national government. Arab governments generally lacked clearly distinguishing cultural bases, and they were aware of their failure to cultivate cultural traditions that would be sufficiently interested in the fate of the polities that presided over them. To the contrary, such polities were usually experienced, especially by the middle classes, as owing their very being to their unwelcome disruption of former links and freedoms of movement.

Whereas processes of integration affect *substantive* dimensions of governance, namely, those having to do with the range of its legitimate operation, processes of constructing similitude address its *formal* character—that is, the structural appearances and tales of legitimacy it must exhibit in order to generate recognition from within its borders as well as from without. In this sense, examining similitudes essentially means examining the globalization of standard forms of governance. In particular, the idea concerns the degree to which governing systems come to resemble each other across the globe in terms of their structure, logic of operation, and social role. In some sense, communication among various systems of governance may itself be premised on the prior accomplishment of such institutional similitudes. Here, political governance becomes fundamentally a *model* whose basic features are rooted not in local traditions but in its more glorious manifestations of itself on the global scene. It is an example, a learned practice, an emulated system, a transmitted idea, whence it becomes as it is today, a ritually referenced factor in the tales of history and society.

This is not to say, however, that governance has always been a model, to be exported and imported like vegetables out of season to places where it had no sufficiently supportive local environment. Rather, in terms of transnational implications, what concerns us is the discovery of governance as a *transmissible* and hence semistandard form across the globe. It has been fashionable in political theory for some time to think of "transmission" of ideas as involving little more than the appropriation of procedural principles like dictatorship or democracy. More fundamentally, I think, the notion of transmission under modernity has involved orders of governance learning from available models on the world stage how to amplify their *magnitude in society*, not how to become more "enlightened" or "benevolent." The essential form of this modern culture of governance in both dictatorships *and* democracies was and still is totalitarian—not in the traditional and widely misused sense of the term but in reference to a vision of governance as an *embodiment in the last resort* of the meaning and mission of a collective social body. The globalization of such a vision ossified governance over society in a standard form, which made it ill suited to creatively handle the variety of challenges that have and will continue to confuse its sense of mission.

Today political governance operates amid an eroding sociocultural exigency and purpose. Even in its heyday, its single-minded formula of representation, expressed in the state system that was itself one product of global modernity, was never immune to contestation. Yet forms of affiliation that transgress political borders (for example, global religions, internationalism, global movements such as feminism or environmentalism, continental solidarities such as pan-Africanism or pan-Arabism) and enjoy significant spiritual force, intellectual support, and centers of cultural reproduction have so far not succeeded in enshrining alternative centers of political governance in their competition with the state. Even in countries where advocates of such broader frames of solidarity have taken over the power of the state (such as Iran since 1979, Ghana under Kwame Nkrumah, or Egypt under Gamal Abdel Nasser), the subsequent behavior of those advocates ultimately became locked into the limits of their states' interests and fate. Conversely, at a subnational level, secessionist movements that threaten the unity of the territorial reach of state power do not usually succeed without an extraordinarily hard-fought battle (as in Eritrea). And whenever state systems have fragmented, such as in the former Soviet Union, Yugoslavia, or Czechoslovakia, the products have been nation-states that specifically rejected the cosmopolitan or multicultural ideology of their former hosts and proceeded to model themselves according to the hypostasized normative correspondence between nationhood and statehood.

The international state system thus continues to *appear* well entrenched as the normative ideational fountain of a specific and otherwise historically contingent form of governance within global politics, in spite of the fact that the economy has become increasingly global, subsequently undermining the ability of parochial orders of governance to place it under strict control. This form of governance also persists in the face of burgeoning transnational communications and travels, which would be expected to give rise to or reinforce frames of solidarity that are not conterminous with the cultural requirements of parochial governance. Finally, this state system persists in spite of the fact that it has been forced to make serious accommodations to transnational forms of governance (notably in Western Europe, which is inspiring models of accommodation to transnational governance in other world regions). On the other hand, it is obvious enough that some of the older international organizations, such as the United Nations, the Organization for African Unity (OAU), the Organization of American States (OAS), or even the European Union (EU) in its earlier phase as the European Community, never did anything to challenge the state system. If anything they reinforced it by both giving international legitimacy to officeholders in various territories and by excluding nonstate entities (citizen groups, nongovernmental organizations, nonstate peoples, and so on) from recognition as equally legitimate loci of governance.

Another source for the seemingly continued relevance of such polities emanates from a *limited* role they could fulfill in terms of the current structure of world economy. Saskia Sassen, for instance, highlights the fact that in spite of its global reach and orientation, capital continues to be embedded in one state or another, primarily due to a still unresolved question of guaranteeing rights in the global arena.[2] This argument implies that the state survives only to the extent that it services some economic pillar, in this case the question of property rights and, secondarily, safety of deposits. The state, and the political system in general, is seen here as subordinate to the requirements of a more organized economic system. This element of subordination of the state to something other than *raison d'état*, in turn, results in a political system lacking in consistent political rules. In one important study, Justin Rosenberg observes that the anarchical patterns of relations among states theorized extensively in the field of international relations flow from capitalist trajectories that, according to Marx, ultimately cause a decoupling of political and economic structures of action. Marx observed that capitalists, as they resist political control and regulation but simultaneously pursue economic centralization in their own enterprise, introduce anarchy to the political realm and order to the economic one.[3] Placed in today's transnational context, in which states operate in an environment shaped by an economy that is more integrated globally than are states and in which transnational corporations seem more rationally organized and purposeful than political units, one can readily detect one source of the fundamentally anarchic logic of relation between states today,[4] lacking as they are in a strategic logic that would be expected to inform the wide variety of intermittent actions that are expected of them.[5]

What must not be forgotten, however, is that this anarchy also emanates from and advises the structure of much of modern political science itself, which has become a self-enclosed science of power embedded in a self-enclosed world of politics, with only the most superficial links to more-integrated systems of inquiry. At one point, Stanley Hoffmann argued that the very existence of a field of inquiry like international relations was part and parcel of the practical imperatives of U.S. foreign policy after World War II. This proximity to the "dirty world" of political imperatives further detached the field from any serious cultural or philosophical concerns, as it became relegated to an advisory role and structured largely around predictive and applicable theories.[6] But it is also symptomatic of these times that the heritage of the realist paradigm in international relations, with its emphasis on states as autonomous players acting on behalf of their own interests *as states,* has been repudiated and assaulted even within the realm of political theory itself.[7] States could reduce global political anarchy by redefining the role of the state in society and vis-à-vis other states. The various attempts at transnational integration show that under certain circumstances orders of governance are willing to negotiate a partial surrender of their sovereignty, in such a way as to reduce the range of their claims and obligations, and thereby the potential for anarchic and accidental calculations in their relations with other states. But as will become apparent later in this chapter, the motivations for such moves are less likely to emerge out of the innate logic of governance than out of processes in economic and cultural life that invariably reduce the degree of control that would be exercised by a system of governance over society.

One of the major political aspects of global modernity has been that every state in the world had to regard itself not only in the context of other states but also as a unique institution with rules that are innate to it. The struggle of polities for survival in a world teeming with other polities follows the dictates of a modernist understanding of the art of politics, which sets it as a realm of self-sufficient logical necessity. Michel Foucault argues that Machiavelli's *Prince* marks the foundation of a notion of externality of the prince to the principality, with the two existing without a "fundamental, essential, natural and juridical connection." The art of governing then becomes an art of guarding against dangers implicit in this logical disjunction.[8] Extending the argument, Colin Gordon documents the growth of a notion of a state as its own self-referential mystery, with a self-generated basis for being *(raison d'état).*[9] In one sense, the sufficiency of *raison d'état* expresses the lack of necessity for the political to be structurally rooted in any origins exterior to politics proper.

If philosophical ideas express the spirit of their times, then perhaps one can argue that the disjunction of the political is simply one aspect of the disjunctions in the spheres of reason, which Max Weber outlined earlier in the twentieth century. One interesting example of the implications of such disjuncture is given by the late structuralist thinker E. W. Ardener, who once offered a general illustration of the indeterminacy of "structure" through the example of a chess problem: By looking only at the problem, one cannot determine whether the current setup resulted from a game that had actually been played (that is, out of an actual "history") or whether it had simply been constructed for its own sake.[10] At the moment it is given the chess problem looks the same *regardless* of where it came from. Its presence is not affected by whether or not it has a history or logical roots in an evolutionary process. Ardener does not consider the possibility that one source of indeterminacy concerns the "rules of the game." That is, the very ability to analyze the given game presupposes a knowledge of its rules. By invoking the rules, one can begin to chart out the problem's past trajectory, only to realize that such rules are insufficient for ascertaining the problem's historicity. The indeterminacy is thus built into the rules of the game. The function of the rules is to create a game and give us the capacity to play it. In other words, the "rules of the game" bring the game into being by ensuring its future, *not* its history. The players are expected to use the rules to play, not to ponder the essential link of the game to the larger world. That is to say, with the acquisition of a set of rules for its presentation and performance, the game becomes a *self-sufficient substitute for the world* rather than its logical embodiment or a representation of its essence.

If we apply this principle of the game to the rules of relations among states within the existent international state system, we come to recognize the lack of necessary or logical connectedness of these rules to any ground exterior to the game proper, or even to economic determinations. One can only describe rules of playing that are fundamentally transnational in character. In the international state system, states use a specific set of rules to relate to other states (prefigured in the codes of sovereignty and domain; agreements and treaties; representation, diplomacy, and negotiations; and balances of power, up to and including war calculations).[11] In this kind of world, sovereign governance is defined primarily by a sharp distinction between an inside and an outside. The outside—for which Machiavelli, Karl von Clausewitz, and modern day realists constructed their models—is governed by the rules of a global game with no organic, exclusive, or unique links to historical, ontological, or even socioeconomic grounds. From a global perspective, the ubiquity of the state system as a locus of governance must be seen as being embedded in the nature of the rules by which the state is expected to play vis-à-vis other states rather than as the result of any inborn nature of the state itself. The inside, also seen from a global perspective, is governed by the imperatives of constructing similitude, whereby local transformations are ultimately geared toward creating a globally *recognizable, that is, legitimate, player*. Some will insist on evidence for even this elementary point. I can here do no more than point out once more that the world gives us no shortage of examples of postcolonial states that are more meaningful from the perspective of the "international community" than from that of their constituents. In a more general fashion, in what follows I would like to chart briefly the contours and transformations of these two dimensions of inside and facade leading up to the contemporary scene.

Historical Contours of the Inside: Magnitude and Multiplicity

One of the most obvious but nevertheless overlooked facts regarding the internationalization of the state system of governance in modern times concerns its remarkable unevenness along such crucial dimensions as internal legitimacy, cultural support mechanisms, or need of constituents. The unevenness can be traced to the spread of globally standard rules of collective embodiment of an imagined constituency. As outlined in Benedict Anderson's theory of nationalism, the need for new rules for such an embodiment flows from the replacement of vertical loyalties with horizontal solidarities.[12] What is not emphasized as well in Anderson's outline, however, is the opportunistic role of governance in promoting such a horizontality[13] and its differential capacity to push such a transformation through. The widespread use of the term "nation building" in development literature in itself testifies to this fact, namely, that a nation frequently has to be "built" so as to correspond to an institutional structure that developed *ahead* of it.

The impetus for modern state formation in the colonial world was by and large initially exogenous, and it has remained largely such. In Europe, by contrast, the diachronic precedence of the political institution over the collective identity represents indigenous historical developments in which the institution and the "spirit" eventually came to support each other. In this way, there was a dialectic rather than a purely voluntaristic, unidirectional process of national emergence. Modern systems of governance, expected to rhetorically represent a general will for which they stand, amplify that will beyond what it would have become if governance could have been found in cultural idioms other than those of collective will (for example, if governance corresponded more to a divine dictate from above or if it were expected to assume a merely arbitrative, administrative, or purely technocratic function). Of course, the emergence of ideas of representation or embodiment did not follow a smooth or unopposed trajectory. Rousseau's well-known ambivalence toward mass representative democracy—on the ground that the populace exercises its voice only at the moment of election rather than continuously—points to an early point of struggle over the question of whether the state as a political structure can ever succeed in representing such a thing as "popular will" in a pristine or unadulterated fashion. But Rousseau does not rule today.

The genesis of the modern state system as a standard form of embodiment capable of playing on a global scene required the aggrandizement of two fundamental internal rules: that there was horizontal solidarity in the polity and that a political structure could stand permanently *on behalf* of such solidarity in the larger world. These claims, of course, are used regardless as to whether the system is a "democracy" or a "dictatorship." Before modernity, the "magnitude" of governance—meaning its self-understanding of its role regarding society—varied widely through history. On the one end of the spectrum we see forms of governance that understood their role as especially transformative, extractive, or interventionist, often with divine blessing. This kind of understanding of governance's prerogatives and essentiality can be seen in the wide range of historical systems to which the term "absolutism" is usually applied, although these forms of government are not confined to absolutist experiments. The antithetical model, in which the idea of governance meant some variation on the idea of arbitration and minimal social regulation of a self-organized civic society, has its famous historical prototypes in ancient Greece or Carthage, as well as throughout nomadic societies down to the present.

Similarly, if we consider other indicators of the role of governance in society, such as its legal claim to monopoly over power or representation, we also find a great deal of premodern diversity. On one extreme are those experiences in which several sources of governance simultaneously exercised recognized rule over the same population, such as in early medieval northwestern Europe, where competing claims of governorship (communal, feudal, and religious) maintained a negotiated balance in contiguous and overlapping territories for several centuries after the fall of the Roman Empire. Conflict between those sources of governance, though not uncommon, rarely led to challenges to the principle of multiple sovereignty until the late-medieval period.[14] In this sense, the idea of the gemeinschaft did not spell out sharp distinctions; rather, it included the possibility of multiple levels of loyalty and solidarity. Loyalty to medieval kingdoms, as the historian Susan Reynolds argues, could exist side by side with loyalty to local community or church. The idea of distinct peoplehood, which she otherwise argues was the basis for kingship, did not apparently presuppose that that distinction had by necessity to be expressed exclusively through the state.[15] The contemporary discourse of "autonomy," which in many ways also spells out the practical need to reduce the weight of the overarching singularity of governance, may thus be prefigured or even fruitfully modeled after an ancient idea of multiple sovereignties.[16]

Seen from "above," however, an openness to a principle of "multiple sovereignties" may, over time and given the right conditions, be sublated into a principle of "multiple peoplehood" exposed to the same sovereignty. Experiences of ruling that were more universal in orientation had little problem in seeing that it was in the nature of things that a *diversity* of population groups can be exposed to a singular source of governance, to the extent that such governance exhibited confidence in its imperial claims and possessed the capacity to act upon them. These models are well known throughout history, since tales of successful domination beyond linguistic, ethnic, or territorial lines tend to be memorable precisely because they are so exceptionally luminous and also because they become coterminous with the production of a wider cultural identity that we call "civilization." Articulations of this transcultural and civilizational basis of real or potential systems of governance vary in terms of its ideational association: from a notion of general order *(Pax Romana),* to the transnational aristocracy of the faithful (the Islamic *umma*), to the universalizing ethos of "white man's burden" under colonialism.

Although those are noisy large moments (a farcical copy of which we today endure, with the usual vulgarity and intellectual dullness one has come to expect under *Pax Americana*), it is worth keeping in mind that the aforementioned model has also been articulated on smaller scales, such as in the European *Ständestaat* or the Netherlandic and Swiss federations. These smaller variations on the idea of "multiple peoplehood" amended the imperial vision, notably by entertaining a notion of governance that recognized the diversity both of its sources and of the population groups subject to it. The flexibility and demure scale of these non-imperial variations on the model is perhaps responsible for its presence under very different historical circumstances, such as in African polities that were proximate to the occasionally precarious southern Saharan trade route. One can mention, for instance, Uagadu, which functioned as a court of tribal arbitration for several largely independent population groups, or Songhai, which entertained a creative combination of arbitrative, authoritative, and multicongregational roles. Similar understandings of the nature of governance can be found in the much grander Mogul Empire in northern India, which in spite of its legendary reputation for despotism throve as long as it adapted itself to religious diversity. It began its long disintegration only after Aurangzeb (d. 1707) reinforced Islamic orthodoxy and dismissed Hindus from the court and, by extension, from cogovernance.[17] For most of its duration, the Ottoman Empire maintained an arbitrative and intermittently interventionist role over a multiethnic domain that also included different, even rival sources of governance. Again here, disintegration directly correlated to the imposition of a more monolithic, interventionist, nationally inspired orthodoxy that undermined the system from within and facilitated its ultimate defeat in World War I.

Though it served as the standard modernist form for expressing the spiritual role of governance vis-à-vis society, the nation-state did not entirely obliterate all traces of the earlier variety of forms of governance. But this is not its main concern anymore. When it looks deep into its dark and lonesome soul, the nation-state now asks local questions whose roots are transnational: How can governance today relate to society in light of new or unavoidable transnational realities? Should its purview be reduced to mere arbitrative or judicial tasks? Should it be redefined as a pure technocratic machine? Or must it continue to be infused with moral authority from which guidance is expected? Is it still essential that it continue to be seen as being endowed with a historical mission, a depository of a collective spirit of some nonnegotiable sort?

In the recent past the pressures of model emulation across the globe condensed many of the above functions together, so that governance assumed the highest common denominator in social life, to such an extent that all civil societies referred to it as the ultimate goal of their deliberations rather than seeing it as simply another institution in a decentered sociopolitical life. Today a new vantage point opens up as the state becomes less able to fulfill expected obligations toward constituents, due to both fiscal hemorrhage and various transnational pressures. Thus the question of state *in* society, rather than that of state *over* society, can be recast anew in the hope of reaching a more diverse range of answers than it has so far been possible to entertain within the restrictions of the modernist straitjacket. I will come back to this question in the later segments of this chapter.

Historical Contours of the Facade: Realm, Empire, Enclave

Summarizing in his own words an ancient observation rooted in Aristotelian thought, in which the idea of political community appears in a tripartite form, Thomas Aquinas distinguished among *civitas vel regnum, civitas vel gens,* and *civitas vel provincia.*[18] Only the first refers to a form of community brought about by the reality of governance; the other two are more implicated in *alternative* ideas of peoplehood and territoriality.[19]

In some way, that observation anticipated that the path toward the creation of one global standard of what governance should look like would be paved by a chaotic admixture of elements characterizing three methods by which governance approached or organized itself in order to deal with the outside world. The most obvious of such structures, implicated in a notion of distinct peoplehood, characterized what might be called the *realm:* socially self-organized, self-enclosed, self-referential. In the case of the realm, a system of governance usually emerged out of a growing symbiosis between cities and countrysides whereby the production of agricultural surplus, coupled with complexity and challengeability of claims to land, brought forth a system of arbitration and protection. Outsiders to the norms of such systems, as evident in the cases of the Mesopotamian and Greek city-states, were decried as deviants and barbarians. That form was also clearly evident whenever systems of governance developed not under direct influences from larger or imperial political systems but, rather, on the model of more-resilient notions of hierarchy. From precolonial sub-Saharan Africa to central Java, widely dispersed systems of governance emerged from and operated explicitly as parallels to structures of authority found at the level of the household. This parallelism to kinship was in itself a universal ground for otherwise elusive legitimacy. Aristotle, for example, explicitly rooted the moral superiority of Greek kingship over Persian despotism in the ascription of the father image to the Greek king. For Aristotle the proper role of governance in that comparison was prefigured in Homer's attribution to Zeus of familiar patriarchal prerogatives among the gods. By contrast, the tyrant assumed the more detached image of the master rather than of the patriarch.[20]

The image of the father did not merely signify the right to exercise and expect obedience to normal authority, nor simply the ability to intervene as a credible judge in disputes. At a more fundamental level, the image pinned authority on a certain conception of universal nature. In the context of political upheavals in medieval Japan, the political philosopher Chikafusa (1293–1354) readily traced the conditions of the people's physical health to the failure or success of governance in reflecting the order of nature for which the image of household relations stood. He found it useful to use Indian mythology as a proof of the universality of the belief that the restoration of legitimate rulership could only restore nature itself, for example, could restore ordinary people to the legendary height and longevity they enjoyed in times past.[21] In that case, the detachment of governance from everyday social values was evidenced in the deviation of the people from ancient bodily perfection. Governance in this case is not simply embedded in some abstract idea of "society." Rather, it is represented as nothing less than *organic* inflow into and outflow from the very bodies of its individual constituents.

Whereas the realm thought of itself as *the* world, the empire knew that the world was translocal, and it planned accordingly. Imperial expansions are those in which *civitas*—large scale and thus more imagined—is formed largely by the imperative and due to the requirements of governance. There are of course the exceptions, where the rulers themselves confront already formed transnational *civitas* or older traditions of governance. They may accept these as models and adopt the customs, manners, and faiths of subject populations. A famous example of this kind of transformation characterized later periods of Mongol rule in central and western Asia. But as a distinct political structure, an empire's consciousness of the "world" is both detrimental to its survival as an empire and constitutive of its raison d'être, even when it remains self-referential in terms of culture, manners, and symbols. The Ming's fabled isolationism never prevented them from continuing to conceive of the world most familiar to them—Southeast Asia, Korea, proximate central Asia—as by nature a constellation of tributaries to the Middle Kingdom. An empire's system, due to its translocal, transreligious, transethnic, translingual, transterritorial reach, must operate at a much higher level of abstraction than the realm, even when the empire does not possess the requisite knowledge system or philosophy to sustain such a domain.

But looked at from "below," the empire is significant in another respect, namely in that it introduces a specific variety of governance—and sometimes its very idea—into peripheral regions and population groups regardless of local custom or need. By definition, imperial governance comes to most of the world from outside rather than as a response to local developments. And it is this feature that distinguishes it most from the realm. Empire carries with it one of the primary and most direct instances of transmission of a culture of governance. Transmission, in this respect, does not necessarily entail an exact replication of the nature of governance as it is exercised in the center of the empire. Aristotle, for example, advised Alexander that whereas the Greeks were more properly ruled by a leader *(hêgêmon)*, the more distant barbarians required the rule of a master *(despóts)*.[22] Yet the fact that empire may recoil from integrating the barbarian outsiders into a culture of governance seen fit only for core "citizens," as happens under colonialism, does not mean that the outsiders will easily forget the model of governance that so successfully subjugated them. Once introduced into regions far away from the empire's center of gravity, imperial governance frequently continues to nourish vestiges and replicas of itself, some feeble, others triumphant, long after the empire's grip has been removed from such peripheries.

Between the realm and the empire lies a third model of governance, which may be called the transnational *enclave*. The enclave has existed in a variety of forms and under a myriad of ideological justifications for millennia. In the context of transnational models of governance, the enclave most typically exemplifies Aquinas's territorial dimension of political community, since that dimension, rather than its hardly exclusive culture—the enclave can scarcely keep the door shut in the face of cosmopolitan spirits and affiliations—tends to be the enclave's main asset. In general, two major types of the enclave can be distinguished, and both are distinct from the realm in that they emerge more as an outcome of global forces than of indigenous developments. One can identify first the kind of enclave that comes into being primarily due to an evolving local awareness of the world at large; its incentive for coming into being is to guarantee both an independence from and profitable relation with an encroaching world. Those experiments are generally lauded in a rich tradition of political theory running from Aristotle to St. Augustine to Rousseau, in which small *reichs*, city-states, and cantons are preferred to larger systems, or are otherwise paraded as the norm from which larger systems deviate by necessity.

Second, there is the enclave that is created by or organically embedded in transnational developments. This enclave is frequently a small locale carved out of an antecedent territorial or cultural sphere, with precious little in the way of self-sufficiency. Its meaning and survival are tied to its outwardly oriented perspective. World history and contemporaneity teem with examples of such enclaves, from Aden to Mecca to Malacca to Zanzibar to Brunei to Hong Kong and Singapore, not to mention the little oil sheikhdoms, among many others.[23] The Caribbean is usually a good place to study the most pristine forms of this idea type. Karen Olwig's extensive work on Nevis, for example, concludes that in studying such an enclave, so clearly a creature of global forces and so dependent economically on the remittances of the global community of its migrants, it makes little sense to outline the enclave's culture in isolation from its global connections.[24] That is because the enclave usually offers the clearest example of how inessential culture is; in an island so consciously tied to global contexts, nothing is essentially Nevisian. The enclave knows that, unlike the economy of the locally oriented realm, that of the enclave came into existence almost exclusively as an outcome of world *demand* for its services, location, or single raw material. The independence of the enclave, therefore, is displayed primarily in its self-expression as a political entity, less in terms of its culture, and certainly not in terms of its economy. Yet even insofar as its political outlook is concerned, the enclave frequently knows that it may have difficulty surviving without the military protection of a global empire, as we see in the Persian Gulf today, for example.

By its very nature the enclave must downplay any association or identification with its immediate surroundings, as it consciously seeks to distinguish itself from them. In contrast to its immediate surroundings, the enclave monopolizes the attention of the world. In the ultimate analysis, the enclave (the oil sheikhdoms being the most extreme example) is a nervous institution, acutely cognizant of its precarious position in the world: an enticing weakness, an illegitimate novelty, a detested monopoly over some valuable resource. Tirelessly using what it knows to be a passing advantage, it labors to ascertain that as an institution, it remains more than a transient phenomenon upon the face of an otherwise perpetually abandoned landscape. The enclave usually lapses back into oblivion upon the expiration of its largely parasitic role in the world system.

As ideal types, such varieties of governance are not mutually exclusive; nor are they incapable of transforming over time or possessing a dual character. Realms can and have throughout history *become* foundations of empires or enclaves, and enclaves have frequently fallen back into the local realms from whence they emerged after the world lost interest in them—for example, Zanzibar, Malacca, or Hong Kong, but not Kuwait, which continues to be interesting on its own largely from the point of view of its transnational associations. And empires, after their dissolution, have often left their imprints on the realms and enclaves that sprang from their decomposing shells. Thereby, even after their death empires left behind cultural reservoirs that could be drawn upon to justify a wide variety of subsequent political orders (for example, Christianity after Rome, Islam after the conquests, Confucianism after the early Hans). Transmutations and overlaps notwithstanding, realm, empire, and enclave can be fruitfully analyzed as ideal types, because each produces a culture of governance rooted in its own specific conception of its standing in the world at large.

In recent times, these ideal types have continued their presence in various discourses of political culture, although such discourses are invariably flavored with the requisites of national rhetoric. For instance, while the nation-state imposes limits on the articulations of imperial ideas in the old sense, one finds the empire in the attempt to imagine the universality of some aspect of national culture. Such claims—frequently heard from politicians—as the assertion that "American culture" is global culture, or that "French civilization" inspires far beyond the mother country, paradoxically wed a feeling of national distinction to a belief in its universal character. The illusion here is that the empire is the source of universal ideas, since universal ideas are seen to emanate from a center of power rather than from the logic of the world system at large. Regardless of how the world adjusts to or produces variations of modernity, the logic of empire today is inscribed in this will of one political center or another to see itself at the source of all such metamorphoses.

Transforming the Facade

In recent history the imposition of the straitjacket of the nation-state on these diverse origins must be understood in terms of the predominance of the Eurocentric attention to the question of nationalities after World War I. The transformation processes show a great deal of variety, and it is possible only to suggest the most general of patterns. But if we keep in mind the three models just introduced, then we can approach the global trend toward the nation-state at a lower level of generality, that is, by proposing three models of transformation into nation-states. That is, the global convergence toward the nation-state model can be charted along pathways commencing from three different points of origin rather than along a single route. It would follow, then, that to the extent that we see it expressed in a singular form, the nation-state can be approached as a facade covering up a variety of more salient, yet now disfigured, older conceptions of governance.

That would be the case to the extent that one is addressing transformations in the facade rather than in the essence of governance. The globalization of a *single* facade of governance was related in complicated ways to the dynamics put into motion by the victors' division of the spoils on a global scale after World War I. But the idea was also a fruit of several centuries of expanding international communication systems and quasi-anthropological knowledge, which finally "revealed" that the differential entitlements to sovereignty were based on the evolutionary status of political communities. Here, modern wars on a global scale, whether "world" wars or colonial conquests, must be understood as being struggles over political languages as much as over material spoils. The Wilsonian principle of self-determination, which identified nationhood with statehood, encapsulated the ideal form of globally *standard* political structure that would emerge out of the smoldering heap of the old systems. The principle itself was closely observed largely in Europe, where the political map was redrawn along lines of nationalities, at enormous human cost.[25] Elsewhere the combination of this "emancipatory" principle with the requisites of imperial domination resulted in an opportunistic redefinition of the European colonial heritage away from pure possessions and into a form of "mandate." The mandate was extended by the League of Nations to colonial powers for the explicit purpose of "preparing" their colonies for nationhood. In theory, the mandate was understood to consist of laying down the administrative, intellectual, and infrastructural background for *transforming* colonial possessions into nations, since it was only then (at an indefinite point in time) that the colonial possessions could be entitled to their own statehood.

Of course, it is never prudent to assume that the political field exhibits harmonious symmetry between expressed and real intent. It is hardly worth demonstrating once more the cynical maneuvers of the victors around such a redefinition, and their attempt to keep the colonies under various pretexts. The important point here concerns the introduction of a new kind of political language to justify transnational domination, after the old language of bombastic imperialism had been buried in the ashes of World War I. The legitimacy of the new language of the mandate was predicated on an already established teleological vision of an abstract, institutional state structure as the final and most appropriate embodiment of a collective, whereafter such a structure could play with similarly typified states on the international arena, using provided rules of playing and representation. Various formulations of international cooperation of that period, from the League of Nations to the Olympic Games, refer precisely to this understanding: namely, that various peoples could be captured through a universally standard form of representation, as either standing for a national body or being definable through it.

The universalization of the "rules of the game" is one possible response to the emergence of one game played by a particularly powerful player. In this case, the model that was transmitted through the operations outlined above emanated from the European historical experience, in which the principle of the nation-state was finally established after calamitous devastation and ethnic cleansing. From there, this model spread to engulf what had essentially become a Eurocentric world. This rather traditional narrative of transmission leaves out so much, since new rules of play do not establish themselves everywhere without a struggle, occasionally to death, with the advocates of the different games. The vanquished game is either obliterated, pushed underground, or reoriented toward a wide range of political and cultural practices (for example, precolonial frames of belonging, transnational religious affiliations, internationalist workers' solidarity, nativist mythologies). The growth of nationalism and the nation-state in Europe, and its transmission as a global game, is the subject of abundant research.[26] It is not my goal here to reiterate or examine this rich body of work. Rather, I would like to focus for now on the globalization of a formalistic facade of political governance and to examine the ramifications of that accomplishment in light of contemporary transnationalism.

The discussion above addresses forms of political representation that emerge in the context of expanding domain and expanding knowledge of how other polities—especially the relatively powerful ones—define themselves. The world system that gives rise to this emulation is also a world system of *ideas*. In the aftermath of World War I, the understanding of the state as an entity that should embody a nationality *everywhere* was inseparable from the definition of the war itself as a *world war*, and the subsequent definition of the rules of governance as world rules. At Versailles, Eric Hobsbawm tells us,

> [g]iven the official commitment of the victorious powers to Wilsonian
> nationalism, it was natural that anyone claiming to speak in the name of
> some oppressed or unrecognized people—and they lobbied the supreme
> peacemakers in large numbers—should do so in terms of the national
> principle, and especially the right to self-determination. Yet this was
> more than an effective debating argument. The leaders and ideologues of
> colonial and semi-colonial liberation movements sincerely spoke the lan-
> guage of European nationalism, which they had so often learned in or
> from the west, even when it did not suit their situation.[27]

This would indicate that the dynamics by which the idea of emancipation from colonial rule was universalized in terms of *national* independence emanated not entirely from processes of autogenesis in the political
life of the peripheries. Part of the impetus can also be readily traced to
the cynical manipulations of the great powers, which sought during the
war either to destabilize their opponents by parading the idea of independence before the latter's colonized subjects or to stabilize their own
colonies by promising eventual independence. Many of the major dislocations sustaining perennial crises in today's world are rooted in the
heritage of such promises. Most of these were either contradictory or not
intended to be fulfilled. In India, for instance, British emissaries found
themselves during the war offering promises of independence that they
hoped would be forgotten after it. Similar pledges were offered, with
more catastrophic consequences, in the Middle East, where the unful-
filled promise of Arab independence was coupled with the contradictory
promise of a Jewish homeland in Palestine. Thus, to pursue the short-
term imperatives resulting from their conflicts with their peers, the great
powers frequently precipitate regional crises that become interminable,
especially since their sources are rooted entirely in exogenous games
rather than in local dynamics and thus are not subject to local, customary, or established rules of conflict resolution. This story is continuing
even today. Comprehending the recent Balkan crisis, for example, requires comprehending not only the internal history of Yugoslavia but
also the international context, which, even without direct interventions,
made it possible for local antagonists to act upon larger expectations of
alliances, support, and international prestige than would have otherwise
been the norm in a local conflict.

That the national principle should have emanated from a Eurocentric
world refers precisely to the decisive cultural appendage to a global system

characterized by "center" and "periphery": The center is so not only because it is decisive in economic and political matters but, moreover, because it is capable of inducing the peoples of the peripheries to entertain its discourse on collective identification as a means of legitimizing their claim to emancipation and empowerment. At the height of the struggle he was leading against colonialism, Amilcar Cabral noted that the struggle in itself gave rise to a new (but not arbitrary) form of collective identification, which required programmed accumulation of existing reservoirs of that identification: "[T]he liberation struggle is, above all, a struggle as much for the conservation and survival of the cultural values of the people as for the *harmonizing and development* of these values within a *national* framework."[28]

Despite not having existed as such before, Cabral's "nation" is nonetheless called upon to assemble itself in response to subjugation. The struggle here is carried out with the intention of severing a realm from the tentacles of an empire. The struggle itself becomes possible because the modern "empire" is seen by its distant subjects as it actually sees itself: not an empire as much as just another realm that has run amok. As renovated in European nationalism, the idea of the realm was in one sense self-referential, in another outwardly oriented. In its modernist European reformulation, the realm resurfaced in the principle of nationhood-as-resource, and Cabral used that principle against its own inventor. In the first place, this new realm justified struggle against external enemies on the principle of exclusive national prerogatives rather than the principle of inclusive imperialism. In the second, it no longer confined the requirements of prevailing in such struggles to the discipline imposed by formal governance, or even to the material richness upon which it was based. Rather, this new realm placed at the forefront of its arsenal the requisite of superior cultural organizational capacity. This capacity entailed both inventing national culture and making it serviceable to the designs of the state.

The assimilation of this lesson by liberation struggle leaders is succinctly summarized in Cabral's line of argument regarding the logic of national emergence. A nation emerges directly out of a struggle for power with the colonizer, using the *same* cultural reservoir: "[T]he liberation movement must be able . . . to achieve, step by step but surely, as its political action develops, the *confluence of the cultural levels* of the various social categories available for the struggle. The movement must be able to transform them into the national cultural force."[29] Thus the organizational underpinnings of this drive required the input of organized agencies of liberation (such as the envisioned independent state) rather than relying exclusively on the resources of popular nationalism or noninstitutionalized folk identities (or, in Hobsbawm's terminology, "protonationalism"). That vision of the state corresponded to the Hegelian vision of it as a vehicle for the embodiment and regularization of an otherwise amorphous or passing collective spirit. In general, therefore, the nation-state represented less an institutional adaptation to the "maturity" of national spirit than the stage of maximum mobilization of resources available to assist the nation-state in displaying itself in a world of governance occupied by like states.

This appropriation is expressed now in a vast array of measurements that are collected and have meaning only in the context of nation-states. For example, the much-criticized term "gross national product"— (GNP)—as a measurement of national might, wealth, potential, and standing in the world—was and still is unimaginable without an image of society as an *institutionally* bounded entity. Through this measurement, activities that have more accidental than logical connections (for example, making shoes, cultivating tomatoes, printing books, consuming beer on a hot afternoon) are conceived of as together producing a total, measurable meaning that a monetary sign signifies and singularly evaluates. The fact that this abstraction became a credible measurement of well-being refers less to an innate or generally felt condition of happiness than to the rootedness of the nation-state in a drive to mobilize all the resources it could to reproduce the totalitarianism of its meaning as the norm of political community. The more recent experimentation with and debate about alternative measurements of well-being can perhaps be regarded as indicative in one sense of the erosion in the scope of credible state claims regarding the general welfare of society.[30] After all, GNP played itself out as a *comparative* measurement mostly because the *total* meaning of the nation-state was premised to a great extent on its assumed sovereignty over economic as well as other pillars of national distinction. GNP has much less indicative meaning when various sectors of "national" economies are discovered to be more meaningfully integrated across rather than within state borders.

Looked at from another angle, the purely political meaning of such abstract measurements is evident in the impossibility of adjudicating fundamental individual experiences, such as a sense of communal belonging or happiness, in their terms. The evidence for this disjunction between measurement and experience is already provided in the heritage of economic anthropology. Marcel Mauss's pioneering study of the gift in archaic societies, Lewis Hyde's examination of the persistence of the gift in modern societies, or Marshall Sahlins's outline of how the leisurely life of the hunter-gatherers was premised on perpetual discarding of property seem to suggest that the experiences of belonging and happiness are premised, in fact, on the destruction rather than the accumulation of material wealth. The disjunction between the experience of well-being on the one hand and its measurement in terms of capital accumulation on the other can be further problematized by observing the historical rise of psychotherapy, which was unimaginable without the bourgeoisie as its client and the bourgeois family as its cultural model. This, of course, is beside the point and not the real question from the point of view of total measurements of well-being in society. In a global game of representation, the total and abstract measurements summarize for the state feelings and mental conditions in a format useful for its worldly battles, for it has learned that in a world of total polities, ultimate status belongs neither to the most rational, nor to the most "civilized," nor to the most dedicated but to the most relentless organizer of all potential totalities within recognized domains of sovereignty.

The Master's Simulacrum

The rise of total polities in modernity thus cannot be separated from their obsessive attention to each other, an attention that is itself a feature of globalization. The famed German jurist and political theorist Carl Schmitt offers a conception of politics as nothing but continual preparedness against a foe, a preparedness more guided by considerations of effectiveness than of legality.[31] The requirement of effectiveness implied that moral intentionalities were not sufficient to change the context of politics, as that context was by its very nature constructed by an amoral logic. Morality can at best influence discursive expressions permeating the political field; morality cannot influence either its essence or its general course. At a more philosophical level, Alexandre Kojève offers in his interpretation of Hegel a model of self-consciousness premised on a struggle for recognition by the master. This struggle, Kojève suggests, was not over the right to exist as an objective and separate entity in the world *(Dasein)* but, rather, over *recognition (Anerkennung)* from the master. In other words, it is a struggle over "prestige." In such a struggle, the only alternative to recognition is death.[32]

Here, what is to be recognized is *not* the "natural order of things"—since that is the sphere of the animal kingdom—but, rather, the likeness of the slave to the master. This recognition would affirm that the slave is made of the same human qualities as the master, of the same existential fabric, and possesses the same potential for identity. From the perspective of the slave, transgression, up to and including slaying the master, is the just punishment for the master's withholding such recognition. This logic clearly influences Frantz Fanon's psychological interpretation of the therapeutic function of violence in anticolonial struggle. Looked at from a different angle, transgression could be interpreted as a response to the fear that if one is not even more powerful than one's perceived adversary, the recognition of identity that is essential for human and historical life would be withheld.

Thus, in order to gain the recognition of being "like," one occasionally strays "above" (which perhaps explains in some cases the proliferation of fascist or rigid ideologies following experiences of national defeat.) Without the drive for recognition—which presupposes an Other from whom this recognition must be derived—there is no recognition-seeking activity and thus no history. Kojève tells us that history is nothing other than a dialectic process of power relations that molds the existential nothingness of Man into a form of being.[33] The claim to a "natural right" is just another aspect of this longing-to-be-recognized, which in this light is synonymous with the longing *to be.* In Hegel's own rendition of the idea, the struggle is synonymous with an ongoing effort at reconciliation; the master needs the slave for his identity, whereas the slave gains his through his labor in the service of the master. The dialectics of the relationship themselves provide the qualities one must enlist in seeking recognition: the *fear,* ingrained in the inequality of the relationship, and the *discipline,* ingrained in the experience of servitude.[34]

In a further refinement of the logic of struggle for recognition, Axel Honneth charts it out in three distinct spheres: love, right *(Recht),* and values *(Wertschätzung).* These occupy the respective dimensions of emotion, morality, and sociability.[35] While Honneth does not pursue these distinctions in the context of political history, the model he provides is fruitful in showing how the synergy among these three spheres in one totalistic system closely parallels the evolution of the ideological claims of the nation-state. The identity of the nation-state can be said to possess totalitarian features to the extent that it actively seeks recognition on *all* bases: emotive, juridical, and communal. This expansion of the identity of the modern state, Schmitt's thesis implies, can be traced to a single source, namely its preoccupation with a foe seen to be organized likewise—for Kojève, a master. The history of colonial contact clearly illustrates the globalization of this dynamic from its very commencement.[36] Napoleon's abortive yet seminal expedition into Egypt in 1798 allowed such a dialectic to instill itself very quickly: The French victory was decisive enough to cause a basic reconsideration of the very nature of the old regime in Egypt but short enough to allow future political developments in Egypt to originate with the stamp of local authority. The subsequent rise to power in Egypt of Muhammad Ali is generally credited to the lessons learned from Napoleon's short but remarkably sobering occupation. Ali is identified with a massive project of reform, modernization, state centralization, and expansion that at one point seriously challenged the old system of the Ottoman Empire.

Al-Jabarti's contemporaneous chronicle of Napoleon's stay, though written from a traditional local perspective, already condemns the decay of the very structure of the old regime for its inability to stand up to the French.[37] In a striking passage, al-Jabarti even sees in the dedication and organization of the French military, which he otherwise sternly condemns, more resemblance to the noble tradition of early Islamic warriors than can be found among the defeated Mamluk protectors of Islamic Egypt.[38] Indeed, his chronicle anticipates the nature of the system that would emerge out of the occupation. That system would attempt to touch as many dimensions of social life as the occupation itself had. The three dimensions described by Honneth are all represented here.

In the first place, that the emotive dimension could be a basis of governance was spelled out in a recognition of the need for authentic return to religious piety. Al-Jabarti describes in disbelief how *sheikh* Napoleon had already claimed this authenticity for himself, in a remarkable and early display of boundless cynicism.[39] Second, the need for juridical certainty was a running concern on almost every page of al-Jabarti's chronicle. The question of the recognition of basic rights clustered around questions of taxation and merchants' property. French practices in that arena were for al-Jabarti proof enough of the injustice of the occupation, inasmuch as novel methods of taxation were a central concern for Napoleon, who had been cut off from France by a British naval blockade.[40] Finally, the question of recognized unifying values as a basis for the regime was clearly represented in Napoleon's incredible claim to be fighting the Mamluks not on behalf of any French empire but, rather, under the banner of a universal Islam led by the sultan in Istanbul. But it was this same unity of the *umma* (community of the faithful) that al-Jabarti saw to be sorely lacking, on the evidence of the early success of the occupation itself. That recognition was also the basis for Muhammad Ali's project, which began to coalesce on the heels of Napoleon's departure, to bring order and unity to the perilously exposed *umma,* first in Egypt, then through a largely successful yet ultimately abortive military campaign into the Levant and Anatolia.

From the imperial perspective of Napoleon, things of course looked different. Napoleon was obsessed with a different foe than Islam or even Egypt when he went to Egypt: The mission was largely motivated by an attempt to sabotage British links to India. The outcome for the political culture of Egypt could not have been any less intended from the point of view of imperial politics. But as one of the first footsteps in the history of modern colonialism, Napoleon's occupation flowed out of an expansionist outline of international politics, already latent in European rivalries. At least according to Arghiri Emmanuel's interpretation,[41] subsequent colonial expansion into the peripheries can be understood as an outcome of competition between European powers rather than in terms of logics of expansion innate to each European power. After an initial period in which colonial conquest was confined to profitable coastal possessions, river estuaries, and isolated strategic points, between the Berlin Conference of 1884 and World War I it grew very suddenly to encompass entire regions and landmasses. The latter form of expanded dominion, according to Emmanuel, cannot be explained solely in terms of its benefit to the mother country. After all, such expansions were in general less profitable to conquering powers and more costly to maintain than the previous confinement of domination to small but strategic enclaves. Nonetheless, that expansion was made inevitable by rivalries between colonial powers; by laying claim to a vast region (as opposed to a small, easily controllable and more profitable part of it), colonial powers were motivated more by the need to *deny access* to it to competing forces than by the uncertain rewards of such an expensive extension of authority. Eventually, that system collapsed under the weight of its increasing cost to the dominating powers, which had been weakened rather than strengthened by it.[42]

The elementary principle here is that at a certain stage of power struggles, after the local resources are fully mobilized, additional mobilization demands an expansion beyond the local domain, thereby inciting competing forces to do the same. The expansion of governance and of the field of politics in general invariably follows the properties of empowerment discerned from the behavior of the foe. It is in the nature of such a structure of competitive games to reach a ceiling of available resources, which then has to be transcended. At that point, a new descriptive discourse of the game must be found, the range of claims made available by the old one having been exhausted. The *need* for transcending any given ceiling is inseparable from governance's permanent alertness to the possibility that a competitor might reach that ceiling. Processes leading to globalization—which for governance entail the concomitant dissolution of the self-referential realm—have only *increased* the number and scale of foes an order of governance has to reckon with. Today the various stages of national and then colonial consolidation, which were integral to the coming into being of a Eurocentric world, are giving way to a different order of political consolidation, one that is transnational in name, claim, and character.[43] It is no accident that the North American Free Trade Agreement (NAFTA), for example, is frequently described as a response to the EU. What is usually missing from the description is the fact that while transnational economic concerns usually benefit from and support such consolidations, they hardly value them as "responses." The notion of "response" in this context is more *political* in nature than economic, especially in light of transnational capital's continuing propensity to transcend even the boundaries of those politically expanded commercial blocs.

In general, therefore, processes of globalization establish logical contours and orientations that sharpen governance's awareness of its own vulnerability. The general anxiety resulting therefrom has often been managed by summarizing the flood of foes into clearly discernible monoliths, so that a clear strategy of combat could be followed. The ideological terrain thereby becomes remarkably simpler: In the colonial epoch the primary struggle was between "civilization" and "barbarism"; during the Cold War it was between "democracy" and "communism" (or, alternatively, capitalism and socialism). Today the effort to summarize a multitudinous feud on a global scale is taking new directions. The simplest summary articulates global struggle in terms of a dichotomy between cosmopolitanism and nativism. This dichotomy is spelled out nowhere more straightforwardly than in Benjamin Barber's famous opposition of the caricature worlds "McWorld" and "Jihad."[44] A more partitioned but no less troublesome summary is Samuel Huntington's famous sketch of pristine civilizations as the new categories of global conflict. Huntington's schema is not another empty academic exercise. The proximity of his vision of the world to an unspoken official rethinking of imperial centers can be noted in the ringing endorsement it has received from intellectual statesmen no less weighty and no more dissimilar than Henry Kissinger and Jacques Delors, among others. This emerging tradition is to be explored in more detail in chapter 2.

The history of grand political categories, such as those just mentioned, is essentially a history of those struggles defined as *global* tasks. They fashioned alliances and provided discourses by which various orders of governance could reduce the number of their foes through pooling resources against an assortment of enemies, real or manufactured. An order of governance engaged in a global task could thereby further legitimize its encroachment upon civil societies within its borders and its increasing claims over national resources. The peripheries of these grand global alliances provide breeding ground for the political parasite—for example, enclaves, despotisms, or oligarchies that throve in much of the Third World during the Cold War, and precisely because of it. The parasite finds a purpose for existence and a source of international support in the opportunities offered by global struggles in which it can offer some auxiliary support. The ultimate outcome of this dynamic is a political world divided in terms of ideological tasks into three main modes, namely, that of the producer of the vocabulary defining the global struggle; that of the consumer of that vocabulary, who seeks to transform local conditions in order to approximate the description offered by it; and that of the parasite, for whom such a vocabulary simply offers an obvious resource for longevity.

Capital and Coercion

The study of state formation generally follows three main traditions of emphasis. The tradition inaugurated by Machiavelli highlights power struggles and differential coercive capacities. The examination of the economic foundations of state formation developed later as a field of study under Marxist influences and is also currently a ubiquitous perspective. In a distant third place one finds some attention to governability as a form of culture, which some see as a more significant pillar of governmentality than economy or power. Generally, it is easiest for students of history to dwell on the role of power struggles in state formation, since elements of power differential tend to be the most visible and documented dimension of the story. The merciless process of eliminating competitors in early modern Europe is frequently cited as a fundamental prototype in the genesis of the modern state. The wars of the Reformation in the sixteenth century, the Thirty Years' War in the first half of the seventeenth, the peasant and urban revolts of the eighteenth and nineteenth, the Napoleonic Wars—all precipitated redrawings of political maps. They also precipitated redefinitions of the meaning of the authority enshrined in the peace agreements ending many of these troubles, such as the Peace of Westphalia in 1648, the Peace of Utrecht in 1713, the Partition of Poland in 1773, or the Conference of Vienna in 1815. European state wars continued well into the twentieth century and were punctuated only by military adventures outside the continent, such as the expansion into the Americas (where European states continued to fight each other) and into the colonies of Southeast and south Asia, Africa, and the Middle East (where prior agreements on spheres of control somewhat contained further European rivalry for the same colonies). Whether in or out of the European continent, one can chart nearly four centuries of uninterrupted and explicit rivalry, which frequently broke into full-scale wars.

The historic connection between state formation and war is a subject of extensive research.[45] It is not my aim here to argue whether the state emerges out of military needs or whether its very structure presumes a violent drive to eliminate competitors from the geographic and spiritual domains it seeks to occupy. With respect to the history of governance *as a creature of transnational forces*, it serves more purpose to chart out some of the processes by which powerful states, once obsessed with the image of the adversary, create unintended political worlds and sometimes embark on catastrophic miscalculations on a global scale. In one systematic critique, Jack Snyder analyzed the trajectories of imperial expansion in terms of concepts that, misleading as they are with respect to the nature or motives of the adversary, become integral to the cognitive repertoire of policy makers. The most pivotal of these include a cumulative understanding of gains and losses, the myth that expansion is fundamental to regime security, an image of the adversary as a "paper tiger" subject to intimidation, and a domino conception of frontiers and "vacillating societies." Snyder found such justifications of both disastrous and successful expansionisms in paradigms of international relations, which were premised on a vision of an abstract and standard actor equipped with universal, utilitarian rationality. These paradigms were also rooted in what Foucault would call the science of governmentality, that is, in the cognitive attempts to force *uniform conceptual order* on data, reports, and conditions of diverse sorts and origins.[46]

Although such processes of political expansion have frequently been tied to the spread of capitalism, governance must not be understood as simply a vehicle through which capitalism spreads its tentacles across the seas. (The classical theory of imperialism, which made much of this connection, will be revisited in the next chapter.) Capitalism, as Fernand Braudel argues, spread *ahead*—sometimes centuries ahead—of the systems of governance that came to be associated with it.[47] Janet Abu-Lughod demonstrates that in the medieval world system a global capitalism existed that was characterized by the lack of need, aspiration, or capacity of most participants to politically dominate others, a condition that furnished a spirit of coexistence that prevailed until the arrival of the Europeans.[48] In a recent work, which stresses an Asian centricity in world economy that endured up to the eighteenth century, Andre Gunder Frank came to similar conclusions regarding universal similarities in economic outlooks. Unfortunately, however, Frank's otherwise illustrious project suffers from a woeful lack of attention to the pivotal role of state and coercion in the establishment of a Eurocentric world. It therefore fails to register the role played by new types of states that emerged in Europe after the Thirty Years' War in gradually (although not always consciously) introducing dynamics of connection between capitalism and coercion that had not been known before.

Apart from safeguarding certain trade routes, premodern states' projects of expansion were largely met with suspicion or even outright opposition by the mercantile class. It is remarkable, for instance, that the immensely profitable gold trade of the Sahara remained beyond the reach of most of the states that knew of it and sought for so long to control it. One of the most illustrative premodern attempts in that line, namely, the ambitious Moroccan expedition in the late 1500s, was strongly resisted by the local merchants and the populace at large, and the sharif had to rely for the task on an army consisting largely of foreign conscripts.[49] In that classic case, the mercantile opposition to such a grandiose state project stemmed not merely from the project's anticipated cost but, more importantly, from the fear that the state might eventually come to control the lucrative trade in ways detrimental to mercantile interests. In that case, the state competed (unsuccessfully) with, rather than furthered the interests of, commercial capitalism.

Although in many instances, such as under later forms of European mercantilism and colonialism, capitalist expansion was aided by the resources of imperial governance, in others it was capitalism itself that provided the model of stable and predictable governance. The fabled histories of the Dutch and British East India Companies constitute two of the greatest historical episodes of such a transformation. In North American history, on a somewhat smaller scale, the "company town" provided a comparable model of the total social reach, capacity, and responsibility of the capitalist enterprise. The classical capitalist company was often more stable—in terms of endurance, structure, leadership, and flexibility, among other attributes—than the many systems of governance it had to deal with both in the precolonial world and in the world of the frontiers, where the state was yet to venture. Such a company, in an important sense, was also a proto-state, with full-fledged administrative apparatuses, explorers, and foot soldiers. The Dutch East India Company (VOC, 1602–1799) was a fundamental factor not only in founding entire new countries, such as Indonesia and South Africa, but also in stabilizing its home base of the seven Netherlandic provinces in the seventeenth and eighteenth centuries. It was a major player in the histories of India, Ceylon, the Bengal region, and Southeast Asia in general.[50] And as such it often displayed a cultural resourcefulness that could to an extent mitigate the recourse to coercive practice. For example, there is an interesting eighteenth-century Javanese rendition of the reign of Jan Coen, the first Dutch governor-general of the VOC in Batavia, in which he is interpreted not as a company man or even as a foreigner but, rather, as the son of a Javan princess who was predestined to bear authentic kings.[51] The company, thus, could be incorporated into local culture, which itself furnished the raw material for a nascent mythology of governance. Local culture, therefore, was capable of infusing itself into new and subsequent social organizational models, which in turn had been inspired by the company.

Today, efforts and debates everywhere regarding the privatization of historical state functions, up to and including social security, hark back to a belief typical of that classical capitalist era, namely, that the logic of free enterprise is inherently more efficient, or even more in tune with interpersonal realities, than that of state bureaucracy. Thus, political debates once again articulate social concerns more in terms of *economic* principles (such as efficiency, cost/benefit analysis, or human capital investment) than in terms of *political* concepts (such as justice, community, or harmony). In many ways, the history of the classical capitalist company shows that contemporary multinational enterprises that enjoy significant transnational influence and virtual immunity from national control are not without precursors, roots, or models that were experimented with in a long-bygone era. Moreover, the classical company provided a *model* for stabilizing the phenomenon of governance itself, both in its home territory as well as overseas. The expansive company has been the direct or indirect founder of many enclaves. Those, in turn, proved to be the most profitable political creatures from the point of view of capitalist accumulation. They allowed for a great concentration of profit and extraction, with minimal outlays toward social services and coercive structures, as the size of territory and population was usually relatively small. In advising the realm, the company offered a model of stable hierarchy channels, orderly personnel turnover, and essential continuity of policy objectives (thus predictability). It also offered a superior knowledge system; it organized, periodized, and catalogued the company's far-flung network; its developing awareness of cultures; its investment in communication technologies; and its cross-fertilization of agricultural species, thereby subordinating local or theological systems of knowledge to secular, investment-oriented taxonomies.

On all such fronts, many systems of governance that came into regular contact with such a grand sociopolitical company were impressed with its meritocratic norms of hierarchy, predictability of objectives, and systems of abstract knowledge. It is no accident, therefore, that the realm tried to emulate the company. It assumed for itself the structures and functions that typified the company and ended up learning from it, to a great extent, how to govern a populace. In Abdelrahman Munif's epic historical novel *Cities of Salt*—far more accurate in capturing ideational developments than any sociological account of the sociopolitical history of oil in Arabia—the company is portrayed as being always a few steps ahead of the local "government" in terms of its knowledge of material resources, dynamics of social change, and capacities of existent or possible modes of social organization. Here, governance in effect transforms its nature through social dynamics put into motion by the company, and it is often propelled into action or into restructuring its modus operandi according to the model of rational planning and control freely provided by the company.[52] But as governance begins to operate in that fashion, it also becomes, as though half-dreamily and without any specific grand plan or purpose, an expansive power operating at a much grander scale than the company would have ever found profitable. Sometimes, when governance has accumulated so much power that nothing in the world seems to be able to teach it the forgotten virtue of modesty, it becomes an overtaxed empire that can justify itself only by continuing to imagine new purposes. The transnational world of today no longer provides an abundant supply of such purposes. How much longer can they still be imagined?

Transforming the Inside

If one considers Muhammad Ali's Egypt as a prototype attempt to transform a precolonial realm into a modern state, one can isolate two pivotal characteristics of the regime's program: first, the invention of a socially interventionist state, which placed charitable functions under its jurisdiction; and second, the territorial extension of direct rulership so that it was no longer confined to a capital city from which power radiated through uneasy local alliance into the countryside. In Europe, similar dynamics of state expansion into society were coupled with a bourgeois penetration of a growing bureaucracy at all levels, and at the same time both the bourgeoisie and the modern state consolidated their territorial connectivity.[53] The basis of such a state thus consisted in part of a tenuous symbiosis primarily with the outlook and secondarily with the interests of a class that was more profuse and globally oriented than the feudal and religious aristocracy that had furnished the pillars of the old regime. Yet the tenuousness of that symbiosis was bound to reveal itself in the course of time, for such a state had to be rushed into being everywhere, without having had the time and resources to accumulate sufficient sociocultural and historic foundations in contemporaneous Africa, India, central Asia, or the Middle East. Although one can detect a nascent intellectual fervor in favor of the new state in many of those regions, the fervor was largely born more out of intellectual contact than out of social transformations that paralleled European social developments in the nineteenth century.[54]

It may be argued that in a hypothetical world typified by regular contact but little coercion, variants on the emergent model in Europe, namely, of state-society symbiosis, would also have developed in the course of time in the peripheries, with strong local imprints upon them. However, in the real historical world the fateful acceleration of the process of state emergence in the peripheries owes much to their contact with a nascent imperial project, which upset the ancient balance among peripheral political actors and encouraged immodest ambitions by introducing new military technologies, visions of alliance with great powers, and novel ideas of governmentality and power. That kind of contact contributed to experiments greatly varying in results, from Muhammad Ali's regime in Egypt, to the Meiji restoration in Japan, to Chinese nationalist modernity. As far as the realm was concerned, national "restoration" was frequently accompanied by a variably successful imperial expansion modeled after that of a conquering power; Muhammad Ali's abortive attempt to take over the Ottoman Empire followed and went further along the route that Napoleon had taken; the Meiji restoration, carried out amid the great alarm over Commodore Matthew Perry's awakening of the insulated Japanese realm to the games of global power, inaugurated a slower but more sustained effort at empire building.

Where domains of local sovereignty were relatively small or parochial, exposure to the outside world entailed some fundamental misunderstandings, which expansive colonial powers were to "correct" in their own way. That correction usually entailed the local domains' transformation into enclaves of the modern world system. The sultan of Dar Sila in northeastern Africa, for example, did not at first fully recognize the epoch-making difference between the French, to whom he offered allegiance in 1909, and his former suzerains of the neighboring states of Darfur and Wadai. Nor, apparently, did the French fully realize how incompatible the sultanate would be with the requisites of incorporation into a European-led world economy. In particular, the French demand for cash taxes not only magnified the money economy to a level never before reached, but it caused hardships and famines for which the traditional tax system had made allowance. As in the Americas after the encounter between the two worlds of Hernán Cortés and Montezuma, the ensuing conflict of values ended in the demise of a reclusive order that had been a perfectly interwoven fabric of stability—an order that could be sustained only by dogged parochialism—and its replacement by a tributary system of the world-oriented discoverer.[55]

By the time of decolonization, the colonial world was given back as parcels of territories governed by new institutional shells, which could already enlist some intellectual and class foundations for their internal support. There was also a prevalent suspicion that the system of governance delivered "back" to the natives by colonialism had the outside world to thank for its being more than autochthonous history. As is well known, one of the first decisions made by the OAU upon its founding in 1963 was to respect the arbitrary colonial borders. That decision expressed an awareness among the new political elites of the fact that other and older models of collective identification were still very much alive. The new elites feared that opening up the question of borders would mean inviting an unrestrained cycle of disintegration of postcolonial polities. Thus, borders had to be tolerated in spite of the lingering contempt for their capriciousness.

As later conflicts and instabilities demonstrated, the *Realpolitik* expressed in the OAU's foundational decision about colonial borders did not experience a smooth career. Though strong states like Nigeria or Congo managed to retain Biafra and Katanga, respectively,[56] equally strong states like Ethiopia failed in the long run to keep Eritrea from seceding; some states, like Somalia and Liberia, decomposed into smaller, de facto self-governing territories; others, like Angola or Uganda, continue today to experience difficulties in exerting a meaningful level of control over their territories. Of course, many of these fissures were magnified by the involvement of major global powers in supporting local claims. But such claims could not have been so magnified to begin with had they not been so rooted in memories, traditions, and cultural networks not corresponding to the institution of the nation-state that they were able to resist being willfully eliminated. Long-established traditions and identities, after all, do not readily conform to the dictates of purely diplomatic agreements. The legitimacy of governance consists of the degree of correspondence between the governing and administrative apparatuses' language and practice on the one hand and a collective cultural self-understanding and collective cultural interpretation of the world on the other.

If this is accepted, then one rule for measuring legitimacy presents itself: Legitimacy can be said to exist to the extent that the claimed correspondence between governance and society endures, pace Weber, through resources *other than* an authority's capacity for coercion. The more coercion is referenced, the less secure is the claim to legitimacy. The more coercion is referenced, the more evidenced are the inaudible, substate spheres of representation, spheres in which an autonomous and largely ideational (as opposed to institutionally generated and structured) culture is produced and reproduced across generational lines. That certain parochial frames of reference survive inaudibly means precisely that given the right combination of factors it is always possible to reactivate frames in one form or another, even though the presence of state governance—with its institutions and its incentive to keep the appearance of legitimacy—prevents them from revealing that they endure on the political map. Governance, however, perceived those subterranean forces as ultimately absorbable or neutralizable; this understanding flowed from the philosophical outlook underpinning the organizational imperatives of the modern state, to which we now turn.

Totalitarianism and the Documentary Philosophy of the State

Until recently the received wisdom was that a healthy institution of governance would invariably resolve any issue of cultural dissonance, either by creative assimilation of the problem or through corrective education. The totalitarian nature of the modern state, partially inspired by its self-understanding as the sole product and guardian of "national culture," was epitomized in, though not entirely formed by, a notion of governance as a culmination of a historical logic. Though not always cited in this regard—especially today—the philosophical expression of this idea was already in full bloom in Hegel's view of the state as the site of the eventual embodiment of a spiritual process of historical maturation. Several of the founding texts of modern social science also articulated that ambition in one form or another. Auguste Comte's *Cours de philosophie positive*, to pick an influential example, articulated positivist rationality as a product of evolutionary progress toward a coordinated social system that would impose some order on the spontaneity of earlier forms of social and intellectual life. The combination of the key terms "order" and "progress" in Comte's treatise spelled out the grand integrative grid anchored in positive science, of which "politics" was the crown: "No real order can be established, and still less can it last, if it is not fully compatible with progress, and no great progress can be accomplished if it does not tend to the consolidation of order. . . . The misfortune of our actual state is that the two ideas are set up in radical opposition to each other."[57]

In Comte's case, the *political* category of order is brought into harmony with the *economic* category of progress in a single system explicitly imitating the complementarity of contradictory qualities of matter (static and dynamic) in physics. The total systemic harmony brings together an economic realm characterized by dynamism, change, and flux and a political one formed by an essential structural stability. Significantly, this conception inverted what until modernity had been the accepted model of the relation between politics and economy: It was economic arrangements, whether seen in the vision of timeless feudal relations, caste positions, or trade route regularity, that had been seen as characterized by essentially stable forms, mores, and relations. From antiquity until the rise of the bourgeoisie and the realistic novel, the best illustrations of the dynamism of human relations were provided not by the steady economic patterns of life but, usually, by the quintessentially "political" tales of treason, loyalty, power, and stratagem.

By Comte's time, that referential cosmos had already changed beyond recognition. Comte made it clear that the political field was the ultimate objective of his general positivist science, a science designed to coordinate historical, scientific, and social knowledge toward the task of informing political actors.[58] For him, the vast field of responsibilities entrusted to government encompassed material, spiritual, and moral dimensions, thereby necessitating that it be informed by scientific knowledge of society, that is, "positivist" science. Comte saw the phenomenon of governance itself to be rooted in nothing other than the "natural disposition" of intellectual superiority to rule. Some five decades later, that same intellectual basis of modern governance, as formulated in Albert Schäffle's social theory, included mastery over documentary, communicative, and written embodiments of popular traditions. All such traditions were seen to symbolize, in the final analysis, political ideas.[59] The contours of totality seeping gradually into political theory were usually articulated in universal rather than culturally specific terms. Comte's theory even culminated in his construction of a tentative vision of a global (European) system, which would coordinate divergent historical experiences so that they would come to approximate the sociopolitical ideals of positivist science.[60]

Thus one of the ethical foundations of the modern state revisited the old question of how to integrate into it pertinent mores of social hierarchy. This was hardly a novel concern—constructions of behavioral parallels between political governance and household relations had been attempted in different ways as early as the times of Confucius and Aristotle. The novelty in the new representational ethics was something else: It consisted primarily of subtracting from the notion of politics any expression of its modus operandi as a self-referential "game," exterior to all ethics. It was in an important sense a rebuttal of Machiavelli, who was neither the first nor, to be sure, the last spokesperson of a tradition that regarded the representation by political players of general social morality to be at best a nonessential ingredient to success. That line of thinking can be found in such an ancient compilation of tales as the Indo-Persian-Arabic *Kalilah and Dimnah*, in which governance is portrayed as little more than an allegorized art of survival in a world bustling with potential adversaries and claimants. *Kalilah and Dimnah* was far from displaying an exotic, specifically Oriental politics. In the West the very same theme permeated countless literary representations in a long tradition interrupted only by brief doses of Kantian, Hegelian, or Comtian schemes of integration and totality. From Shakespeare to Franz Kafka, there is hardly a shortage of literary representations of the art of political domination as little more than variations on ancient games of illusion, intrigue, and tragedy.

To be sure, the intellectual resources for an organic as well as game-like understanding of politics were always available. In the history of political theory and in widely differing situations, the legitimacy of a political hierarchy was frequently premised on its reflection of or parallelism to smaller and more customary levels of hierarchy in society, notably that of the household. The theme is abundantly clear in Aristotle's *Politics,* in which the city is above all an integral constellation of households and the idea of fatherhood itself legitimizes benevolent governance, in the same way that Zeus's *fatherly* status underpins a pantheon of other authorities.[61] Educational manuals for princes and royals liberally make such parallels. Foucault cites in this connection a Renaissance manual that distinguishes between three arts of governance: "[T]he art of self-government, connected with morality; the art of properly governing a family, which belongs to economy; and *finally* the science of ruling the state, which concerns politics."[62] This articulation obviously involves more than simple analogy. Rather, the arts of governance are arranged sequentially, with each level mastered by learning from the previous one, albeit the respective spheres (morality, economy, and politics) remain logically distinct.

As a form purporting to represent a distinct national community, the modern state thus came to confront some of the same ethical questions as had the old, self-enclosed realm. In both cases, the attempt to resolve the logical split between ethics and power consisted of an effort to append a cultural corollary to the phenomenality of governance as a pure form of power. For Confucius the model of imperial governance consisted of an expansive ethicism whereby the empire learns its ethics from the realm: The emperor displayed toward feudal landlords those manners of hierarchy that they themselves had already displayed toward their serfs. Ceremonials were intended to reveal signs of "awe-inspiring majesty," so that governance could become, without force, "the wind beneath which bows the grass."[63] This "awe-inspiring" quality gradually came to be seen not as a property emanating from the needs of governance itself but, rather, simply as a reproduction of other social hierarchies already enshrined in society and outside of the domain of governance. In the Confucian Vietnamese realm, the Lê monarchs actively supported ideas of obedience and loyalty that ran throughout the social fabric in a way that made loyalty to the empire seem a simple extension of already accepted mores. Central to such a system was a tripartite notion of bonds *(tam cuong)*, with children being obedient to their parents, wives subordinate to their husbands, and, explicitly drawn as a parallel, ministers loyal to their emperor.[64] Thus, side by side with widely dispersed representations of governance as essentially a grand game of illusions, a different tradition outlined the idea of political hierarchy as the ultimate translation of and even model for *preexistent* social relations.

The transmission of such mores—processed and shot through with statist ideology—back into the populace completes the story and marks the specificity of political modernity. Foucault argues that the replacement of the family by more general concepts as models of governance occasioned a postmercantilist emergence of "population" as a statistical category in the eighteenth century. Such grand patterns as marriage and death rates could neither be interpreted within the framework of nor reduced to an analysis of a single family unit.[65] Vehemently rejecting the notion that "society" could be reduced to individual atoms, this perspective eventually became the hallmark of Durkheimian sociology.[66] The heritage of political modernity cannot be understood apart from the process of the emergence of those measures that facilitate totalistic thinking.[67] There can only be a short distance between conceiving of "society" in terms of irreducible aggregate measures and conceiving of legitimate political authority as the outgrowth and guardian of an irreducible fabric of solidarity. The mass transmission of such new tropes, as is well known, uses various channels of authority (media, literature, education, bureaucracy and administration, the legal system, and so on). It succeeds most effortlessly when its dialectics of power find a receptive populace—which in Ernest Renan's terms daily rediscovers its symbols of togetherness—and couples that with a transgenerationally repeatable educational cycle.

The continuous, daily renewability of this stale, tired identity obviously offends the sensibilities of the cosmopolitans among us, many of whom despise both the conformist citizens of mass society and their cynical government. But the renewability of the identity instills the propagated themes of power, governance, proper channels, and representation into a mass, everyday consciousness. These become, therefore, part of a system of predictable behaviors, in which Norbert Elias sees one of the fundamental drives behind the growth of "civilizational" common denominators across great distances. In Elias's formulation, civilization appears as nothing but the *predictability* of ordinary patterns of life. This need for predictability, which in one's own psyche becomes translated into self-control,[68] is tied to the acknowledgment that one is involved in increasing societal interdependencies and concomitantly to one's need to invoke the categorical imperative. Here the social grounds of Kantian rationality are directed at allowing the intentions and actions of others to become readily interpretable to any individual involved in the same civilizational grid.[69]

As one of the essential grounds of common civilizational patterns, general predictabilities are not the exclusive property of governance, even though their establishment is clearly one of its expected tasks. The impressive spread of world religions, without the benefit of modern communication technologies, can be understood in terms of the need to ascertain or display the predictability of the manners and behaviors of distant and unknown trade partners. The spread of Islam into east and west Africa, Southeast Asia, and elsewhere, where conversions emanated more from local tendencies than from fear of the political sword of a remote and disunited empire, is one significant example of this trade-based process of acculturation.[70] Among other things, in that case faith operated as a system of identification, upon which was anchored the trustworthiness of distant partners in a world system. Sometimes this deep-seated imperative of predictability could just as well support governance's claims to guarantee uniformity. Governance esssentially means that predictability depends upon a state's coercive capacity and threat of deterrence, rather than on spiritual communion within a less controlled but more voluntarily interactive world.

In addition to reworking models of traditional hierarchy and safekeeping patterns of predictability ingrained in an older idea of civilization, expansive orders of governance in modernity claimed a third major cultural prize, one concerning a specific orientation toward abstract formation: A geographically, transethnically, translinguistically, and transreligiously expanding economy ruptures a production-consumption cycle to which only the tangible participants are beholden. One of the first steps in that expansion, as Marx, Simmel, and Elias observed, consists of progressively replacing barter economies with universally abstract money economies. Monetary valuation obviously cultivates abstract relations to things and products and also to producers who may be invisible, unaccountable, or uncontrollable. Its prominence can be seen as a symptom of the intensification of abstract activities and reflections that is a fundamental aspect of everyday transactions under modernity.[71]

Abstraction in this sense involves an unconscious, daily affirmation of commonalities with a secular social whole, as Renan famously observed when he defined the nation as a daily plebiscite. If a community of tangible producer-consumers is to define itself as unique in some essential sense, it naturally must attempt to set up identifiable boundaries that distinguish it from the rest of the world. For Hegel, a sense of uniqueness is unimaginable without subsequently transforming its object into a formalism, that is, without translating a momentary and ephemeral condition into formal continuity extending beyond its original context.[72] This abstracted continuity of a trace of uniqueness, then, becomes a guide for an everyday practice of reason, will, and feeling.[73] According to this formulation, governance functions so as to make an *accidental convergence of interests* permanent. As such, governance is an accidental instance holding together a totality of interests that would otherwise eventually disintegrate back into their parochial natures.[74]

That amplified need for an instrument of power to guarantee perpetuity of commonalities can perhaps be traced to the particularity of the European trajectory, in which the convergence of interests that brought parochial outlooks out of their cocoons was hardly voluntary or intentional. An example of a major historical "convergence" is the gradual crystallization over almost four centuries of highly intrusive polities in Europe between 1400–1800, which were an indirect response to the introduction of the putting-out system *(Verlagssystem)*. That system, as is well known, shattered the economic self-sufficiency of towns and cities, whose destiny became increasingly dependent on market fluctuations in distant regions. The increasing scale at which such an economy began to operate led to redefinitions of the sphere of self-sufficiency, whence it was enlarged to encompass novel abstract concepts such as "nation," which, like the old gemeinschaft, was imagined as a unique and distinct entity. In an important sense, thus, the nation can be approached as one of the conceptual attempts that sought to arrest an expanding economy and in so doing to reincarnate an imagined sense of communal control over collective destiny. This sense of communal control was prefigured in the self-enclosed medieval town.[75] The explicit denial of the contribution of "outsiders," which was often foundational for such a system (and which at a later point was to be spelled out in such terms as "independence" or "*self*-determination"), attests to this primacy of self-enclosure as an essential founding leitmotiv for the nation-state paradigm, whereby an enhanced form of self-reference is underwritten by a cultural armory added to governance.

Paralleling that paradoxical development of systems that were both large in scope and self-enclosed in their rhetoric was another dynamic contributing to the growth of an abstract, documentary philosophy of the state. This dynamic was connected to the emergence of the economically accountable "tax state" in Europe out of the old feudal *patrimonium*.[76] Joseph Schumpeter's analysis of that phenomenon placed it in the context of feudal rivalries, recurrent feudal challenges to the weak center, increasing costs of the unavoidably patrimonial court, and external imperial threats—notably the Ottoman. All such dynamics forced the prince to go back more frequently to local suzerains and ask for more in tax revenues to meet such needs. In turn the prince had to become more and more beholden to and regulated by the demands and expectations of the local authorities. Out of that process emerged a model of governance that entailed a stronger sense of answerability to a variably defined realm of constituents and that engendered a rethinking of governance away from the model of private property. Far from remaining aloof, self-referential, sporadic, ephemeral, or purely formal, governance was now understood as the system by which an enlarged and abstracted community could continue to imagine and demand control of its destiny.

In the nineteenth century the transfer of the three endowments described above (hierarchy as a mirror of society, predictability as a civilizational entrustment, and abstraction as a logic of embodiment) to the culture of governance was concluded. The emergence of the body of thought just outlined in essence signaled, among other things, the silent abandonment of the Social Contract as a model of reciprocity in politics and its replacement with a secularized version of an older conception of a *corpus mysticum* as a model of sociopolitical integration. Down to the present, the "democratic" notion of national embodiment in the state has followed far more the dictates of indissolubility that defined the old theological-political notion of *corpus mysticum* (as represented, for instance, in the social philosophy of Johann Fichte) than those of the fabled (and theoretically revocable) Social Contract.[77]

Even though none of the theorists of irreducible society and total governance readily used, or even seemed aware of the similarity of their constructions to, the model of *corpus mysticum,* the evidence here that history sometimes repeats itself almost to the letter is abundant. Throughout the nineteenth century the enhanced scope of governance was expressed in a myriad of theories of posttheocratic totality. Many of these theories saw society as an "organism" that could be literally modeled after the human body, with the state often regarded as its head and organizing imperative.[78] In the 1870s, Paul von Lilienfeld published his multivolume *Gedanken,* contemporaneously with Herbert Spencer's works on social Darwinism, at a moment when organismic theories of total polities were at their peak. Like Spencer's, Lilienfeld's work was significant both because it was a symptom of the new total organizational self-understanding of governance and also because it epitomized the new centrality of political thought to theories of society. Thus one learns from that heritage that one of the main characteristics of the social "body" is *Kapitalisierung,* which consists of amassing, recording, and organizing a sum-total of social "resources" (material, administrative, and spiritual). Such resources are claimed not necessarily because the social "body" needs them to satisfy immediate needs but, rather, because they are of *potential* value for future use.[79] Government, according to this view, is the ultimate organizer of information in and about society and the intellectual trustee of the record of social aggregates.[80]

Within the larger scope of post-Enlightenment cultures of governance—and side by side with the globalization of networks of interdependence, economic world systems, colonial expansions, and their lasting imprints throughout the world—the constituting elements of the culture of governance just described were gradually transmitted around the globe and translated within different cultural contexts. For instance, the increasing awareness that orders of governance had of each other provided new sources for the idea that hierarchy was a fundamental category of governance. In the context of the enclave, the idea of hierarchy had been determined by the need to guarantee the minimal organizational imperative of mobilizing the enclave's resources within the transnational grid to which it owed its existence. Thus enclave governance was particularly attentive to the requisites of *efficient administration.* In the context of the realm, the idea of hierarchy of governance had been grafted onto already existing social hierarchies and thus avoided appearing to be a violation of traditional laws. In that case, governance was expected to display significant *moral dimensions* as its raison d'être. In the third historical model, imperial vision of the nature and value of political hierarchy went beyond local organizational needs or the reflection of cultural patterns. Oriented as empire was to the wider world as a field of expansion, ostentatious and expensive *power display* was a usual and naturally resilient aspect of imperial hierarchy.[81]

In that sense, the idea that governance manifests society in a condensed fashion fueled a drive to copy the models that appeared to be most successful in doing so. The *globalization of the internal structure of politics* essentially meant that the concept of hierarchy as it pertained to governance became outwardly oriented, seeking to *transform* local cultures so that they, like the nations of the "modern" world, would exhibit similitude of essence. The goal of hierarchy was no longer derived solely from the local cultural resources that governance had historically found at its disposal, although its rhetoric and even structure continued to be expressed in terms of such resources. What mattered for an order of governance active in a global world was that it enact the models of successful power exercise, and such models were available *only* outside its borders. In a world typified by inescapable power relations, that enactment was more fundamental for the survival of governance than its ability to reproduce local culture.

Imperial expansion, which in the modern age culminated in colonialism, universalized a notion of hierarchy of governance that began to compete against the models that had predated it in realms and enclaves throughout the world. Many would protest at this simplification, on the ready evidence that some essential features of Western European systems (for example, parliamentary, liberal, or bourgeois democracy) were not always successfully appropriated in worlds formerly dominated by Europe. Barrington Moore, for example, argues that the process of global learning in which adversaries learn from each other, though formative, cannot be linear. He stresses, correctly, that imposing one country's perceived model of "success" on another enjoying a different order of class relations led to vastly contrasted systems:

> The methods of modernization chosen in one country change the dimensions of the problem for the next countries who take the step. . . . Without the prior democratic modernization of England, the reactionary methods adopted in Germany and Japan would scarcely have been possible.

> Without both the capitalist and reactionary experiences, the communist method would have been something entirely different, if it had come into existence at all.[82]

The differences between such systems (liberal democracy, communism, fascism), though clearly significant, must not be overemphasized. The differences can be regarded as purely procedural, different means to accomplish very similar grand goals considered incumbent upon governing modern society. These are, namely, the need to develop a bureaucratized, centralized, and rational administration, which in one context or another would become the engine of modernization. The Eurocentric model of post-Enlightenment governance, as encapsulated in Weber's definition, emphasized an idea of hierarchy based on its *singularity*. Its central nerve-like function in society was independent of whether the procedural rules for governing were democratic or dictatorial. Nor was that sense of singularity threatened by the unregulated playing field allotted to early, laissez-faire capitalism, since that form of capitalism had already been discredited in the nineteenth century amid a barrage of socialist, Communist, utopian, and syndicalist thought and buried in the ashes of the business cycle itself. That logic had to escape from Europe to the colonies and from the American east to the western frontiers. In both cases, however, the government either came after or was pulled into the new quagmire. The resulting dialectic, while hardly threatening capitalist freedom, until recently reduced it to a politically dependent form of economic life (as will be explored in chapter 2). That form, unlike the case of the early chartered companies, required the outlay of substantial governmental inputs into new colonial and frontier adventures.

Remodeling the concept of hierarchy was thus the first item on the agenda of governance as it became exposed to modernist pressures of globalization. The second major cultural endowment of governance, namely, being entrusted with predictability, went through an equally significant transformation. The enclave's obsession with predictability was oriented toward safeguarding its links to the world outside, links over which it had little control. As such, predictability for the enclave was a property of the world outside. It was thus imperative for enclave governance to carefully cultivate relations, to play a balancing game, and to forge alliances in such a way as to maintain the enclave's usefulness to the outside world. For the realm, by comparison, predictability meant maintaining tradition. Realm governance, imprisoned within local walls and inwardly oriented, justified its presence by maintaining a modicum of law and order, which allowed tradition-bound life to go on in communities that were large and complex enough for central regulation but not so large as to have a need or the capacity to carry out imperial regulation or expansion. This story, of course, is complicated and cannot be reduced to the formula of ideal types described here. Some imperial expansions, to be sure, were set in motion largely by an interest in *maintaining* some aspect of already established traditions, although subsequent conquests added more tasks for such nascent empires. This was typically the case with expansions seeking to safeguard trade routes linking different communities across long distances, communities that had been tenuously connected before the emergence of an empire to spread its wings over them. One of the best examples of this process was the Mongol incursion into western Asia, which was to a certain extent explicitly motivated by the interruption of the safety of formerly established trade routes.[83]

The inculcation of new routes, intensification of traffic upon them, "discovery" of new regions and hinterlands, colonial adventures, and the demands of nineteenth-century industry—all such factors complicated the perennial task of making the world a predictable place. That task had been either entrusted to large empires or encoded in a more amorphously structured idea of "civilization" and "civilized behavior." Colonial incursions were repeatedly legitimized by alleging that a traditionalist adversary was "erratic" and needed to be controlled or transformed into a predictable copartner in a world system of common political signifiers. But it was not only exotic outsiders who mattered. The takeover of the historical responsibility over civilization by a particularly active form of governance also rearticulated the idea of citizenship, which Hegelian philosophy captured in a characteristically systematic manner: Hegel noted that the state's legitimacy was based on the citizen's willingness to give up ordinary suspicions and endow the state with his "trust." The idea of "trust," as Hegel articulated it, meant an assumption that the interests of the individual citizen were embodied and invested in the interests of the state.[84] That transformation expressed the notion of governance as a *representation* of a society lurking below it, even though such governance claimed to be, in a legal sense, above the task of reflecting traditions that were held to be "private"—notably, religion.

For the realm, abstract consciousness had entailed the opposite orientation. Even when the function of governance was seen as safeguarding traditional links, hierarchies, and relations, governance in the realm did not represent a society below it as much as a larger cosmic plan above it, a plan to which the realm ultimately belonged by nature rather than by choice. In the enclave, the abstract thinking of governance, such as in Zanzibar, Malacca, or the central African states along the Saharan trade routes, meant the adoption of the spiritual language spoken by the world with which it dealt. That orientation expressed itself in the enclave's abandonment of local spiritual animistic orders (which often continued to reign unchallenged in the immense country just a few steps outside of it) in exchange for the great world religion of its main partners. The transition from local animistic relevance to universal book religions was not so much a move in a game of power as a maneuver by which the enclave, intricately lodged in a global system that was both a menace and a blessing, sought to certify its *belonging* to that system. Thus the enclave, following different dynamics than the realm, still identified itself as a *local embodiment of a universal pattern*. But the abstract order was provided not by cosmic plan, as in the realm, but by the imperatives of establishing earthly identity and trustworthiness within a far-flung world grid.

In contrast to such ancient venues of abstract self-understandings of governance, the modern political systems that have infected the world with their logic of representation highlighted venues that were more typically associated with imperial bids, albeit employing unavoidable variations. Perennial European wars and European colonialism clearly highlighted the dimension of power relations among systems of governance.[85] The elements of power involve not simply technological and military dimensions but also a system that seeks to *organize* the sum total of known, mobilizable, and otherwise amorphous energies in the claimed domain of sovereignty. The requisites of such a system included the inculcation of national identities, the rewriting of history, standard mass curricula, daily and continual presence throughout media channels, claims to "national" literature, and bureaucratic and professional translations of daily life and the public sphere. Once that infiltration of all public spheres and civil societies was completed, even antiauthority trends within modern states consumed their energies with questions of governance: how to petition it, how to penetrate it, how to reform it, how to replace it (by another order of governance), and so on. The gradual defeat of civil society and its eclipse by mass society left no political center as clearly ensconced as national government. Special interests of all kinds can clearly be very effective, but their effectiveness is normally judged on the basis of how much they can impose their views or get what they want *through governmental action.* Their disposition toward governance in itself testifies to governance's success in normalizing its claim to social embodiment, *especially* in mass democracies: It is powerful not because it has the guns but, more fundamentally, because it cannot be ignored within its borders. The noise it produces deafens the ear and dulls the sensibilities toward alternative forms of political self-regulation and regularly strips all episodes of "micropolitics" of energy, impact, and relevance.

The argument thus far has been that the nationhood principle increasingly came to be seen as the most appropriate cultural pillar of the modern state more because of the infectious demonstration of prowess by states that organized their societies according to it than because of the historical maturation of some lurking collective spirit everywhere. There is perhaps no clearer example than that of post–World War I Turkey, a nation-state emerging out of the center of the shell that had held one of the last of premodern empires. The Young Turks actively sought to attach the country to European modernity. They relied on such culturalist moves as latinizing the alphabet and distancing themselves from the part of the world over which the Ottomans had exercised hegemony for several centuries. And, significantly, in the process they could scarcely resist copying the fiercest manifestations of Europe's nationalist discourse in a way that reached calamitous proportions against ancient ethnic residents, notably Armenians and Greeks. Of course, the process was hardly unique to Turkey; Kemal Atatürk was simply importing the logic of "disentanglement of nations" as the defining ground of modern statehood. That principle underpinned the Versailles agreement ending World War I and was represented in the subsequent tendency to draw the map of Europe according to a clear territorial distribution of national communities. As is well known, the task proved impossible without further genocide, mass deportation, and war.

As a corollary to this story, genocide is not simply and purely an expression of preexisting, normal human malice (a reductive theory that became more fashionable after World War II and still finds a substantial audience today).[86] The simple truth is that genocides do not happen every day. In modern times the common denominator among all genocides and mass deportations has been a dogmatic notion of *uncontaminated secular togetherness as a novel ground for national empowerment.* In the case of modern Turkey, the Greek retaliation—expelling Turks from the territory claimed by Greece—completed the lesson of the story: In a great measure, oppressing a group under the principle of nationality itself precipitates the *creation* of that nationality. When Golda Meir asserted in the early 1970s that Palestinians did not exist, she failed to note that though they had not existed historically as a distinct nation, they had already been entrenched as such for about three decades before she made the infamous statement.[87] Though "Palestinians" had lived for millennia in Palestine, without being culturally or juridically very distinct in the general region of west Asia and north Africa, they did not emerge as a national group with an ongoing claim to the right to a state of their own until they had to pay the price for "Israelis" founding an exclusive polity. That polity was modeled after the European nation-state, and its main intellectual foundations were provided *exclusively* by European Jewish intellectuals. In an important sense, the embodiment of amorphous ethnic distinctions in the cast iron of states abrogates an ancient multicultural practice in everyday life, in shared cities, and along trade routes and replaces it with abstract national communities defining themselves almost exclusively in terms of their position within a grid of, or in opposition to, other similar communities. The prophecy in this case is usually self-fulfilling, but its realization does not mean that history can be written in the unilinear fashion presupposed in the fantasies of national "awakening." History is a contorted terrain, whose myriad pathways often collapse in the imagination into phantasms of unilinearity.

A substantial portion of the history of modern nationalism thus concerns its marriage to state power. This accomplishment signaled the defeat of the other alternative, or what Hobsbawm calls "proto-nationalism"[88]— an antecedent feeling of quasi solidarity not historically seen to require embodiment in a state. From a global perspective there is hardly a shortage of evidence for the assertion that the state viewed nationalism as simply another resource in its struggle against foes of various kinds. The nation-state's very success in expanding its cultural power was often based on its ability to permanently swallow up all available public spheres within a consolidated home territory. Bismarck originally saw domestic and international alliances as interchangeable, since both belonged to the *same* game. At one point, when he had choices, Bismarck regarded his alliance with German national liberals as an *alternative* to an alliance with France or Russia, and he saw both alliances (the "domestic" and the "foreign") as ways to counterbalance Austrian power in the 1850s.[89] His international success, in turn, can be attributed not merely to his diplomatic skills but, above all, to his ability to accumulate for his state a permanent reservoir of internal social capital.

This process of transformation within countries was further facilitated by the replacement of *civil* societies everywhere with *mass* societies and by the displacement of enclaves, realms, and formal empires with standard state systems. Governance everywhere became thereby *totalitarian*, in a sense of the term very different from that employed by Arendt. It is perhaps one of the greatest delusions of modern social science to parcel out the notion of totalitarianism as if it concerned someone else. This delusion was fostered in no small part by the rhetoric of the Cold War, but it was also fostered by the fashionable digressions of Arendt and her supporters, whose customary liberal proclivity for self-congratulation led them to look for totalitarianism everywhere except where it really mattered, right under their own feet. The obvious political heritage of modernity is that governance *everywhere* becomes totalitarian, partly in the sense that it understands itself as a *total* representation of society and the ultimate translator of society's will or historic mission, but also because governance in itself possesses the impulse, will, and capacity to place that understanding into devastating practice. *Mass* democracy becomes its ally toward the perfection of that mission, not its corrective guard.

Interests, Common and Special

Modern governance's ability to enlist social capital on an ongoing basis, especially in complex and large societies, depends on its ability to bring special interests into general systemic alignment. The notion of general interest, as a putative *measure of totality* ultimately entrusted to governance, can only indicate a diffuse ideological orientation propagated by the state or populist nationalism; it cannot indicate a timeless sequence of concrete policies, especially in fluid or mass societies. In "corporatist" countries, such as much of Western Europe, the notion of general interest was restrained by an acknowledgment of the intrinsic legitimacy of special interests—except during episodes of virulent nationalism. In such modern mass societies as the United States it is commonly observed that special interest groups shape a political landscape increasingly formed by disparate initiatives that do not correspond or give rise to any total or strategic vision of governability. This state of affairs has become an explicit source of expressions of disenchantment from "the system" as a whole. The general complaint is that "the system" is approached by interest groups as an opportunity to be used, as a marketplace of spoils to be parceled up, or, to the extent that some forces are regarded to occupy

That is because a modern political map reflects only formal similitude, and thus international recognition *by states of each other,* rather than by peoples of each other or of their states. Despite their occasional and usually opportunistic resort to the rhetoric of "human rights," the paradigm of similitude requires states to hold to the fiction that there is a natural correspondence between statehood (but not necessarily specific governments) and peoplehood in already established states.

Wherever this modern state emerged more due to the imperatives of emulation than to relatively autonomous processes, as in much of the postcolonial world, one can readily document a greater amount of effort needed by governing orders to ensure peace, regime survival, law enforcement, and public cooperation with regulation emanating from above. But in terms of the ideational pillars of the postcolonial world as seen from the outside, an alternative to the state as such is unthinkable (and, wherever it is vocal enough, could invite violent suppression). Note, for instance, the low repute in diplomatic circles of the demands of Muslim movements, from Algeria to Malaysia, to establish various versions of "theocracies" within or across borders built to accommodate "nationalities." The avowedly cavalier approach of such movements to the very notion of the nation-state, like the internationalist slogans of socialism in its heyday, induces much fear precisely because such calls explicitly refuse to acknowledge the nationality principle for which such polities had been built.

But in general the challenge tends to be inaudible, namely, the property of those who had been thought of as the weak and the vanquished in the emergence of the modern state system. Whether the challenge to the idea of the nation-state is conducted according to local (for example, "tribal") or cosmopolitan (such as Islamic) frames, its practical translation would entail a fundamental subversion of a standard set of rules born out of a prior exposure to exogenous models of governance, models that radiated from powerful centers of world politics. How far the challenge succeeds depends on its connection to the deepest roots of the modern system, roots that had various claims to civilizational linkages. Those roots, in turn, are significant for authenticating transformations in governmentality; in order for processes of emulation resulting in the state system to appear to be the result of a world historical mission, rather than simply an outgrowth of a pure question of power, the emulation had to be clothed in the more serene mantle of a civilizational program.

As the old world was gearing toward self-destruction in the great wars, theories of civilization were supplied in relative abundance. In the late 1920s, in the aftermath of World War I and amid the rise of fascism in Europe, Sigmund Freud offered a thoroughly pessimistic assessment of human nature in *Civilization and Its Discontents,* echoing thereby a widely felt disillusionment with the rationalizing promise of modernity. That view was also adopted by Norbert Elias and by cultural pessimists elsewhere on the Continent; it asserted that no society could survive without rechanneling individual drives or regulating individual behavior. It must be kept in mind that even then the appraisal was far from original, although casting it in psychological principles certainly was. The theory of primordial parricide, first outlined in *Totem and Taboo,* offered Freud a way to trace the genesis of sociability in the *recognition* of violent drives: The band of brothers discover their collective power through their murder of their father. In other words, they discover that as a "society" they could transcend the power and authority of the patriarch. This violent liberation from the tyranny of the father introduces a chilling fact that subsequently becomes the basis of civilization: Without maintaining the murderous collective into perpetuity, the culprits of which it consists cannot protect themselves against a reenactment of their brethrens' already demonstrated capacity for boundless transgression.

Working within a tradition completely different from psychoanalysis, Max Weber came to identify the legitimacy of the state itself not only with the capacity for a higher degree of violence but also with a monopoly over its exercise toward or on behalf of its constituency. The state, according to this view, exercises violence not for its own sake as an element extraneous to society but on the behalf of and for the benefit of its members. For Weber the legitimacy of the state is premised on the acceptance of this principle by constituents. Maneuvering between those two positions, Jürgen Habermas argues in an early work that when "private people" consent to public violence exercised on their behalf, they regard themselves as "owners" *(Eigentümer)* of that violence, even though they do not exercise it themselves.[93] Legitimation, in this sense, is evidenced in the willingness to give over to a trustee of a collective what must otherwise be regarded as one's property. Such a voluntary transfer is an articulation of Hegel's concept of "trust," whereby the state is understood as an embodiment and container of one's interests, indeed, as a teleological culmination of a historic effort to embody the spirit of a collective in a singular instance.

In a grand synthesis of the views on civilization of Hegel, Weber, and

Freud, Norbert Elias argues that with the coming into being of a more or less stable monopoly over the right to exercise physical violence, other sociocultural dynamics begin to cultivate a sense of civil order in collective life. Such dynamics result from and accentuate individuals' interdependencies, which manifest themselves in a more elaborate division of labor, more intermediary chains of interaction, and greater functional reciprocity across society. The sum total of such realities, together with the entrustment to the state of a monopoly over violence, protects one from *sudden* accidents and outbreaks of lawlessness and forces one to hold spontaneity in check, to impose self-controls, and to live not for the day but with an eye to the future and to the consequences of one's actions. Conscience, reason, and superego are for Elias various names for this growing proclivity toward self-control. In spite of the normative undertones of Elias's outline, what is most interesting in it is this unification (attempted around the same time by the sociologist Talcott Parsons at a very abstract and even more normative level) of cultural *and* institutional spheres under the assumption that both belong to the same story of civilizational evolution.

Parallel to that tradition of thought, which described an evolutionary civilizational trajectory, we can detect a different tradition of structural theories that described state behavior at any epoch in terms of an eternal repetition of a very old story. In this tradition the rise and fall of states is usually described in terms of recurrent transhistorical dynamics rather than in terms of a perpetual evolution through which civilizational ideas unfold as history turns its pages. S. N. Eisenstadt argues that a state's collapse does not indicate social (or for that matter civilizational) disintegration as much as a continual redrawing of the boundaries of social organization.[94] George Cowgill extends the argument more concretely by delineating two main troubles that states confront (and which one can argue tend to recur with every growth of "civilization" as described above): (1) The first trouble facing the state is acquiring income, especially for its maintenance and expansion. This acquisition is hampered by the recurrent resistance and avoidance of powerful forces or elites, the relative enrichment of peripheral or intermediate centers within the state's domain at the expense of the overall center, and the declining productivity over time of activities that generate taxed incomes. (2) The second trouble consists of the increasing costs of doing what is expected of the state. This is often the case when the state is challenged by powerful outsiders, when it is called upon to do more to offset social and environmental problems, or when it suffers from destabilizing increases in population, increased expectations in general, and associated increases in the cost of bureaucracy and governability.[95] Such perennial troubles are largely internal, but in some way they are implicated in externally imposed conditions, since these too influence what the state can afford to do within its claimed domain of sovereignty. Indeed, one can argue that one of the most pronounced effects of globalization today is the enhancement of the organic link between internal and external causes of state decomposition, to such an extent that the two can hardly be discussed apart—as is still customary in some circles in international relations.

The causes of state decline just summarized have only been aggravated by processes of contemporary globalization, as was discussed earlier and as will be further elaborated in the next chapter. In the case of many postcolonial polities, one must add to those causes a severe crisis of legitimacy, engendered by the loss of even the facade of self-reliance. Created largely through arbitrary colonial borders and denied the capacity to unleash the equivalent of the historical transformations that have otherwise given their mentors their independent stature in the world, such polities remained structurally incapable of finding credible discourses expressing their embodiment of their constituents' interests. The many military takeovers are symptoms of this crisis. Their frequency and tenacity must be regarded as signs of the *lack* of an entrenched or recognized culture of governance within the affected polity or, alternatively, as signs of the polity's *saturation* with an unintegrated polyphony of identities, each having underwritten something akin to the old realm's idea of small-scale but essential distinction. Of course, military takeovers are necessary consequences of such a state of affairs only to the extent that the state is expected to rule actively in the realm of everyday life, to transform society, and to extend meaningful authority beyond the capital city. Thus, ironically, the current and still uncertain "wave" of democratization in states formerly ruled by military oligarchies, notably in Africa and Latin America, may be related to the *decline* in the meaning and acknowledged capacity of the state.

The world system may have required strong states (imperialist at the core of the system and coercive at its periphery) at some point, but the same system today seems to require weaker ones. Janet Abu-Lughod observes that the world system does not rise and fall in the same way as states or civilizations do, since it rises with increasing global connections and declines with the decline of such connections.[96] It must be kept in mind that expansive empires were usually "strong" along the main trade routes, but they were much less visible or consequential at the local level. In India a succession of powerful empires could not alter the ancient village rule system *(panchayat)*, which survived the stormy fates of mightier and more cosmopolitan rulers, some of whom (for example, the British) were apparently unaware of its continued existence.[97] The same can essentially be said of the old informal governance system in Albanian villages, which moved underground after its prohibition only to resurface recently. Even in its clandestine form the Albanian system continued to regulate everyday common concerns, ranging from the use of telephones in the village to harvest rules, and it included non-state-oriented regulations of mutual aid, of which the central government of Enver Hoxha was naturally wary.

Transforming the inside of the national household can thus be considered a "success" to the extent that governance succeeds in penetrating society, so that the legitimacy hitherto conferred upon other forms of association is transferred to it. However, the cases just outlined suggest that in many quarters of this world, the tremendous effort to transform the nature and scope of sovereignty in order for governance to fit a global model of legitimacy has succeeded only in transforming the *facade* of the sovereignty. While some parochial or substate systems, such as those of the Indian or Albanian village, may be long enduring, they do not necessarily constitute an unalterable norm. There is no reason for them not to persist as long as grander political systems fall short of replacing the range of lifespan and everyday concerns covered by their practical, traditional, yet pastoral wisdom. Modernity and developmentalist logic, however, have posed a fundamental challenge to systems so resonant of the old, self-enclosed realm. They must either surrender to the modernist model outright or else live for a little longer under siege by an encroaching world, which will in due time become the center of gravity of all localisms.[98] Where local self-reference is lost, its memory may yet survive through a variety of narratives. Some of those narratives simply nourish the tragic part of the soul, recording that once upon a time someone persisted but was eventually claimed by large systems. Others offer the imagination new ways to humanize existence in a large world. Neither of these stories is over.

Chapter 2

The New Imperialism:
Six Theses

Since the inception of modernity the phenomena of global power collectively known as "imperialism" have been seen largely as outcomes of grand economic logics and interests. As such, imperialism signified the extension into the realm of global politics of what had gradually become a defining feature of modern governance: that is, governance as custody over a new sense of national communion, formed by the integration of economic questions into the heart of politics and culture. Modern states, including those with little capacity for imperial extension, had until this moment derived both legitimacy and purpose from furthering large economic interests overseas, and from successfully harmonizing the relation of such large interests with smaller economic interests domestically.

Some commentators, like Foucault, argue that the process of absorbing the economic into the political began in the sixteenth century, a period in which "the essential issue in the establishment of the art of government [was the] introduction of economy into political practice."[1] From the time of Xenophon until that point, the term "economy" itself had connoted little more than practical extrapolations from household relations, and as such it had scarcely any political implications. The rise of the economic as the pillar of the political can be seen to be connected to the rise of a new philosophical paradigm that occasioned the genesis of modern capitalism. Albert Hirschman identified it in the move from the paradigm of "passions" to that of "interests." While Adam Smith is generally credited with elucidating the connection between pursuit of interests and general happiness, earlier commentators, such as Montesquieu and James Steuart, went as far as asserting that only the pursuit of interests could impose checks on despotism.[2] That shift from heroic pursuits to a pursuit of interests did not simply occasion the rise of the bourgeoisie and the decline of aristocracy. More pertinently, it foreshadowed the incorporation of economy as a regular, negotiable part of the science of governability and, further, the consignment to economy itself of the task of making governmentality follow regular and predictable paths of action.[3] From that point on, answerable to a demand from here and a demand from there, the refashioned *corpus mysticum* assumed one clear purpose, formed by an avowed primary concern with the question of earthly, material interests. If it failed, it could be forgiven if it promised to continue trying; functionaries may be replaced, but the pursuit of economic interests, which largely defined the expressed parameters of social action and mobilization, could not be displaced from the heart of politics—until today.

The saturation of the *modern* state with the question of economy was originally shaped by the capitalist ethos as the notion of "interests" required more systematic elaboration.[4] This infusion with the capitalist ethos provided an especially potent combination with politics during times of colonial empire building. The incorporation of capitalism into political programs on first a national and then a world scale, it must be kept in mind, was not a product of a straightforward unfolding of historical inevitability. The role of the state varied from one situation to another. In U.S. history, for example, the Civil War is frequently credited with providing the building blocks of modern, expansive capitalism, namely, by protecting the interests of the industrial North, by making available to capitalist enterprises all the hitherto inaccessible reservoirs of wage labor, by justifying a subsequent role for a strengthened federal government in building the infrastructure of capitalism, and by allowing further capitalist territorial expansion into the West.[5]

In all cases, it seems that the territorial expansion of governmentality laid down foundations for the consolidation and further expansion of capitalism (for example, the earlier consolidation of England itself as a "national market"). Yet more careful attention would reveal that the emergence of this communion was an outcome of experimental processes in which originally different models presented themselves. To illustrate the point, we may contrast two basic models of colonial expansion: British and Dutch on the one hand, and Spanish and Portuguese on the other. In the first model, the company went first and the state followed; in the second model, the trajectory proceeded in the opposite direction. In the first model, a union of interests was forged or conceived between a political order at home and capitalist adventurers in the wider world (a process also evident in the expansion to the U.S. West). In the second model, governance itself claimed a monopoly over extraction, so that the representation of capitalist interests through it, though at times substantial, could only appear as an accidental or secondary appendage to the power of the state rather than as its indelible defining feature. In political theory, the genesis of this split trajectory is already evident in the works of Machiavelli, who may be seen to have articulated a uniquely middle perspective between them. The *interests* of the prince, around which the science of governmentality is constructed, require a delicate balance between building resources of empowerment that remain sufficiently unique to the prince, and, in measured doses, satisfying the interests of those new forces among elites and "the people" whom he must appease.

It is perhaps no accident that Iberian imperialism, characterized as it was by the centrality of politically controlled extraction, eventually gave way to Western European imperialism, in which the political acted on behalf of capitalism rather than being itself the locus of capital accumulation. The Iberian model displayed the dynamic propensity of all kinds of imperialism for overextension, a propensity that ultimately undermined Western European imperialism itself when the latter began to copy elements of the old Iberian model with unreflective vigor after 1884. In the Iberian case, the state's centrality to extraction required an expensive extension of direct control over large continental tracts distant from the imperial center. By contrast, *early* Western European imperialism garnered great profit by confining itself to small, easily controllable, and strategically situated enclaves.[6] It is a testimony to the exceptional productivity of such enclaves that they were the last imperial possessions to be surrendered; many have been in imperial possession until very recently. If we look at the Americas—where the story began—to compare the early fate of those two types of imperialism, we readily discern the pattern: Large and well-populated colonies were the first to be lost, both by the Iberian powers in the south and the British empire in the north.[7]

Ultimately, until recently the first model provided the prototype of the political as a form of tutelage, domestically and internationally, over a broad range of economic interests. The nature of that union was abundantly clear by Marx's time, when it seemed apparent that the entire logic of history was anchored upon the harmonious synchronization of the wheels of economy and politics and that the ideas of the ruling classes were the ruling ideas, in the same way that their interests were the ruling interests. That thesis presumed that throughout history (and not just in modernity) the connection between governance and the welfare of specific groups or classes defined the *essence* of governance. However, it can be countered that this symbiosis between governance and specific economic interests is contingent and that that contingency reveals itself the more the system experiences the onset of any of the following three conditions: (1) fiscal bankruptcy of the state, making the state less and less able to afford expensive tasks; this is especially the case when the demands upon the state expose it to an increasing spiral of financial obligations;[8] (2) consolidation of the power and legitimacy of the *purely political* in the system, so that the political, rather than deriving legitimacy by acting on behalf of specific interests, becomes more confident of its continued existence regardless of its abrogation of obligations that only yesterday had seemed fundamental; and (3) the collapse of any ideological alternatives to the system, a phenomenon that no one alive today can fail to discern as a prevalent attitude (which is different from saying that one must necessarily accept it as unalterable fate). All three conditions have of course been operative with various degrees of intensity for some time now. It is not that they lead to a "weakening" of the system, which bankruptcy suggests, or to a "strengthening" of it, as suggested by its increasingly self-referential legitimacy. In terms of outcome, the convergence of the three conditions in recent history has enhanced the *autonomy* of the political from other spheres of social life—including culture and economy—as will be explored shortly.

One of the central dilemmas of our age will continue to be precisely the danger inherent in the autonomy of power detached from fields of rationality exterior to it. (I am not arguing that economic logics or cultural patterns necessarily provide "better" rationalities, merely that a world typified by a disjunction among rationalities poses unexplored problems. My focus concerns only one such problem, namely, that inherent in the new dynamics of power.) With this kind of autonomy, power can be unleashed unexpectedly and in order to attain purely symbolic aims. When capitalism was more wedded to specific policies and governmental strategies, and even in the instances where it led to imperialist adventures, the general course of power exercise and its aim were to some extent predictable in light of the rational cosmos advising the imperial state. Thus there existed some rules that allowed those subject to such power to negotiate it, and opponents were thereby provided with mechanisms by which they could adjust to or even belong to the global domain ruled and regulated by this kind of power. Under modernity, imperial power has been a global game with bases in some *economic* discourse possessing universal potential.[9] The final victory of capitalism everywhere means among other things not only that the capitalist state has also lost its mission and meaning but also that we are left with a far more threatening spectacle than capitalism could ever have provided on its own as a purely economic system. If one accepts that the state was the ammunition of some economically based ideology in a global battlefield, then it must also be accepted that what is left, now that the battle has been fought and is over, are empty cannon shells everywhere. The menace of the state after the end of this war stems precisely from its unpredictability, now that it is devoid of all ideological grounding. Its *raisons d'état* are once more its raison d'être. This time around, however, history is repeating itself with all the trappings of tragedy: In its long journey back to where it came from, the state has also managed to accumulate much more instrumental power over society.

Furthermore, one can detect three emergent sociocultural and economic megatrends, in which this development is implicated: (1) There has been a decline in the meaningfulness of what can be called "measurements of social totality" (evident in, among other things, the disjunction between GNP, or aggregate social wealth, and cross-class feelings of economic security and well-being[10] or in the displacement of unifying cultural symbols by multicultural claims emphasizing essential difference).[11] (2) "Intelligent" governance based on knowledge of the world in which governance is doomed to operate has become increasingly impossible or impracticable, especially on a global scale. (3) A triumphant, global capitalism has become increasingly disjoined from all systems of governance, including those systems that had supported its globalization. It is this last development that I would like to focus on in what follows, for it is both fundamentally detrimental and also circumnavigable within the scope of an essay.

How Imperialism Lives On When It Has No Purpose

One of the basic problems with much of the contemporary critique of globalization, both from the Left and Right, is their single-minded focus on its rapacious economic aspects. The solutions offered are thus little more than warmed-up versions of statist regulation and concomitant calls for *strengthening* the state. It is surprising how much the world can change, while some remain faithful to their old habits. Given the threat of a new form of *purely political* imperialism, globalization mandates far more vigilance to the ideological underpinnings of global politics than has hitherto been usual. It is not as though economic globalization offers no new challenges or problems. But for now, it is perhaps more pressing to contest and be attentive to new deployments of power rather than to familiar deployments of capital. For capital, as Marx himself observed, always seeks to burst out of its political fetters, and thus today it is doing no more than that which is in its nature. But with respect to global power, one can detect the emergence of a new form of imperialism, an imperialism less attached to economic or other material interests than the traditional theory of imperialism had supposed. As such, the new imperialism is less predictable than the old imperialism. Power, rather than specific material interests of social groups or classes, justifies sui generis the institution wielding it, thereby marking the face of the world with a new form of unanchored totalitarianism.

Of course, imperialism can be approached as *one* of the manifestations of globalization. Imperialism has always been defined with respect to differential power relations among systems of governance and in terms of a more covert mode of economic and political domination. In addition, it has also been defined as organized cultural hegemony. Globalization, on the other hand, is a broader concept. Elements of power, hegemony, and domination are indeed part of its story, but so are voluntaristic associations, codependencies, religious and other cultural affiliations, and trade and other economic venues. Unlike globalization, imperialism is exclusively definable by the primary attentiveness to and regularized exploitation of the power differentials that could exist in any of these venues.

Whereas the traditional theory of imperialism presumed a continuity of interests between political and economic centers of power, the logic of globalization today is introducing a fundamental divorce between the logics of global politics and those of global economy. The fact that global economy and transnational corporations of all kind transcend the parochial limits of the modern state does not necessarily mean that the state will wither away for lack of purpose. Rather, the state—especially a state with a "glorious" modern history—reinvents its purpose, but in an erratic fashion and without recourse to systemic worldviews.

This disjunction results precisely from the triumph of capitalism, a triumph that means in the first place that because it is a global norm for which there are no credible alternatives on the same scale, capitalism no longer needs the support and tutelage of an imperialist state. Of course, we have to distinguish among various states depending on the variable capacity for imperial extension. Those with global imperial capacity, most notably, the United States, tend to exhibit most closely the structures of action described below. Elsewhere, where governments have generally reduced the scale of their socioeconomic responsibilities and their claims for loyalty, one sees the disjunction of politics from all other spheres of life expressing itself in the increasingly symbolic nature of politics, as will be discussed at a later point. Where governing orders have appealed to xenophobic nationalism, as in the Balkans, the dearth of resources available has compelled local imperialism to restrict its target to specifiable communities. By contrast, the peculiar nature of the U.S. polity in the modern world is tied most clearly to the diffuse *globality* of its reach, claim, and power. This globality, in turn, renders it impossible for it to specify a set of adversaries in a way that an ancillary rational cosmos—for example, capitalism—would have been able to identify with any strategic or ideological clarity in times like those just past. In what follows, I will outline six basic and fundamental areas of disjunction between traditional and passing imperialist systems—as outlined in the traditional theory of imperialism—and the emerging logics of power deployment today.

I. Coercion and Voluntarism

The early takeover of coercive responsibilities from chartered companies (in India, Southeast Asia, Congo, and elsewhere) by the imperial systems of their mother countries signified among other things the degree to which modern capitalism required a historically uncharacteristic input of *coercion* for its global propagation. This can be compared to medieval world systems, which, though of vast geographic and demographic spread, were characterized by their participants' lack of need or capacity to control each other.[12] The historical minimalism of coercive structure imposed upon global economies is also evident in ancient global routes, such as the trans-Saharan or the Asian routes that linked various regions and societies. These routes were not products of imperialism—even though merchants usually benefited whenever centralized political control was placed upon them, such as under the Mongols or, earlier, the Romans. Those same merchants, however, had reason to fear too much political control. In the late 1500s, for example, wealthy Moroccan merchants who participated in the gold-salt trade of the Sahara to their south refused to finance the military campaign to their trade regions by their dynast precisely because they feared that his success would result in more of the trade income being transferred away from them and directly into the pocket of the political center.[13] Indeed, unlike in the modern era, imperial control over trade routes was not a sole or even necessary prerequisite for founding such routes. Rather, imperial control usually followed the establishment of such routes through various prosaic and voluntary schemes.[14] In general, participants in historical world systems remained politically independent of each other, until the encroachment of the imperialism of the modern period. That imperialism essentially entailed forcible conquest, whereby world regions would be captured directly and incorporated into the world system *on the conqueror's terms.* Those captured were not necessarily regions that would have invariably failed to join the system. Rather, conquest foreclosed their option to negotiate their own terms of relation to the world system.

Thus under traditional imperialism, as we have known it from the colonial period until the 1980s, political domination was one of the important and conscious means of economically incorporating tributary regions into world systems. Under contemporary transnationalism, however, coercive force is scarcely needed for the incorporation of regions into world systems; the whole world is already incorporated into an interactive economic grid, since embeddedness in a global economic order is sought *voluntarily.* Even amid the recent outbreak of turmoil in global financial markets, only one country (Malaysia) has opted to isolate itself (temporarily) from the global market. In earlier times half of the world would have done so, as during the Great Depression. The common response now to global financial uncertainty is for countries to delve *deeper* into the global economy, to accept currency devaluation, or to link one's currency to more stable ones elsewhere. Under such conditions, political control is needed only for bare-bones system maintenance, since it is expected that a global economic system is (1) either capable of functioning on its own with minimal political support, (2) requires a diminished state role in order to operate properly, or (3) is just too complex for any global-level political adoption of it to be effective. In sum, whereas the old imperialism invoked the necessity of political domination for the expansion and maintenance of an economic system, globalization today structures the economic system so that it functions via its own internal capacity, without the necessity of political support. Transnationalism, in other words, describes a form of capitalism that has *outgrown* imperialism.

Some commentators argue that global capital continues to need certain governmental protections, especially for guaranteeing financial assets, property rights, and contracts.[15] But this role, it must be kept in mind, no longer mandates planning for the eventuality of imperial adventures. In other words, while capital may still need the coercive muscle of the state for the minimal task of safeguarding property and financial assets, it no longer needs imperial conquests. The increasing distance between capital and the state thus results from the fewer coercive needs of the mercurial financial capital, the preeminent form of global capital today,[16] especially in comparison to the old needs of production capital.[17] Compared to the old production capital, financial capital today is far less wedded to location. But even for production capital, location has become less significant: It has learned to parcel up the production process across various global sites and has thus acquired not only flexibility in the face of potential turmoil or opposition in one location but general flexibility— of which, it seems, one can never have too much.

II. Hierarchy and Lateralism

Old imperialism invariably involved a hierarchical arrangement of the world system in terms of core and periphery. This hierarchy has traditionally invited or was accompanied and legitimated by a variety of culturalist discourses of diversity and superiority, as well as by developmental and evolutionary sociopolitical logics, which were also implicated in the differential capacities for conquest.

From the point of view of transnational capital today, however, concepts of core and periphery mean little. Like the old *Verlger* who had "one foot in the country and another in the towns,"[18] transnational capital approaches the whole world in terms of comparative opportunities. Indeed, some of the more notorious theories of economic globalization, such as those based on David Ricardo's notion of "comparative advantage," seem to suggest that at least economically the hierarchy of core and periphery can be naturally balanced out or even reversed in the due course of time. The merit of that or similar theories is not the point here. The point is, rather, that from the point of view of capital accumulation, investment, extraction, and profit making, a *hierarchical* organization of regions and countries no longer serves a clear strategic purpose. While there are clearly both wandering hunters and unassuming game on the global economic scene, as a process globalization consists of approaching different regions in a lateral rather than a hierarchical manner. Imperialism, by contrast, has traditionally wedded systemic economic expansion to the imperative of global political hierarchies.

The lateral organization of capital was first suggested in the seminal work of Scott Lash and John Urry, though they seem to have drawn the wrong conclusion from it. Far from signifying "disorganization," the preponderance of lateral subsidiaries and sites signifies that contemporary global capital has a much higher level of rational *organization* than had been previously available to it. Indeed, the lateral view of the world marks the emergence of the global company as a more meaningful signifier of totality than the customary and increasingly polyphonic and irresponsible national polities. Thus, from the point of view of the company, one of the remaining functions of the custodians of political systems is to acknowledge the expansive nature of the company and thus to act in such a way as to make it possible for the company to assume a transnational and transpolitical character. To the extent that they can be of any further use from the point of view of the company, political custodians should thus invest their energy in fighting for and enshrining global trade agreements against all opposition. When the world is finally its stage, the company operates and builds alliances according to a *more coherent and limited* set of principles than those confronting the nation-state. The latter, which no longer knows what to do with itself, does not confront meaningful and easily summarizable totalities like those confronting the global company. Rather, it confronts a myriad of ideational leftovers from a bygone era—contested cultural meanings, imagined historical mythologies, the clutter and noise of "obligations"—to which it finds itself responding in an increasingly ad hoc and unrehearsed fashion.

Furthermore, the strategic coherence of capital confronts the logical fragmentations of the political in the latter's own playground. Cities and regions within "nations," abandoned or called upon to fend for themselves by the federal center, are forced into playing their own separate games with capital. One of the ironies of the enhancement of federal control, power, and public responsibilities, which had been essential since the nineteenth century for the construction of the infrastructure of a capital-oriented society (building transportation networks, providing metropolitan services, ensuring stable currency, enforcing foreign loan repayments, extending protectionism to nascent industries), is that it actually shielded regions from the specter of financial insolvency while periodically exposing the center to large deficits. In recent times the rhetoric of the devolution of "power" from the federal government to states in the United States follows on the heels of this story, as states generally continued to enjoy budget surpluses at the same time that the federal center became swamped with debt.[19]

Such devolutions only enhance capital's capacity to negotiate various terms with competing regions. It is a world that fits the logic of capital's increasingly lateral approach to the world. Within highly advanced countries, the regions, provinces, states, and cities now actively compete with each other to lure various international enterprises, which therefore enjoy an enormous advantage in negotiating good terms. In this new grid, "global cities" are increasingly more connected to each other than to their hinterlands as they become the favored sites of highly competitive enterprises. Among commentators on globalization, references to new, deterritorialized "geographies of power" have become common currency. They are generally implicated in capital's ability to provide for itself through increasingly complicated schemes that transcend territorial boundaries of parochial sovereignties. For the company, the new geography is not the old political map of the world but an array of such transborder associations and techniques as offshoring, electronic-space transactions, international arbitration centers, and international bond-rating agencies.[20]

The fact that the transnational corporation—unlike political orders—has little use for the hierarchical segmentations of the world system, is evident in the configuration of the transnational corporations, whose "index of transnationality" has been rising continuously in modern times.[21] Financial capital in particular, because of its fast-paced nature greatly enhanced by new communication technologies, shows that it is more attentive to the healthy functioning of the network of its own globally connected communities[22] than to any vision of global hierarchy premised in parochial political power. The latter remains the domain of the state, which has little connection to or incentive to learn from the logic of financial capital as it operates today. Of course, it may be argued that hegemonic advantage accrues to corporations that benefit from a home country's ability to globalize its business law, manufacturing standards, or accounting norms (consider, for example, the globalization of U.S. standards in these areas). Yet even this last service to the corporation by the national center may not be all that crucial for its prospects, since corporations, and especially those that are truly transnational, have by definition learned to adjust and do business with remarkable flexibility in a variety of world contexts, and even to benefit whenever possible from the diversity of standards and practices in the world—a diversity that smaller competitors may not be as capable of adjusting to as resourceful, large predators.

III. General and Special Interests

The traditional theory of imperialism was in many ways persuasive because it made imperialist behavior predictable. The old-fashioned predictability of imperialism stemmed from a clear strategic vision fed by a
totalistic conceptual outlook. Under old imperialism, an expansive economic ideology blended harmoniously with and informed grand political
behavior in the larger world. Thus a General Motors executive, who in
the early 1950s also occupied a U.S. cabinet position, could at a very famous moment state that what was good for General Motors was good
for the United States. His statement was so memorable precisely because
it forthrightly articulated the strategic, total, and consistent vision of
traditional imperialist ideology at its height.

The assertion that what was good for the company was "self-evidently"
good for the country cannot be understood in terms of simple rhetoric,
nor can it be seen as an expression of unthinking malice. It is part and
parcel of the logic of recurrent times, when custodians of political systems
seek to perpetuate feelings of common national purpose, feelings that
would have been inculcated in some euphoric experience (such as a "great
moral war"). In such a context, the company was by no means the only
source volunteering a formula of general purpose, clustering around its
own interests. Parallel to that statement, we also see extra-economic efforts to ensure continued unity of purpose, most evident in the same era
in the United States by the McCarthyist witch-hunt. For McCarthy, the
enemies of the system were pariahs to both the system's economic logic
and its principle of citizenship (that is, Communist *and* un-American).

While not exactly similar, the invocations of commonality of interest
in both cases to which I just alluded pertain to specific eras when an imperial system sought to entrench its foundations. Once it has succeeded
it no longer needs such ideological supports and can indeed show signs
of liberalism and tolerance, that is, precisely when such gestures of openness have no obvious consequences detrimental to the survival of the system. Of course, this search for a clear definition of general interest is part
of the logic of modern governability, not necessarily just of imperialism.
Hegel had already noted that it is indeed part of the dialectics of institutional life to ensure into perpetuity the accidental convergence of interests that would otherwise diffuse back into their own particularity.[23] He
did not note, however, that after its introduction, "common purpose" can
only devolve into a myth that, no matter how beautiful, will eventually

wither away as particular interests resume their own separate journeys into the larger world, a world beyond the grasp or comprehension of the institution into which they are supposedly organically fused.

Beginning with Bismarck in Germany and culminating in the New Deal in the United States, that obvious truth was vigorously contested by states eager to show that they could indeed act in the interests of downtrodden classes at the same time that they could make the world safe for the trials and tribulations of capital. Amid the romantic serenity of the rebuilt world of the 1950s, T. H. Marshall attained immense acclaim when he argued that the idea of citizenship involved social and not simply civil and political components. Here, the *modern* citizen could expect material rewards bestowed by authority, and such rewards were incumbent upon the very definition of the individual as citizen.

Ideas such as these usually represent the horizons of their times. Marshall's idea was as much hailed in his time as it is derided today. While the structural adjustment plans of the International Monetary Fund (IMF) have effectively prevented many Third World governments from placing such a model of citizenship into practice, First World governments could adduce no equivalent stewardship restrictions as they looked for ways and justifications to dispense with the weight of having to cater to more social interests than they could bear. It is no accident that in the United States, where the idea of social citizenship has historically had the lowest regard in the Western world, the "citizen" is being promoted as a perennially self-reliant, hard-working, low-cost patriot. Such a citizen does indeed have "rights," but they are carefully distinguished from "entitlements," since "rights" are more likely to cease their solemn advance when they reach the government's purse. The retrenchment of the range of economic interests serviced by the state has taken place in the context of streamlining governmental budgets so that they could be brought into line for the purpose of promoting "competitiveness" or politico-economic integration. Kennedy's "Ask not what your country can do for you . . ." finally rules unabashedly. Ask not what your country can do for you, not just because it is unbecoming of the definition of citizenship to do so. In an age doubly haunted by globalization and budget deficits,[24] with each of the two monsters demanding the sacrifice of the other, your country has made its choice: It has decided it can do nothing for you.

The ideological ramifications of this move thus consist of once again decoupling the political and the economic. Political authorities may still act on behalf of specific interests—and today those tend to be the interests oriented toward open markets everywhere. Domestic politics therefore no longer designates an isolated field of sovereignty that can reliably shield the citizen from the impact of inexorable global forces. Devoid from instrumental connection to action, politics today becomes more than ever an obscene game of vanity. Those who win offices frequently advance slogans without having any practical resources to implement them, and are replaced only when the tired electorate savors the faint smell of difference; Gerhard Schröder, Tony Blair, or Fernando H. Cardoso can do no more than *improve* on their predecessors' adherence to neoliberal orthodoxy. This point is still vigorously contested by some liberal and left Keynesians, who nonetheless can offer no more than hopelessly outmoded, largely exhortative recipes. They ignore the fact that the logic of globalization has made politics into a self-enclosed universe, from which the economy is largely autonomous. The field of politics continues to harbor some capacity to act on behalf of certain major interest groups. But as a whole, it is much less able to credibly display the model of the "covenant"—a slogan raised for its charm and then dropped unceremoniously after the recent successful presidential campaign of a well-known chameleon. Politics today cannot symbolize the mystical harmony of social interests, since global capitalism offers such interests no way to approach it with a unified perspective.

The point is that *large, complex societies consist not so much of "people" as of special interests.* The dialectics of an open world are likely to correct any miscomprehension of this principle in due time. Today, no General Motors official could conceivably state again, with any sense of confidence, what the company may have actually believed in the 1950s. And therefore the problem of rational guidance: Save for their heavy involvement in the political aspects of trade, major global companies have less of an incentive than they had during the Cold War to invest energy in systematically guiding the international behavior of government. What is good for the company now is far more likely to be good for all of its transnational subsidiaries and branches than for a polyphonous and fragmented national entity. The removal of the economic clothes leaves us nothing but the naked body of politics.

Seen from a different angle, such a state of malaise has been alluded to under a variety of resonant rubrics, such as "the end of politics," "the end of ideology," or even "the end of the state." All of these have been in circulation for some time now. The basic contours of the argument regarding "the end of politics" are well known and can be readily summarized. First, in an age of complex global networks through which "interests" of all kinds are exchanged, the idea of solidarity has no natural reference point in territoriality.[25] And it is fundamentally territoriality that has provided the existential basis for the modern expression of nationality and, subsequently, for its embodiment in statehood. More important, however, the internal decline of the state's ability to shield *all* of its constituents from the impact of global forces becomes the ground for the rediscovery that in any complex society, the state can only be either a battleground of various special interests, if it is to be truly pluralist, or little more than a representative of one of those interests against the others, if not.[26] As such, "the end of politics" is certainly not a new thesis. The transnational challenge, however, provides a new meaning for this recently recurring observation. Under conditions in which recognized political entities in the world are increasingly incapable of alleviating domestic anxieties and when nothing they can or are willing to do could found a higher institutional instance to control global capitalism, the only thing left is naked politics, politics for its own sake, as a pure game of power, where power can exist only for itself rather than as a venue for material interests.

While such theories may be overreaching in different directions, in various forms they are symptomatic of the growing attention to the orphan status of politics after capital abandoned its guiding role. In its place, one sees the rise of disparate initiatives as sources of advice to and bases of governmental thinking. These are represented in the ceaseless activity of a mushrooming community of tens of thousands of lobbyists in Washington, the increasing role and indispensability of campaign contributions from all kinds of single-issue political action committees, and the rise of erratic initiatives as the dominant style of political life, all at the expense of bodies representing strategic and integrated styles of thought and outlook.

IV. Hegemony without Logic
The decline of totalistic strategic vision leaves a political scene typified by directionlessness and by illogical and nonsystematic invasions and wars, where it is difficult to discover a common trend or thread other than sheer and unanchored political opportunism. Instead of exercising hegemony for the purpose of influencing specific directions, the imperialism of today has only an irrational attachment to the principle of hegemony.

The irrationality of contemporary hegemony is evident in the lack of any strategic unity in its manifestations, and even more so in the absence of any clear ideological logic for its exercise. Indeed, many policy thinkers have come to openly decry general strategic directionlessness. Some even compared this state of affairs to the logic of contemporary courtship, based as it is on instant gratification with no commitment.[27]

However, though a term like "hollow hegemony," employed by the system apologist Fareed Zakaria, may describe perfectly the kind of power amassed and exercised without clear, long-term strategy, it does not describe how the objects of such hegemony are chosen. The fact that the collapse of the earlier, total ideological vision renders the world conceptually inaccessible means that only what is known about the self can serve as a guide for ascertaining the intentions and character of others. Thus, in a classic case of Freudian projection, the very irrationality of this nascent imperialism evidences itself in the innate and irreducible irrationality it ascribes to its imagined, mysterious, and globally ubiquitous adversaries ("rogue nations," mad "terrorists," faceless "fanatics").[28] Compare this messy, unfocused paranoia to the more orderly designations of the Cold War, where paranoia could at least be tamed by the system's rational capacity to assume a rational cosmos governed the behavior of the adversary, and thus that the adversary's behavior could be modeled, albeit with mixed results. The new adversaries, by contrast, are typified by total unpredictability and possess a mysterious capacity or desire to strike at random, anywhere.

When did this descent to illogic begin? If a date and place is to be assigned for the last clear exercise of the logic of old imperialism, it is possible to locate it around the overthrow of Salvador Allende in Chile in 1973, when Kissinger acknowledged that capitalist interests were the prime reason the CIA supported the military in their takeover. That event can perhaps be regarded as one of the last manifestations of a close coordination between political and economic logics.[29] More recent imperial ventures, notably the second Gulf War, in 1991, or the Kosovo war, seem to flow from the logic of the new imperialism. In the former case in particular, the protagonist was not especially opposed to capitalism as a system or even as a set of concrete interests, which were always negotiable without a war. Furthermore, the defeat of Iraq was not followed by the customary capitalist rapprochement (as had happened, for example, in Europe and Japan after World War II), whereby the devastated country would be either opened up to be rebuilt at great profit by corporations based in the victorious country or allowed to develop in such a way that it became indissolubly integrated into the global political logic informed by global capitalism and the outlooks associated with it. Rather, the profit-making potential was forsaken for a lengthy embargo in which few benefits accrued to global capital interests in the West. In this case, the more accommodationist policies of countries like France or Russia, which are here at least less wedded to the logic of the new imperialism, resonate better with the logic of global capital. But in the case of the real power in that war, namely, the United States, which represents the apogee of the unconscious irrationality of the new imperialism, the response to the war itself has been characterized by nothing short of sickening intellectual malaise. It is clear now that the war was fought with no rational or strategic planning for its aftermath, in sharp contrast to 1944–1945, when acute intellectual effort (however misguided) was called upon to chart an approach for an ongoing engagement with the enemy *after* the war, an engagement that enlisted both, victor and vanquished, in the *common* camp of one global ideology.

In many respects the recent war in Kosovo illustrates the dynamics and propensities of the new imperialism. At least three catastrophic miscalculations are readily apparent in the NATO strategy: In the first place, the entire campaign was premised on NATO's refusal to consider the alternative strategy of in some way nurturing local resistance to Serbian authority. Rather, its insistence on claiming for itself a monopoly over violence can scarcely be understood apart from its primary attachment to the principle of hegemony (rather than, say, to such moral principles as "human rights," "self-determination," or the like).

In the second place, this attachment to the principle of hegemony was coupled by a paradoxical lack of resolve, masked only by the extensive deployment of warfare technology and now happily forgotten amid the current suspension of hostilities. That is, nowhere in the modern history of warfare do we see a similar example of one side telling the other that it has no intention of using all of its arsenal—in this case, NATO's early and repeatedly expressed decision that no ground troops would be sent in for the purpose of fighting and that the entire war would be waged and won from a distance. The remarkable public stance spelled out more than anything else that the *objectives of the war were not seen to be worthy of any domestic political cost for the imperial center.* In other words, the modus operandi of the new imperialism consists of acquiring those technologies that make its action possible, without regard to any principles that can be contemplated apart from its pure capacity for action.

Under traditional norms of capitalist calculations, pursuit of objectives requires a more integrated assessment of costs and benefits and, to the extent possible, a clearheaded appraisal of the many dimensions, risks, and opportunities attendant on one's actions. The logic of the new imperialism, however, does not have this calculative vantage point. Its wars must be cost-free precisely because they are waged without an integrated vision or moral conviction. Yet they are capable of producing gratification, which can lead to commitment only accidentally, but not as an outcome of integrated strategic thinking.

In the third place, we can detect in this war a classic failure on NATO's part to see clearly by-products of the war that should have been obvious from the start: namely, the catastrophic human devastation, the unexpected length of the war, the destruction of Kosovar society, and for the time being the strengthening of the regime of Slobodan Milosevic. It is hard to see how this failure of vision could have come about unless the entire operation was based on NATO's self-inflated expectation that the enemy, faced with demands it deemed for some reason impossible, would simply surrender without a fight. Capitalism never had such an expectation from its enemies.

As a guide for strategic action, therefore, what remains is the murky notion of "geopolitics," but geopolitics as a referent to pure power, that is, power in its own service rather than as an appendage to an integrative complex of economy, culture, and polity. What we see is the waning of the influence on government by such strategy-minded bodies as the Council on Foreign Relations, which had best exemplified through its history, from World War I to the present, the happy marriage of business and political elites.[30] Whatever else it may have done, the guiding role of capital did provide a rational cosmos for political conduct, surrounding it with limits and purpose. The withdrawal of that rational cosmos today leaves us a form of imperialism that can only be a self-referential system of power.

V. Strength and Weakness of the State

Under traditional imperialism, capitalism throve because of the protective power of a *strong* state. Marxist and left-liberal critics have long noted that, thanks only to governmental intervention in both economic and social life, boom-and-bust cycles failed to bring capitalism down. A further extension of political cover for capitalism was provided in the Cold War, when the battle between capitalism and socialism was waged between political-military entities whose feud was *explicitly* on behalf of economic paradigms and interests. The perennial fiscal crisis of the capitalist state—resulting from having provided twin shields for capitalism, one social (to protect it from its internal enemies) and another military (to protect it from external ones)—was in many ways unavoidable. There was no choice but to operate under the burden of such fiscal crisis, until today.

Under globalization today, by contrast, capitalism thrives because of the *weakening* sovereignty of the state. Global capitalism now requires a less socially overbearing state, a state offering a "competitive," deregulated environment to lure an already secure, globally flexible capital. The state thus opens up its domain of sovereignty through free-trade agreements, which involve an unmistakable acceptance of reduced sovereignty—at least the part of sovereignty that deals with *economic* responsibility. This occasions and often explicitly justifies a global trend in national politics toward removing *one* of the two main historical shields of capitalism, namely, the social shield. Ostensibly, the fiscal crisis should be resolved thereby.

What remains in place, however, is a military "shield" that like Frankenstein has, over the years, become gradually autonomous from its political creator in its thinking and mode of operation. Thus it does not now wither away from lack of purpose; once the monster is here, it can only be redesigned with a different function in mind. Recently a budgetary proposal that elicited an immediate consensus among the policy-making elite in the United States outlined a strategic *increase* in military spending—already by far the highest in the world—in spite of the lack of any clear enemies to justify maintaining even the existing military capacity. A recent military manual, furthermore, begins by noting that "specifics of US future interests are nearly as uncertain as future threats and opportunities." It then proceeds to develop what is therefore described as a "simplified conceptual approach" for use by strategic planners. The scheme is conceptually simplified because "national interests" are likely to be determined on a case-by-case basis rather than according to a rational, ideologically guided, long-term plan. The many recommendations, which generally emphasize the imperative of maintaining an exceptionally lethal military force, include expansions of objectives and definitions of national interest to include efforts against terrorism and international organized crime, various "operations other than war," more-extensive surveillance capabilities, and protection of information. Without apparent irony, the manual asserts the need for such extensions of military dominion *at the same time* that it argues that the world, especially that of the "First Tier" states, will be typified by greater cultural homogeneity, increasing governmental attentiveness to the needs of business, and a *dilution* of national interests, boundaries, and sovereignty.[31]

Thus the old military shield no longer protects a mercurial capitalism that exists everywhere, a capitalism that is furthermore much less vulnerable to ideological threats than in the past. One sees a transformation in the vectors of strength of imperial polities. Whereas the old imperial state was expected to found its strength on both military and economic might and then to employ those strengths in a complementary fashion, it is now expected to be strong militarily but uninvolved economically. Thus one finds a political field increasingly typified by symbolic posturing,[32] since the state is no longer expected to actually offer its constituents any tangible benefits. Richard Armey, one of the most prominent Republican leaders in Congress today, articulated this widely held and influential line of thought with characteristic candor: "Social responsibility is a euphemism for individual irresponsibility." What does this mean? Evidently that governments exists only for the sake of those responsibilities that are *not* social. This may be compared to Kennedy's famous statement ("Ask not what your country can do for you . . ."), which though certainly more memorable, entailed far fewer practical consequences that Armey's edict. The latter, more than three and a half decades after Kennedy, condemns the "entitled" portion of citizenship in equally unambiguous (though mercifully less patriotic) terms. In decoupling the notion of citizenship from any sense of social entitlement, the government does not reference the original author, whose era did not allow the political to be as independent of the social as it can be today.

Global capital's diminishing need for the state, and the state's lack of ability or desire to shield more humble constituents from the unpredictable impact of what may seem to them to be erratic twists of fate brought about by largely autonomous global forces, both leave in place a state structure devoid of much of its grand social purpose. Today totalitarianism no longer consists of incorporating the individual into the body of a grand social machine; it is, rather, exactly the opposite: The machine has become oblivious to all individuals. It continues to work for its own sake, as a purely habitual exercise of self-propelling dominion. It still has all the teeth, all the arsenal and an enormous capacity for mass destruction, but it has no logical plan, guide, metanarrative, or long-term vision for the logical cosmos to which it would wed such inherited resourcefulness.[33]

The weakness of the state in the economy, however, does not relieve it from the fact that socioeconomic demands and grievances will continue to be made. With fewer resources and less will at its disposal, it can either appeal to the spirit of voluntarism or else respond to the trouble symbolically. In order to direct national energies and vision away from troubles it cannot resolve, it may invent adversity, display prowess against others, test bombs, or appeal to national sentiments to support great and largely symbolic causes. Thus, elsewhere in the world one increasingly encounters impossibly parochial slogans that could never be followed to the letter in practice because they contradict the inexorable spirit of globalization. Hobsbawm notes, for instance, that the strong nationalist spirits observed in some Eastern European countries, or even in regions inside Western European polities (Scotland, Lombardy, Flanders, and so on), are ironically coupled with the wish of such "countries" to join the European Union as one of their *first acts of freedom*. They would thus immediately give up any hard-won sovereignty.[34] What this trend indicates is that slogans emphasizing cultural specificity or diversity, which seem on the surface so ubiquitous in our era and which are possible precisely because of the weakness of the state, nonetheless hardly define any essential resistance to the underlying global spirit of the times; but they do illustrate for us how politics has become increasingly symbolic in an age when it can do no more than that.

VI. From Economy to Culture

Under traditional imperialism, and especially from World War I until 1989, nationalist frames of identification were pitted on a global scale against class solidarities. While in theory *capitalism* was sold as an inherently universal system applicable everywhere, *imperialism* in particular required a certain investment in nativism, ideas of cultural difference, evolutionism, developmentalism, and a self-confident sense of national exceptionalism within imperial nations. In contrast, Marxist and socialist thought usually provided an antidote to the notion of essential cultural difference by highlighting class solidarities as *transnational and natural* embodiments of real material interests. Both capitalism and socialism were thus in theory cosmopolitan ideologies. Imperialism, however, throve on the active and systematic manipulation of nativist identities, wherever such a practice yielded the desired results (a practice of which "really existing socialism" was not entirely innocent either, albeit in a far less pronounced fashion).

Today, the scene has once again changed on that score. Under the ethos of globalized culture, the main struggle is alleged to be between cosmopolitan and nativist forces, albeit in a new kind of way in which neither class nor nationalism prefigure prominently. The alleged struggle, at least according to Benjamin Barber's highly popularized thesis, is between the forces of "McWorld" and "Jihad."[35] Both are deemed to be general attitudes vis-à-vis globalization. McWorld represents outward-looking, global mass culture unified by consumerist optimism and common icons and facades of fashion, music, and the like. And Jihad epitomizes reversion to local traditions and local history and a determined resistance to globalism on culturalist rather than economic ground.

While both are ill-chosen metaphors loaded with banal culturalist assumptions, both "McWorld" and "Jihad" can be seen as products of modernity. Much of the distinction between the two models is indeed haphazard, ignoring the fact that, far from fanatically resisting global modernity, the rhetoric of many of the movements identified with the Jihad trajectory is in fact formed by suggestions to link up to it. Area specialists have long noted that "nativist" revivals, including the "jihad" variety, are peculiarly peppered with modernist slogans, emphasizing *tradition as a way to achieve* modernization, progress, industrialization, and democratic mass participation rather than tradition as a simple veneration of the past. Proponents of Barber's distinction tend to simply ignore the fact that even the most retrograde force of tradition-bound fanaticism in the world, represented best in the Saudi royal family, has also been more than hospitable not only to an impressive level of economic modernization but also to imperialist penetration of the worst kind. That system can scarcely be said to be "closed" to the world—it is closed only to the extent that the imperial arrangement warrants necessary for the survival of a regime, a regime that in fact represents a disfiguration of rather than a continuity with a whole array of earlier, more voluntaristic traditions of trade and governance.[36]

Thus one can say that the distinction between so-called nativist and cosmopolitan outlooks is only skin-deep, as it is inconsequential insofar as the globalization of modernity is concerned. The distinction is highlighted now primarily from the perspective of the *new* imperialism, which is determined to crush (albeit with characteristic inconsistency) what it has already constructed as Jihad world. This perspective is most pronounced in the United States, where the logic of the new imperialism exercises an unchallenged reign, although one finds it in milder forms in Western Europe. The difference is significant, especially because the rigidity of perspective seems inversely related to the degree to which various societies have surrendered sovereignty for the sake of regional integration. While the rhetoric of a fundamentally distinct Western culture also prevails in Western Europe, the difference stems from something other than a more enlightened and educated public sphere. It also stems from the fact that in an age of regional integration, national culture, while cherished, is no longer seen to be so distinct as to foreclose integration. While there is no society without "rules of exclusion," as Foucault reminds us, the very proclivity to give up old habits of solidarity also incubates a view of the world as variegated, changeable, and depolarizable in essence.[37] Furthermore, from the perspective of global capital, the struggle between such caricatures as Jihad and McWorld makes little sense. More than imperial state functionaries, capitalists everywhere know that once in power, adherents of nativist ideologies have traditionally proven themselves to be just as eager to play the global economic game of foreign investments, joint ventures, economic liberalization, and free markets. In other worlds, *the cultural target of the new imperialism is not the nemesis of global capitalism as such.* Once decoupled from capitalism, imperialism roves the world like an undisciplined bandit in search of ever new windmills to conquer.

This divergence in perspective has everything to do with the divergence between the political and the economic, which is the prime feature of the nascent imperialism. When the two were coupled together, as they were under traditional imperialism, we encountered a plethora of modernization theories, all of which had their basis in an assumption of an evolutionary cultural universalism. That universalism presumed that all societies would eventually come to exhibit common economic outlooks, along with concomitant cultural and political habits. Now, however, we are confronted from all sides with theories emphasizing the irreducible essentiality of fragmentation. It is indeed ironic that the antitotalistic trends commonly known as poststructuralism, along with slogans emphasizing multiculturalism and autonomies of all kinds, have actually occasioned a world more united than ever by a *single* economic logic, namely, that of capitalism. What goes unnoticed amid the jargon of difference and the particularism of authenticity is the fact that the global economic norm is becoming more and more entrenched as time goes by, irrespective of all culturalist sloganeering. As institutional guardians of this form of capitalism, the IMF and the World Bank issue structural adjustment plans and economic blueprints that are essentially *uniform,* regardless of religion, culture, ethnicity, or the like, and sometimes even regardless of the consequences of such plans for political stability[38]—the assumption, of course, being that the political, however boisterous, will eventually follow the economic, whether peaceably or kicking and screaming.

The most vocal articulation of this notion of essential difference, however, has come from a source that ultimately makes the thesis serviceable to the logic of the new imperialism. Samuel Huntington's much-debated thesis regarding a coming clash of civilizations serves as an epigraph of the times, in the same way that George F. Kennan's thesis of containment foreshadowed the coming of the Cold War.[39] The basic assumptions of Huntington's thesis—that the world consists of largely insulated civilizational categories, that these provide members with a relatively uniform world outlook, and that civilizations are more involved in conflict with each other than within their own domains—are remarkably ill supported. What is interesting about Huntington's thesis is not the merit of its substantive claims, which have already been roundly criticized,[40] but its troublesome proximity to the ears of policy makers, eager as they are to map out the unknown contours of conflicts after the unexpected end of a perennial Cold War left them with no strategic cause. Here is a theory perfectly packaged for those who throughout their lifetime have known little other than a world of global conflicts. Contouring the world in terms of conflictual civilizational spheres speaks perfectly to well-established habits of thought. Like the packaging of the Cold War, the clash of civilizations thesis provides the three basic elements of a credible global narrative of conflict.

First, the clash is expressed in terms of transnational ideologies rather than as a struggle for power among states. States are mere agents of global ideologies. Power struggles among significant polities are clothed in grand principles and ideas, allowing them to seek alliances on a world scale.

Second, the language of the struggle allows clear and strategic behavior, since it allows participants to focus on a limited number of central tasks and to subordinate "smaller" struggles to a central mission. Global struggles generally require a limited number of grand categories (e.g., capitalism versus communism), which act as organizing principles of alliances and as guides for long-term planning in the conflict. (And the range of possible alliances in the Cold War, it must be kept in mind, was far more flexible than the theory of the clash allows now, with its stress on *innate* rather than *acquired* sources of action of protagonists.)

Third, global clashes have important domestic ramifications, since they provide governmental powers with justification for putting their house in order, for enlisting resources at their disposal, and for subsuming civil society; they also provide them with ample ammunition to combat domestic opponents. In other words, the global clash has at least the promise of consolidating ranks at times when national purpose may not be clear, as is bound to be the case in the global era. It is therefore no accident that Huntington himself ultimately attacks multicultural education in the United States precisely on the basis of his global theory.[41] This echoes similar fears in Europe—where they are apparent in the electoral politics of more than just the far-right parties—that the influx of non-European immigrants, especially, would dilute the Western identity of host societies. Just as the Cold War offered an opportunity to purge (real or imagined) leftists and system critics from various positions of influence and to marginalize them in civil society, there is now a similar campaign against those who would dilute the civilizational integrity of the "West," at the very time that it is supposed to be preparing for global civilizational struggles with unified ranks.

There is hardly a need to reproduce here voluminous historical evidence demonstrating what must be obvious by now: that cultures or civilizations are not watertight compartments but, rather, adapt to or assimilate each other when they come into contact; that the most frequent and detrimental clashes are those that transpire within rather than across cultures; that cultures are not transhistorically pristine worldviews but can house incredible paradigmatic shifts. But the availability of information never causes enlightenment just by itself, as must be well known to anyone involved in teaching and also in these kinds of debates. Thus Huntington's book ought to be viewed as itself a symptom rather than a diagnosis of the spirit of the times. It is obvious that theories of civilizational clash, in which the idea of "civilization" is reduced to a rudimentary culturalist outline, are being widely received today. But as symptoms, theories of cultural clash suggest three major ideological contours attendant to the new global era:

1. The shift in the categories used to describe global conflicts away from economic categories such as "capitalism" and "socialism" and toward "civilizations" and "cultures" suggests a paradigmatic shift *from economy to culture* as the ground for the organizing principles of conflict and coexistence.

2. In an important sense, the shift to the cultural may be related precisely to the victory of capitalism (its local variations notwithstanding) as a global economic norm for which no credible alternatives are visible on the horizon. In other words, the *removal of the need to protect capitalism* (or socialism, for that matter) from its global enemies does not just leave governments with no global cause. As capitalism busies itself with building similitudes everywhere, governments find themselves presiding over eroding grounds of national distinction. They can either surrender to the faceless behemoth roaming the earth or retreat to a hitherto murky and less heavily fortified castle of culture.

3. The theory of the clash retreats from the modernist equation of peoplehood with nationhood and concomitantly adjusts to the fact that globalization has weakened the nation-state. The shift to such more diffuse formulations as "culture" or "civilization" signals the end of a modernist conception of the fundamental structure of collective identity propagated by nationalism. It also signals the end of any hope of capturing such similarly structured collective identities in a standard institutional format; while a nation can be embodied in a state, a civilization or a culture has much grander missions and sources of fruition than can be serviced by parochial statist systems alone.

The fact that the clash is being predicted by someone with a history of producing ideas "useful" to sympathetic officeholders may in itself make it a self-fulfilling prophecy. History has no shortage of tales showing that the relation between prophecy and its materialization is more dependent on the powers and associations of the prophet than on the inert or substantive merit of the prophecy itself. If the purported clash were indeed to materialize exactly along the predicted lines, one may suspect that that would be due partly to the connections of those predicting and preparing for it and partly to the existence of a receptive ear. Once the incendiary materials for the clash have been pulled out of their deep storage and assembled around the porous castle, all that is needed is someone to start the fire and fan its flames.

In this light, an organized clash requires institutional promoters as

well as theoreticians capable of making the problems of cultural disloca-
tion in their own society appear to be problems originating elsewhere in
the world. Machiavelli clearly thought of war against outsiders as just
another means for the prince to consolidate power over his own fractious
and potentially rebellious constituents. He approvingly cited Ferdinand's
war against Grenada—paraded in those distant times as a yet another
clash of civilizations—not because of the publicized cause but because of
the war's less obvious but more lasting accomplishment: The nobles who
enlisted or found themselves compelled to enlist in Ferdinand's cause
either did not realize or could do nothing about the fact that that "clash
of civilizations" was allowing Ferdinand to gain permanent power *over
them*.[42] The Crusades can indeed be thought of as an episode of a civilizational clash. But to discuss them only as such ignores a more important factor behind their duration, namely, the attendant remaking of political alliances within Europe. "Civilizations" themselves do not clash;
only institutionalized bodies do. Those, in turn, are not simply driven by
a civilizational mission, even when the rhetoric of civilization becomes
inevitably part of their armory. An institution willing to launch and bear
the risks of a grand clash is an institution that generally has little time for
studying civilizations—including its own.

It is in the light of such a magnificent transformation that certain old
habits and myopias must be reexamined. In particular, I am referring to
the old leftist habit of focusing on global capitalism as the worst enemy
of humanity, and in that focus ignoring the problem of the state. It is not
uncommon, for example, for left critics of globalization to call for
strengthening the state so that it can regulate global capitalism. How
this is supposed to work, no one ventures to say. Nor do any of those
commentators venture to consider the totalitarian prerequisites entailed
in such a cavalier proposal. If global capitalism has become much more
flexible, entrenched, and widespread, then a regulatory state would need
to be equally entrenched and even more far-reaching in its power than
has ever been attempted. You might fantasize that that might not be a
problem if *you* were the state. But "you" are not the state, nor are you
likely to know how to use such a state in the highly unlikely event that it
is handed over to you. There is no guarantee, instrumental or otherwise,
that under current or conceivable conditions the state can or would use
such enhanced power to govern on behalf of some "common interest,"
especially since there is *no common interest against globalization*. This lack

means precisely that the state will use any enhanced power to play the only games available to it now, namely, that of the new imperialism in the international arena, if it has the means, or that of symbolic power domestically.

Indeed, if there is an adequate response to the new imperialism and concomitant new forms of power deployment, it is to *weaken* the state. When global capitalism was more closely associated with imperial politics, it succeeded to a great extent in disciplining imperialism, since conquests and interventions had to have a calculable benefit. Also, *refraining from conquest* and decolonization were connected to the subordination of imperial logic to economy. This subordination was usually expressed in the political field by the rationalizing capitalist ethos that mandated restricting expensive political adventures to those that were absolutely necessary, especially where capitalism had become already established or could continue to thrive just as well without conquest. That disciplinary impulse suddenly disappears once the capitalist entrepreneur opens his eyes with amazement at how open the world has become. He packs his belongings and begins traversing charming and distant lands—no longer dangerous—multiplying profits here and there. In his frenzy he unfortunately forgets to tell the state that while he is away, it should continue to abide by the same old dictum: Its exercise of power must be guided by a coherent notion of profitability. He may not even care whether the dictum is followed or not, especially if he has reason to believe that in neither case will his business be affected, or that only the world is truly his stage, or that he may never return.

This is not to say that there is no hope for imposing any sense of order, regulation, or control over such a vast system. My argument is simply that existing state structures are not suitable, capable, or desirable agents of such control. In any case, it cannot possibly be more wholesome to substitute imperialist tyranny of a new and unpredictable sort for an unimpeded global capitalism. As outlined earlier in this essay, the fetishization of control is particularly prevalent in contemporary rather than older accounts of the "world system." The idea of a "system" does not necessarily presuppose that the system is controllable from a central instance. But it does include elements of self-regulation, to the extent that participants want the system to sustain itself. These elements are not necessarily all "structural"—in other words, they do not consist only of bureaucratic or coercive institutions. They also include, as Norbert Elias demonstrates in a different context, cultural developments ingrained in the establishment of codependencies and methodical and mannerist expectations.

These developments invite us to think of "order" not in terms of coercive potentials but as a product of thousands of small negotiations and organized voluntaristic interventions, themselves made possible by globalization and the weakening of the state. Some of these negotiations can be detected in the activities of the nascent "global civil society." This expresses itself in a myriad of grassroots and nongovernmental organizations; in the growth of global movements such as feminism, environmentalism, and other so-called lifestyle groups; and in the growth of the Internet and other communication technologies—all of these transcend the ideational horizon of customary state jurisdiction. These activities and their influence introduce different venues from which the globalization of the world economy can be adjudicated from non–economically determined points of view. The emergence of the global civil society can be seen as a refreshing antidote to the virtual absorption of much of *national* civil society first by the modern nation-state and then by the welfare state. While the nascent global civil society may indicate the commencement of liberation from such a statist logic, one must not think of this civil society as simply another possible mechanism for placing the world under control since it is obviously not equipped to do that. Much more importantly, civil society invites a more demure manner of living in this world, apart from the dictates of total governability or instrumental tyranny. This way of living leaves one more open to fate and insecurity but also to the yet to be used possibilities of freedom from large, deadly vacuities.

Chapter 3

The Cultural Landscape of Globalization:
Historical Notes

For our purposes, the notion of "culture" needs to be respecified in terms of transnationalization.[1] With respect to globalization, three basic elements readily stand out as major relevant ways of circumscribing the field of culture. One concerns the cultural status of national borders. Borders are interesting culturally insofar as they are transgressed, or inversely, insofar as they hold back an infusion of cultural signals from without. The notion of borders here, it must be stressed, refers to *culturally* meaningful borders rather than to simply political, colonial, administrative, or enclave-like ones. Borders are culturally meaningful to the extent that they house a special and distinctive *solidarity*. (The dream of the nation-state was of course to evolve impregnably as such). This means that one of the approaches to examining the role of culture under transnational conditions involves reconfiguring solidarities at levels beyond, below, or beside national borders.

Second, the idea of culture refers to those elements of everyday life possessing an *expansive* character, such as lifestyle patterns, consumption habits, and expectations in life. In this sense one can speak of a "cultural economy" in the same sense that the notion of solidarity just mentioned packages what may be called "cultural politics." Thus any examination of transnational culture will also have to consider the degree of globalization of lifestyles and associated conceptions of well-being.

Both vertices of cultural politics and of cultural economy, expressed in *common* solidarities, habits, standards of behavior, and norms, presuppose a *common* knowledge system by which they are communicated across vast distances. Transnational media is obviously one of the potential pillars of such a system. Mass travel and the audience for travel reports is another. Similarities between educational curricula—to the extent that formal education plays a formative role—provide further potential support for the transnationalization of culture. In addition, one could point out common modes of communication, such as languages that are widely taught or understood beyond specific cultural borders (for example, English or French), although these could be regarded as symptoms rather than causes of transnationalism.

Thus, in addition to the production of solidarities and lifestyle commonalties, the third crucial category that is of interest in cultural transnationalization is the degree to which common systems of knowledge spread. The following pages will therefore be devoted to assessing the transnationalization of these three components of cultural practice.

Solidarity and Conflict

As a concept, "solidarity" can be thought of as a useful alternative to suggestions of the essentiality or "authenticity" of collective cultures, proposed in the theory of the clash as well as in better-intentioned visions of "diversity." A foundational aspect of the idea of solidarity is *common* exposure to a formative experience. For instance, the common exposure to colonialism of vastly different societies established in itself a genre of transnational solidarities against a common imperial enemy and invited further theoretical explorations into the ontological grounds of such solidarities. The discourse of pan-Africanism, for instance, is more readily traceable to a common exposure to the rhetoric and practice of colonialism than to preexistent tropes of an essential "African culture."

This is not to deny the significant similarities within various families of African cultures. The point is that only after their common exposure to colonialism did such similarities provide an accentuated rhetorical fodder of a *new* pan-Africanist discourse. Thus it is not prudent to suggest that all forms of global solidarity are simply based on constructed links. Emergent national or "pan" identities (for example, pan-Africanism or pan-Asianism) may also be based on an attendant observation that cultural differences within the community imagined pale in comparison to those separating them from more distant cultural groups. Yet these grand constructions ignore the similarity *everywhere* of the cosmopolitan outlook of major historical entrepôts, which were usually more systematically linked to other historical entrepôts than they were to their immediate hinterlands. In the age of nationalism, the hinterland's exposure to the world led it to sacrifice rather than adopt the nonchalant cosmopolitanism of the neighboring entrepôt.

Generally, the notion of solidarity is defined in terms of feelings of community, togetherness, or similitude. Furthermore, Foucault suggests that every society requires not merely symbols of commonality but, more importantly, "rules of exclusion."[2] Every sense of impregnable parochialism requires its borders. The reality of exclusion calls for a theory to account for its formation and maintenance. Foucault offers no clues regarding the criteria or dynamics by which rules of exclusion come to be, why they take particular forms of expression, or how or why they change. In sociology the concept of exclusion has rarely been theorized adequately, particularly in terms of nationalism. At one point Max Weber suggested that in the economy the exclusion of competitors may take more than simply economic forms: A group may be shut out on the basis of such "externally identifiable characteristics" as "race, language, religion, local or social origin, descent, residence, etc." Weber, however, offered no particular theory as to why certain external characteristics are chosen over potential others, or why they arrive at particular points in time. Instead he suggested a practical process whereby the characteristic that was ultimately chosen to delineate exclusions was the one that worked best.[3]

This pragmatic theory of exclusion offers little enlightenment. First, it is restricted to those acts of exclusion that are clearly economic. Second, it offers little clue as to why one category of exclusion works more effectively than another at a particular point in time. Third, it leaves out the question of how a certain type of exclusion disseminates and becomes acceptable across other lines of division in any community (in the case of nationalism, for instance, the exclusion of "foreigners" across potentially hostile class lines). Such difficulties require a digression into the philosophical basis of the concept of exclusion.

In one of the first sociological outlines of the concept, Émile Durkheim suggested that the principles of solidarity in society do not refer to the *content* of its culture. Rather, any set of norms, beliefs, or cultural practices could contribute to the formation of a sense of community to the extent that they become *social facts* through ritual reenactment. A believing society, as it appears in *The Elementary Forms of Religious Life*, worships not God as much as its own capacity to perform a cultural task (in this case, to worship) as a collective. Any society, Durkheim suggests, is motivated by its need to normatize the event of its togetherness by constructing and adhering to common symbols, beliefs, and practices. Those common symbols, beliefs, and practices do not exist, therefore, simply for the sake of their intrinsic value, truth, or logic. In other words, they have no intrinsic essence.

This lack of essentiality in principle suggests that there should be little basis for any systematic resistance to transborder associations. The logical conclusion is that there can be nothing other than time standing in the way of the emergence of a transnational culture. William McNeill, who uses the term "polyethnicity" to refer to something akin to what is being described here as the solidaristic elements of transnational culture, stresses that this polyethnicity is a natural function of interactive civilization, propagated by the forces of conquest, disease, and trade. For McNeill, monoethnicity is an attribute of barbarian or marginal societies, which lack the capacity or the resources to interact regularly with transnational civilization—a condition characterizing much of northern Europe before 1750.[4]

The accumulated record of several millennia of cross-cultural encounters, however, shows that in practice the diffusion of cultures is often not as straightforward as the theory of cultural inessentiality suggests. A parochial culture's lack of an intrinsic essentiality does not in itself indicate it is immediately ready for cultural fusion with "outsiders." While cultural fusions have indeed transformed societies and solidarities as a result of transnational expansions (for example, European city-states into nation-states), very often such expansions—especially those of secular identities—ceased their advance at some imagined border of the culture (whether the state itself reached that same border is a different question). At what point does the logic of fusion give way to the logic of distinction?

In his critique of anthropological reason, Johannes Fabian suggests that visions of cultural or civilizational distinctions have their roots in a spatiotemporal reconstruction of the real world. For him, "*geopolitics* has its ideological foundation in *chronopolitics*," which means that inasmuch as the "West" (a fundamentally *geographic* category) needs space to occupy, it needs "[t]ime to accommodate the schemes of a one-way history: progress, development, modernity (and their negative mirror images: stagnation, underdevelopment, tradition)."[5] Such a ranking of Others by their position in a *single* universal story of evolution serves only to deny the coeval nature of the world. This scheme establishes chronological difference and *at the same time* affirms the universality of one evolutionary trajectory, to which all are assumed to belong. Theories of social modernization and economic development have grown out of this paradox.

In Fabian's theory the Other is a namesake for more fundamental oppositional categories; a state of "development" needs "underdevelopment" to become definable, visible, or otherwise meaningful. The positive category (that is, "developed") is that to which the rest of the world is assumed to yearn or gravitate, since without a universal hope for it, it must be seen as purely accidental or local rather than as a foundation for a scheme of ranking in a world system. The main founders of sociology have variously formulated this centrality of developmentalist logic in the modern world; Durkheim, for instance, had much to say about the evolution from one form of solidarity into another. Max Weber, whose work was replete with binary oppositions, was partially motivated by the need to find out why other parts of the world had *not* exhibited the European model of progression toward capitalism. For Marx, by contrast, such a progression was basic to the arguments of dialectical materialism, with materialist history suggesting universal categories of class positions from which consciousness, organization, and action would ultimately flow.

It is no accident that such a method of knowing, with its paradoxical affirmation of both difference and universality, occasioned an increased European awareness of the "world" from early modern times onward. In European philosophy, notions of the "world" as a conceptually processed total reality have gone through several metamorphoses since the "Age of Discovery." Hume's famous invocation of the Aristotelian rule of induction, for instance, posited the possibility of obtaining knowledge about the world by generalizing from a *particular* experience. The well-known corollary, namely, that knowledge so obtained is unverifiable, is perhaps less telling than the fact that in spite of this major handicap, this method of knowing was posited in the first place. The inductive method was *symptomatic* of an immense interest in open horizons that were still unfolding. The concept of the "whole world," whose *gradual* emergence was detected by Braudel, was confronting parochial consciousness everywhere; that is, the concept of the world appeared *before* there was much knowledge about the world and in an era when the world seemed vast and open.[6] In that case, one was left with the resources already available at hand, that is, one had to extrapolate from the field of the already known. Hence induction, with all its logical shortcomings, as a possible and legitimate method of knowledge.

By Hume's time one channel of knowledge about the world comprised a growing body of travelogues and geographic manuals. Many of those had been attempts to bring the great Age of Discovery to a conclusion, and thus they frequently appeared as digests of available information. A typical example from a large body of works is Roger Barlow's *Brief Summe of Geographie,* published in 1541, consisting almost exclusively of navigational and economic information. The work lists primarily coordinates, wind directions, ports of trade, and location of precious metals, notably gold. Habits, religions, and governing systems in various locations were at best listed in passing, if at all. In other words, while fragments of knowledge about routes and overseas wealth were slowly accumulating, cultural knowledge was virtually absent. Furthermore, the difficulty of obtaining the resources needed for travel from, or even within, Europe restricted its practice either to well-financed expeditions or to the aristocracy. It was not until the middle of the nineteenth century that the ascending bourgeoisie began to popularize travel and break down its elite nature.[7] By that time induction in various forms was, as it still is, a well-established method for producing and organizing knowledge, but it was being joined by a growing body of anthropological discoveries, by translations of non-Western classics, and by a whole industry of professional interpreters of the cultures of an enormous but circumnavigable world.

Formal logical structures, such as Hume's, introduce possible ways of approaching universal knowledge in the actual absence of such knowledge. But if the "world" is interesting as a *cultural* category, then a purely logical interest alone may not suffice for its grasp. The need for a ground deeper than logical formalism was ultimately addressed in Kantian philosophy, where the knowledge of universal totality was inspired, rather, by *moral* categories. Pure reason, for Kant, already supplied a priori principles of universal morality, irrespective of local circumstances. Central to that conception was a hypostatized rational being, capable of existing everywhere and applying the principles of pure reason regardless of the peculiarities of local circumstances. While Kant was aware of the practical difficulties of such a proposition, he felt that it could nonetheless be posited, apparently because pure Reason itself could be posited. The innovative direction that Kantian philosophy opened up concerned precisely the possibility of offering a post-theocratic argument for universally binding morals. The specter of cultural multiplicity in an expansive world motivated a search for standard norms that could be referred to regardless of local particularities, such as locally specific gods, rituals, practices, or traditions. Indeed, one may fruitfully consider the post-theocratic outlook in the context of the fanatic European traditions that had unleashed the Crusades and the Reformation wars. Kant's transnational morality was introduced in terms of common ethics rather than in terms of common religions.

That paradigm has been critiqued directly or indirectly in many ways, most recently in the vociferous debates regarding the heritage of Victorian anthropology in particular. Culminating in the work of Clifford Geertz, Johannes Fabian, James Clifford, and many others, the debate can be traced to the late 1950s, when the original salvos, now seemingly inane, were fired by Peter Winch. Winch's arguments clustered around what came to be known as the "charity principle." In spite of later criticism, the approach advocated by Winch continues to underpin, at a basic level, an ethic of gnostic pluralism. The foundation of that ethic consists of suspending one's referential system when one meets the incomprehensible, in order to consider whether an other-than-customary order of rationality can account for it. In his voluminous discussions of communicative ethics, Jürgen Habermas refutes this stand by arguing that it is more hermeneutic *severity* that matters here than hermeneutic *charity*. In other words, when meeting the incomprehensible Other, one must apply interpretive rigor to one's own method rather than seeking alternative rationalities. For Habermas, the advantage of severity over charity is that it preserves the interpreter "from exercising criticism without self-criticism."[8]

Habermas's position involves a return to a Kantian notion of ethical commonality, but one in which the ethic is confined to communicative procedure and maintained by communicative competence. If standard communicative procedures are synonymous with the foundation of culture, then it follows that universal communicability is transnational culture itself. This is especially the case if the notion of "culture" refers to noncoerced participation in adhering to norms, as Kant himself affirms: "[I]n order that an action should be morally good, it is not enough that it *conform* to the moral law, but it must also be done *for the sake of the law*, otherwise the conformity is only very contingent and uncertain."[9] This formulation makes an obvious distinction between retaining a common culture and simply living with others under a common order of governance. The existence of a binding law produces in itself no sense of community, since the pure existence of law is not sufficient to elicit rational impulses and responses among those affected by it. For Kant, what matters more is when the common rationality ultimately translates *itself* into common laws.

Thus, although this formulation is couched in terms of rationality and pure Reason, it clearly shows that universal *cultural* commonality should precede and itself give rise to universal *legal* commonality. Separating Kant from us is a long historical record showing that transnational phenomena have more often than not proceeded in exactly the opposite direction. The colonial epoch, postcolonial states, international law, and even the United Nations could all be understood as direct violations of this pre-scription. While such events and institutions do have the potential to develop universal forms of cultural communication, as is evident in the rhetoric of global modernity, they often lead to the perpetuation of cul-turally vacuous institutions, such as many postcolonial states. While these facilitate the functioning of economic and political world order, they may in themselves engender little public enthusiasm, sense of citizenship, or solidarity.

Whereas the Kantian framework was responding to the interactions on a universal scale between culture and governance, further develop-ments, especially nineteenth-century capitalism, clearly showed the role of a hitherto less highly regarded dimension, namely, that of economy, and with that revelation came the evolution of economics itself as a sci-ence and the rise of the intellectual species aptly described by Robert Heilbroner as "worldly philosophers." While the potential impact of that genesis on the possibilities of global culture had already been noted in some of Kant's works (notably *Zum ewigen Frieden*), nineteenth-century economic philosophers were becoming increasingly more interested in the dynamics of the emerging capitalist system, industry, labor, and money than in the cultural ramifications of that system. They were happy to leave that enormous burden to the ascending genre of the realistic novel.

Yet the growing attention to economy did not mean that all cultural ramifications were ruled out of the court of transnational thinking. Marx-ism, for instance, presumed an economically determined ground for transnational culture in the comparability of class consciousness across the globe. The famous distinction between "class in itself" and "class for itself" already spelled out this universality; wherever there was no class consciousness, wherever schemes of solidarity existed that did not high-light class positions, we were likely to be dealing with some variety of consciousness diverted from the material basis of solidarity, which could be rectified in due time by working out the contradictions produced by capitalism. Here, the *potential universality* of class culture is premised on the *actual universality* of class societies.

Obviously, the idea of "class" did not furnish the only economic cate-gory to ground global ethical commonalties in the nineteenth century. Utilitarian philosophy saw in the interdependence of interests a founda-tion of such commonalties (though—as with all of the philosophies discussed here—without couching this explicitly in terms of culture, much less in terms of transnationalism). As defined by John Stuart Mill, utilitarianism prioritized not abstract principles regarding the Good but, rather, those deeds that were likely to increase *universal* happiness. That view therefore deducted from the idea of group solidarity all those practices that had no necessary relationship to increasing happiness, such as heroic but pointless self-sacrifice.

At that time, the actual face of universal culture was—as it still is—yet to be seen. Nonetheless, Mill could detect its basis in the notion of "interdependence," whose cultural ramifications he described along strict lines of utility. Then as now, global economy developed at a much faster pace than global culture. One could only hope to hurriedly stitch together cultural clothes to fit, even if only barely, the otherwise naked body of the economy. And as is not so uncommon in the history of cultural tasks performed under emergency, the source was found to have already been supplied long ago, indeed, since biblical times: the commandments "'To do as you would be done by,' and 'to love your neighbor as yourself,' constitute the ideal perfection of utilitarian morality." Adherence to those dictums being unpredictable in an age of self-interest, Mill proceeded to propose further institutional supports for that connective morality, a morality whose applicability was truly global; "laws and social arrangements" could seek to eradicate any disharmony between the happiness or interests of the individual and those of the whole. In the same way, "education and opinion" could instill in individual minds a method of thinking through which individual happiness could no longer be conceived of apart from universal happiness.[10]

Thus the perception here is that an economic drive, encapsulated as the pursuit of individual interests, could no longer be arrested by any common cultural norms. Those norms would then need the support of such influencing media as "education and opinion," which are clearly involved in the creation or maintenance of cultural standards not readily provided by an ethic of progress. It was this declining ability of "culture" to provide its own support mechanisms that Durkheim and Ferdinand Tönnies detected as the price of admission into more complex society. For them, an existing frame of normative solidarity decays in response to the multiplication of economic interdependencies across different cultures, thereby creating new conditions of life, new fields of interest, new associations, and new schemes of valuations at such a pace that the antecedent or parochial cultures are caught off guard. In the case of utilitarianism, a cultural reconstruction was proposed that would essentially meet the economy on its own terms. That was done by shedding all pretensions to cultural categories that were aloof from the world and replacing them by a single category borrowed from the heart of economic discourse itself: utility.

In sociological literature, many of the schemes outlined above were woven together in the universal story given us in Norbert Elias's magnum opus, *Über den Prozess der Zivilisation*. Although Elias chose Hegel, Freud, and Weber as models for his theoretical inspiration rather than Hume, Kant, or Mill, the latter line of thought provided the basic elements of the intellectual heritage sociologized in his theory of civilization. Elias's story traces the twin processes of the increasing monopoly over the legitimate exercise of violence in society by the state, and the parallel development of a corresponding psychic process of internal self-control. The latter track, according to Elias, gave rise to modified behaviors; widespread, standard norms; internalized interest in self-control; awareness of complex webs of interdependence; long-term planning; and resistance to spontaneity. Thus emerged an individual life conforming to the dictates of what Freud called "superego" and Hegel called "spirit," which for Elias were equivalent terms. The crux of this theory of civilization revolves around the gradual elimination of individual and communal autonomy for the sake of both *political centricity* (manifested in a political center with monopoly over violence) and *civilizational centricity* (manifested in the adherence to standard norms across great geographic divides).

Today Elias's theory may appear significant not so much for its presumption of economically driven "progress" toward civilizational uniformity as for being the epitome of a synthesis of the philosophical and sociological interest in the potential universality of cultural standards and orders of recognition. Taking a position that unmistakably resembles Mill's, Elias proposed that utilitarian rather than altruistic calculations were one foundation of civilization. In other words, standard norms were seen to be possible largely when one acknowledges that one is unavoidably located in a massive chain of interdependence. By adhering to such norms one announces an expectation that others will do the same, thereby ultimately protecting oneself from surprises and increasing predictability in the world. The idea of civilization, as expressed here, weds individual and universal interests in a way more based on the material needs of the individual than on an innate or fate-inscribed sense of loyalty to a given tradition, as would have been expected under feudalism.

Elias's grand sociological synthesis also incorporates important dimensions of Kantian ethics, especially in regards to the organic connection conceived between cultures and formal institutions. The very existence of civilization, as Elias theorizes it, presupposes not only a rational interest in civilization as such but, moreover, a standard form of rationality. The basis of that rationality flows from an evolutionary conception of the idea of civilization whereby it is regarded not as an outcome of decrees by elites or central authorities but as a product of a demand from "below." That demand emerges out of a long history of global transactions and exchanges that lead to long periods of cross-cultural peace and to concomitant traditions regarding secure trade routes and honored agreements. The sum total of such transactions and traditions not only creates globally ubiquitous civilizational standards but also legitimizes their institutional and political by-products, which in turn further solidify this civilization and its ideals.

Finally, the knowledge dimension of universal culture, which the principle of induction had espoused as a process for extracting secular universal knowledge from particular knowledge, finds a distinctive expression in Elias's theory of civilization. In a very important sense, the standardization of norms and manners involves making the world knowable for most *practical* purposes. The possibility of extrapolating from local experience allows one to contour an otherwise unknowable world. This immediate association of the local and the global, the known and the unknown, does not simply express a belief in the superiority of one's own cultural standards. More significantly, it expresses one's rational interest in making the larger world a predictable place as one becomes more involved with it. The desire for stability, in turn, becomes one of the foundations for long-term vision and planning. It tames the wild concept of the "world," furnishing it more as a field in which business could be conducted than as a field of adventures, unpredictabilities, and uncertain knowledge.

The standpoints addressed above are of course philosophical symptoms of a historically emergent awareness of the "world" as an expansive notion. They epitomize various experiments that sought to reassess the question of common values when other dimensions of social life—economy, governance, and information flow—had transgressed parochial boundaries. As outlined above, one can detect a line of development through which questions of solidarity, belonging, and social self-definition were gradually losing their aloofness from more earthly economic transactions.[11] That shift employed different categories of analysis. We see a grounding of universal *knowledge* on the basis of pure logic in the case of Hume, a grounding of universal *morality* on the basis of rationality in the case of Kant, and a grounding of universal *motives* on the basis of the economic language of utility in the case of Mill. In other words, one can detect a gradual transition from a notion of universal culture to which only *logical thought* was foundational, to a further delimitation of logical requisites to those that could inform *action* in the world, to a yet further delimitation of action in the world as an avowed *pursuit of interests*.

The discussion cannot possibly be exhausted here. The philosophers just discussed are certainly not the only ones who ventured into modes of philosophizing that were symptomatic of an orientation toward a universal dimension of knowledge, actions, or interests as bases of expansive culture. They do, however, ground various methods of framing transnational solidarity (although that was obviously not the only or even an explicit reason for their coming into being). Major philosophical trends in the twentieth century, in fact, seem to suggest that visions of solidarity have totally retreated from considerations of universal totality. Existential philosophy, with its prioritizing of existence over essence, has clearly pulled the carpet from underneath the feet of a number of cultural categories that had been foundational for the theme of common culture, such as a notion of "human nature." With the priority of an empty existence to be filled in by self-directed individuals, the participation in a common culture came to be seen largely as an issue of voluntary input by individuals for whom freedom came before community.

In sociological terms this retreat into individualism occasions, paradoxically, the modern increase in the complexity of networks of interdependence, as Durkheim observed in the changing nature of solidarity in complex society, or as Tönnies noted in the transition to gesellschaft, or as Georg Simmel remarked in the emergence of the blasé attitude out of the semiological profusion in the modern metropolis. More recently, poststructuralist philosophy, which is being increasingly articulated in the context of transnationalism,[12] has been characterized above all by its relentless banishment of any notion of representable or essential totality; even the individual is disputed as a locus of coherent identity. Far from producing a common global culture, the transnational phenomenon triggers for postmodern thinkers images of fragmentation, or at best ideas of multiculturalism or cultural pluralism. New types of transnational solidarity generally do not generate strong philosophical supporting arguments or well-grounded cultural justifications. The EU is thus far the best example of this philosophical and cultural lack.[13] The EU is easily identifiable by its transnational institutions, policies, and economies, none of which has given rise to a "European culture," much less to solidarities stronger than national or regional ones. This lack is all the more astonishing when one compares it to the integrative role the great world religions played in times past across enormous distances, and with infinitely more humble means of communication than those at the disposal of modern societies and institutions of governance.

The inability of contemporary cosmopolitan experiences to translate themselves into genuine solidarities is obviously not the result of any lack of communication technology.[14] Rather, it has to do with the exhaustion of the reservoir of theories of universality of culture. But this exhaustion may only express the decline of the Eurocentric world that had occasioned a *particular* forum for ideas of totality. The philosophical underpinnings outlined earlier—Elias's included—refer more to the formative process of European rather than universal polities and concomitant cultures. Civilizational trajectories elsewhere exhibited not only unique priorities but also a diversity of forms of embeddedness in nonstate institutions, such as the family, religion, or community. What was specific to the Eurocentric model was that many of the solidaristic functions of nonstate institutions were gradually transferred to or claimed by increasingly complex institutions of governance.

The seeds of this trajectory toward political centers' monopoly over solidaristic ideals can already be detected in the images of politics in classical travelogues, especially those that contrasted different civilizations. Compare, for instance, two of the most widely read premodern accounts of the world, from two distinct cultural universes, notably those of the roughly contemporaneous world explorers Marco Polo and Ibn Battuta. Ibn Battuta, a Muslim judge and scholar who traversed west, north, and east Africa; the Middle East; south, Southeast, and central Asia; and some of China gave far less attention than Marco Polo to the nature and rituals of political authorities of the lands he visited. Rather, he emphasized personal stories, daily nuances, and local customs. In contrast to Marco Polo, he allocated little space for courtly affairs, and his stories of sovereigns—including the ones he worked for—were replete with derision for them. By contrast, tales of imperial power, political conflicts, political figures, and political possibilities are central to Marco Polo's account.

What is the source for this difference in emphases? In the Muslim world the common faith transcended political jurisdictions, and the allegiance of the people, especially the urban populace, was not as much to any mortal order of governance as it was to a generalized "House of Islam" *(Dar al-Islam)*—any territory or city in which Islam had a firm hold. The flux of travelers along trade and pilgrimage routes, which formed the arteries of the Muslim world, was punctuated after the third century of the faith—about A.D. 900—by parochial jurisdictions, which did not correspond in any exact or irrevocable sense to strongly cherished cultural boundaries. In the words of Ross Dunn, "Muslims on the move—merchants, scholars, and skilled, literate individuals of all kinds— regarded the jurisdictions of states as a necessary imposition and gave them as little attention as possible."[15] Marco Polo's home, by contrast, was a city-state, whose walls clearly demarcated the city from the rest of the world, including much of its immediate countryside. The passion for the universal potential of Christendom and the adherence to the cause of the pope of Rome, which permeate Marco Polo's book, did not translate into ready accessibility to and citizenship in even *Christian* domains outside of Venice. On the other hand, Ibn Battuta rarely doubted that he belonged in any territory of *Dar al-Islam,* or even his own right to seek to change local customs, whether in a town in upper Egypt or in the Maldives, when they violated universally valid precepts of the social life of the faith as he interpreted it.

In the case of European towns, especially after the downfall of the Roman Empire, isolated urban centers served to unite political *and* cultural identities in concentrated nuclei that stood in the world against other cities as well as against the surrounding countryside, from whose feudalism many of their citizens had fled. In such a landscape, divided by both political orders and notions of citizenship, a plenitude of aliens was always nearby.[16] The comparable fragmentation evident in the Muslim world after the weakening of the Abbasids occasioned a different context: The resulting political units, each combining several important urban centers, were larger than comparable units in Europe, and yet they still had to live with a system of culturalist solidarities that disregarded their borders. There were some basic similarities, nonetheless. In both Europe and the Muslim world, major political philosophers, such as Machiavelli and Ibn Khaldun, suggested in different ways that sovereigns were interchangeable, since for both thinkers the realm of politics had its own autonomous laws. But the similarities end there. In the Muslim world the system of solidarities remained largely insulated from the impact of dynastic shifts and quarrels. It was fed by an ancient web of maritime, riverine, and great overland routes, whose reach went far beyond the Muslim world itself, even though that world remained for centuries at the heart of the system.[17]

These routes, like routes everywhere and always throughout the history of trade, had two preconditions: safe passage and accessibility. Lengthy trips contributed to a cosmopolitan culture not only by exposing travelers to cross-cultural encounters over many years but, more importantly, by normalizing life on the road. The protagonists of the *One Thousand and One Nights* are usually on the road or at sea rather than at home, and the worlds they come across are yet to be fully known to them: The world of the road offers wonders, mysteries, adventures, and possible calamities rather than a coherent or already visited cosmos. With so much time spent traveling, the sense of belonging, especially for the merchant class, was informed by paradoxes, ironies, and marvelous contrasts. Here cosmopolitan culture was not a product of induction from the comforts of a sedentary hiding place but an outcome of conducting one's life on a route to a number of destinations.

But well-traversed routes themselves presuppose some history of secured passage, instigated by or coupled with a demand for imported commodities. By pacifying large stretches of Europe and the Mediterranean, *Pax Romana* not only facilitated trade within the Roman domain but also established the material basis for Rome's voracious appetite for luxuries, providing thereby added stimulus to the land routes and sea lanes connecting Europe to Arabia, Abyssinia, India, Persia, and Egypt.[18] The Umayyad and Abbasid caliphates, which inherited much of the Byzantine and Sassanid domains, fulfilled similar roles in safeguarding the routes. Many commentators argue that as a new faith, Islam itself had its basis in the interest of the merchant class in questions of safe commerce. The evidence usually cited includes the fact that Muhammad and many of his early companions made their living through direct involvement in long-distance trade, that commercial terms proliferate in the Qur'an, and that the holy text shows acute sensitivity to such commercial concerns as the status of contracts, sanctity of property, debt regulation, rules of trusts, and, above all, safe passage.

For the merchant class, maintaining safe roads had a higher value than maintaining loyalty to parochial orders of governance, especially when the latter tampered with established rules of the road through unwelcome regulation or in the course of their struggles against competing sovereigns. For example, in his account of the Mongol invasion of the Middle East in the fourteenth century, Ibn Battuta did not blame the atrocious Mongols as much as he did rulers of the eastern frontiers of the Muslim world, who, according to him, had instigated the invasion by undermining the sanctity of transborder commerce.[19] Eventually, Ibn Battuta had the opportunity to observe that some Mongol rulers were capable of (unorthodox) conversion to Islam in Persia and the Caucasus. In a way, he was observing that the road, even more than the sword, carried its own magic of cultural diffusion.

During that period, roughly corresponding to the European Middle Ages and shortly before the plague, international trade routes were gradually recovering from the great stress in which they had languished nearly everywhere since the first Crusade. After nearly two centuries of crusades, which undermined much of world trade and exhausted its protectors, the Mongols—their notorious ferocity notwithstanding—assumed, with a few later exceptions, a significant role in safeguarding the old routes. *Pax Mongolica* could be seen less as a feature of a specific imperial system and more as a *transhistorically recurrent linkage system* of safe roads. Whenever nurtured long enough, that condition disseminated cosmopolitan outlooks and eventually furthered globally oriented discourses of identity or spiritual communion. Under the Mongols, the initial foundations of cosmopolitanism were not the common cultural system of an empire but, rather, the secured condition of multicultural passage. The eventual conversion of Mongol rulers in central Asia and Persia to Islam was an outcome of a long period of experimentation with and exposure to a variety of spiritual suitors. The then-prevailing state of flux and coexistence itself made possible such celebrated careers as Marco Polo's. But that very drive to convert testifies to an already existent model of solidarity, a model provided by the history of global trade. The model highlighted action and potential over nature and essence: People oriented toward the road experience solidarity as expansive rather than as tied irretrievably to self-enclosed and nonnegotiable local systems of reference.

Expansive Solidarity, Vagueness, and Enclave Formation

The notion of solidarity as potentially expansive rather than bound by city walls, however, complicated things in ways that could not have been expected from the vantage point of the "Middle Ages."[20] Since the Middle Ages (with the usual interruptions one would expect in any long story) safety of passage has increased, but there has been a consistent downgrading of another fundamental element of transnational routes: free accessibility. In 1791 the French constitution affirmed (rather than invented) the "liberté d'aller, de rester, de partir," all in the same breath (as if coming, staying, and departing were conceptually coterminous). This relative freedom of movement continued to be the norm in Europe throughout the nineteenth century.[21] It was not until World War I that the passport and then visas were invented, eventually becoming major obstacles to free movement. The Universal Declaration of Human Rights of 1948, according to Robert Goodin's reading, reveals a further restriction on the principles of movement: "The text of Article 13(2) stipulates that 'everyone has the right to leave any country including his own,' but implicitly it is only a national who enjoys a right to return to his country."[22] Thus, while modern passage has arguably become more *secure,* it has also become more difficult. It is obvious but still noteworthy that this restriction has occasioned the rise of nationalism as a secular frame of solidarity, at the expense of older religious bonds, which were, interestingly, less restrictive of the right of passage or, with some notable exceptions, even residence.

These emerging restrictions are grounded in part in demographic pressures, in another part in responses to the technologies that had made mass travel possible, especially for the lower classes. But they are also grounded in the new frames of solidarity expressed through nationalism. For Benedict Anderson, one of the preconditions of nationalism was the spread of "horizontal solidarities" at the expense of vertical, removed centralities (such as a monarch or god). While horizontal solidarities were not necessarily any less abstract than loyalty to distant and aloof centers, certain inventions, such as the newspaper or the novel, fed horizontal solidarities by offering daily renewable media to communicate images of sameness.[23] For Foucault, it will be recalled, a search for sameness is inseparable from a search for signs of exclusion, and exclusion, as we have known since Hegel, is part and parcel of the story of formation of identity.

Such theories of solidarity and exclusion become more interesting, of course, when we use them not as dogmas but as conceptual aids as we explore historical specificities and nuances. The legitimacy of new and untried rules of exclusion in some cases may be simply based on magnifying some aspects of antecedent rules. In Europe, for instance, the history of anti-Semitism already involved both implicit and explicit restrictions on immigration and residence similar to those put in place against other kinds of foreigners in the age of nationalism. But at a more general level, the question of nationalist exclusions cannot be separated from the entrustment of solidarity, hitherto allocated to antecedent systems of religious and kin bonds, to a secular covenant. What distinguishes nationalism from religion most glaringly is its fundamentally horizontal nature, its entrustment of society itself to *like mortals*, who remain strangers to each other nonetheless. The American motto "One nation under God" spells out a paradox that belongs precisely to that point of unsure transition into nationalism. *By themselves*, like mortals—experienced on an everyday basis, error-prone, imperfect, untrustworthy—are less capable of inviting solidarity than is an aloof, omnipresent god. Abstract secular rules and regulations, as Max Weber hinted in a different context, become accepted and expected foundations of rationality to the extent that they avoid appearing to be the creation of any particular individual. In other words, secular bonds, very much like religious ones, require transcendental, abstract, and imaginary sources of nourishment.

This uncertainty regarding the source that is supposed to nourish and keep horizontal solidarities together would be expected to require beholders to be permanently on guard. Horizontal solidarity alone, unsupported by any verticality, is usually fragile, especially if its members are habitually abstract to each other. In the case of nationalism, the character of horizontal solidarity is frequently transformed from fragility to brittleness. The road from fragility to brittleness could indeed be long, and we should not necessarily assume that the destination will always be reached: The road has its own character, which may best be identified as a sustainable aura of vagueness. Indeed, the classical heritage of sociology was remarkably alert to, if not actually grounded in, an increased sense of vagueness in the culture. It commented extensively on the gradual erosion of parochial or antecedent meanings of collective life. Some commentators went as far as arguing that the tropes of uncertainty, vagueness of identity, and cultural doubt themselves constituted the heart of what we call modernity.[24] One need only mention Durkheim's preoccupation with anomie or suicide, Simmel's with "the tragedy of culture," Marx's with alienation, Weber's with the split in rationalities. The classic sociologists were witnesses to new conditions of societal life and new orders of cohesion and solidarity that, as Durkheim pointed out, depart from mechanical formulations to assume more-complex and less-apparent organic forms.

The exportation of European modernity (along with much of its politico-organizational and socioeconomic pillars) to the rest of the world brought about convoluted variations in modes of transition from "traditional" to "modern" society. A recurrent theme in studies of such transitions concerns the introduction of general uncertainties. In his study of the history of a Javan town at the end of the colonial period, Clifford Geertz described an "advance toward vagueness," characterized by increased disorientation in the culture.[25] A comparable state of affairs was detected by one of the subaltern historians of India: Gyanendra Pandey noted an increased sense of profound yet vaguely articulated loss in the history of an Indian town after its exposure to British rule.[26] Many similar studies reveal deeply destabilizing erosions—accelerated, shaped, or magnified by foreign invasions—of the traditional solidary ethos; nor are these ethos replaced by ethos possessing the same sense of self-evident rightness. The resulting disorientation is usually so pervasive, in fact, that the most complete representation of it can only be literary. One of the best-known works in this respect remains Chinua Achebe's *Things Fall Apart*, with its minute portrayal of an emergent feeling of grand disorder as one becomes inexorably enmeshed in powerful colonial influences.

Successful conquests are not just those that simply disempower the adversary. More specifically, in terms of the psychology of imperialism, conquest is an event that reshuffles the cognitive cosmos of the adversary without offering a *stable* alternative in its place. In *The Conquest of America* Tzvetan Todorov identifies the fundamental fissure contributing to Aztec defeat in the utter failure of their gods to speak at all, to provide any guidance for action, in light of the baffling, absolute strangeness of the Spaniards. Likewise, the fulcrum of Cortés's victory was his ability to manipulate the language of signs of his nemesis while keeping his own cards close to his chest.[27] That paramount event is thus significant in this respect because of its seminal instructiveness to subsequent forms of cross-cultural conquest. From then on, ever more stratagems for disorienting the enemy's cosmos were added to the antecedent model of purely coercive supervision, a model of which the Inquisition provided arguably the last major historical episode.

In the nearly five centuries separating us from those momentous events, the twin arts of psychological and coercive conquest continued to be perfected. In contemporary literature, Abdelrahman Munif's voluminous masterpiece *Cities of Salt* offers a far more telling portrayal of the cultural consequences of incorporation into the world system than any sociological, political, or historical treatise could ever hope to deliver. The story reconstructs in rich detail a transformation in values and sociopolitical organization following the discovery of oil in the desolate, hitherto population exporting landscape that eventually came to be known as Saudi Arabia. As a U.S. oil company, with governmental blessing, engendered an uprooting of the patterns of socioeconomic relations that had defined traditional society, prophesies of the coming end of the world began to proliferate. Death and departure loom large throughout Munif's volumes, in spite of continued but meek local resistance to the incursion. What was at stake in the novel, as well as in the actual historical tale, was nothing less than the determination of the company—and subsequently of the colluding political authority—to remake or destroy local patterns of life in any dimension where such patterns stood in the way of incorporating even that great forlorn terrain into a global politico-economic machine.

As a "country" is reorganized in order for it to be digested by world economy on terms dictated largely by outsiders, any new horizontal solidarity emerging as a result could be expected to involve different ingredients than the ones that had occasioned European modernity. Since it is not uncommon for regions and countries to be incorporated into the world in pieces rather than wholesale, it is by extension not uncommon for them to replace "traditional" ("mechanical," if one is to follow Durkheim) solidarity with a disjointed, unkempt national household, supplanted with a formalist facade of collective purpose whose cracks could scarcely be concealed. In *Cities of Salt*, as in Ngugi wa Thiongo's or Achebe's later works, one sees a realistic depiction of the entrance upon the political stage of a policing elite, tied to the outside world and fortified by imported technologies of power—whence it becomes increasingly less rooted or even interested in internal sources of legitimacy. In other words, the conquest-like incorporation of the subaltern into world political economy foreshadows the crystallization of enclaves of global orientation *within* each society (for example, orientations apparent only among specific urban classes or specific economic sectors), much more than it roots a new sense of horizontal solidarity *across* society.

That kind of social world reflects itself in the theories attempting to describe it. In classic sociological theory, there was no consensus as to how to define the new rules of social cohesion incumbent upon transition into modernity. One can argue that such a dearth of unified perspectives regarding the ground of new solidarity was not so much due to conceptual problems with social theory as it was itself another symptom of the ongoing process of social atomization and specialization—which provided further fodder for the aura of vagueness in the culture. Weber's notion of the modern as a condition of split rationalities, for instance, was premised on a posited multiplicity of values within society, which were actively competing for self-expression through a variety of distinct discourses (traditional, legal-rational, instrumental, and so on). The logic of capitalism, however, requires a particular type of rationality, propelled by self-interest, driven to guarantee efficiency and rational production, oriented toward planning, and concerned with a certain degree of everyday predictability in the world. In themselves, none of these elements of capitalist rationality demands a particular notion of belonging, unless it means belonging to any institutional frame that guarantees their exercise.

The transition into vagueness outlined above can thus be accounted for as an outcome of the elimination of those socio-organizational aspects that limit the exercise of capitalist rationality (communal rather than private property, needs-oriented rather than profit-oriented production, cooperative rather than competitive ethics, and so on) as the society in question is incorporated into a global capitalist system. If the elimination of such conceptions produces relative vagueness, and if this vagueness in the culture is not supplemented—as is often the case—by other than consumer culture, then transnational culture could be understood not as a system of solidarities but, rather, as *a globally ubiquitous feeling of rootlessness.*

The road into this rootlessness is still being traveled. But first it is important to specify what in the culture is really being uprooted and whether there can be any resistance to this global assault on parochialism. World systems are obviously not new; they have been around for centuries under one guise or another. What characterizes the *modern* world system, as discussed earlier, is the tutelage extended to it by expansive systems of governance. Modernizing governments in the peripheral world frequently found themselves in a competitive ideological game with non-state-based systems of solidarity, in spite of the fact that such systems did not historically lack an internal capacity to negotiate noncoercive terms of belonging to the world system. Because it was so extreme, one of the best examples of this competition between these two frames of solidarity remains Atatürk's Turkey, which is often held up for its legendary assault on religion in the name of enlightened modern secularism. What is frequently forgotten in that tale is that the Young Turks were hardly the only group seeking to modernize the country (or the empire for that matter). Rather, the second half of the nineteenth century was witness to peculiarly modern Islamic revivalist movements and thinkers, represented most famously by the likes of Muhammad 'Abdo and Jalaludin Afaghani, among many others. For these reformers, revivalism essentially meant explicitly the rejuvenation of the old faith, so that it could creatively tackle the issues and spirit of modernity itself, rather than a reinvention of the past as it had been. Violently aborted by the triumphant Atatürk, that trajectory was prevented from injecting the participation in modernity with an aura of local authenticity. Rather, Atatürk's victory essentially meant that belonging to the world system had to take place exclusively on that system's terms. While we do not know what the untried alternative would have been, the fact that other contending paths were being offered also suggests that there was a time—most of history, indeed—when it was possible simultaneously to belong to the system and to maintain some sense of voluntarism in that belonging.

Atatürk's radical stance against any options other than secular nationalism was obviously based on what he saw to be the European model. However, it was no more than a poor copy. First, in Turkey as well as elsewhere, it advanced a distinction between secularism and religion that was much sharper than any western European country had to entertain. Not only was the internal capacity of religion to reinvent itself thoroughly denied, but any equivalent to a European Christian social democratic party, for example, had to be sequestered into the large cluster of "traditionalist" sectors excluded from power, or at best regarded with scarcely concealed official intolerance. Not only did such a state of affairs introduce perennial ideological polarization, but it further guaranteed that the new ruling elites would essentially remain only narrowly based in the societies they were ruling, *unless* they managed to stir up nationalism frequently enough to rally at least urban populations around the state.

The outcome of such a state of affairs is paradoxical but not surprising; having lost touch with or trust in the unenlightened majority over which they presided, the proponents of secular modernity and enlightenment in the peripheral world had no choice but to run their systems as dictatorships, frequently surpassing in the art and magnitude of repression the premodern systems they had displaced. Today, in fact, it is doubly ironic that the Iranian mullahs, who look anything but modern, have introduced far more participatory democracy to their constituents than did any of their secular predecessors and most of their neighbors.[28] Indeed, as many commentators are beginning to recognize, the rhetoric of Islamic movements today is unusually infused with unmistakably modern notions of progress, development, rights to participation, and science.[29] Here one sees yet another attempt to *join* the world rather than close the door in its face, but to join in a way that would allow one to negotiate one's terms, to normalize the affair a little, to combat the encroaching feelings of vagueness and rootlessness included in globalization's bill. Few understand that in the West, for modernity here has always invoked a single meaning fashioned after the one model of the West's self-image. Its pluralist claims notwithstanding, Western modernity never developed a capacity or a credible *method for understanding options.* If anything, it despised them.

The unavoidability of such issues of culture clearly shows that in spite of the drive toward vagueness, contemporary globalization is far from being a mere economic affair to which the status of feelings of belonging are inconsequential. At the very least, if one wishes somehow to link up to a world system dominated by strangers, then one must see that system as being remunerative. We shall now turn to the ramifications of this pursuit of well-being in a global system rather than in local systems. Namely, what is of concern here is the diverse understandings of well-being, the emergence of a global standard for what it means, how it competes with locally rooted ideas of the "good life," and its role as a component in models of transnational culture.

The Cultural Economy

In a little-known memoir entitled *The Worlds of a Maasai Warrior,* Tepilit Ole Saitoti tells of his educational odyssey between the worlds of Masailand and Europe and the United States, or between the worlds of "tradition" and modernity. In the very act of writing the story, Saitoti shows himself to be keenly aware of the novelty of his departure from the tradition yet fully justified in its violation. The sense of novelty is nowhere more glaring than in a letter he writes to his father as he lands in Germany: "I decided to leave our country without your permission, because when I ran away to the Serengeti and returned, you did not punish me. Instead you told me that it was up to me to decide how to lead my life, since you could not advise your children concerning paths you had not taken."[30] Thus we learn here that from the point of view of the modern son, the father, as a custodian of the tradition, himself possesses a remarkably open-ended attitude toward knowledge, leaving substantial room for what tradition does not provide a priori. And it is this room that allows for the flourishing of a wide range of experimentations—some falling within its cosmos, others leading to new pathways.

But unlike his father's, Saitoti's attitude toward the world must by necessity become more structured. Though the path beyond the certitudes of the Masai way of life had not been charted out by previous or credible explorers, the basic skills needed to negotiate it were already provided in his *traditional* molding as a responsible and observant individual. Reflecting on his education in Boston, Saitoti says, "I had always been a responsible and keen herder when I was growing up. The same discipline went into my schoolwork now."[31] In fact, Saitoti seems to suggest that both modern and traditional education replicate some salient general patterns in the life of the individual: "In a way I was repeating the night of initiation I had gone through. College was similar to treading the rigorous path of achieving manhood in Maasailand."[32] Saitoti is aware of the complexities of his position, since he goes on to reflect on whether his assimilation of "Western ways" would make him unfit for his earlier society and wonders aloud about the status of the half-breed he is in the process of becoming. But the fact that in his traditional upbringing he had already received the armory of self-discipline, the gift of observance, and an entitlement to status through initiation means that the basic building blocks for a universal assimilation of stimuli and knowledge are already in place. Modernity does not come to tradition from without; it is tradition itself that supplies modernity with its universal foot soldiers.

The path into the modern, however, was generally charted out in theories that until very recently labored to set it clearly apart from the traditional. In contrast to the received vision of the traditional as local and self-enclosed, the modern was presented in terms of inherently transnational tropes. The heritage commonly grouped under the term "development theory" was one of the biggest salvos in socioeconomic thought on the desirability, feasibility, or inevitability of an upcoming global standardization of styles of life and consumption. While the legacy of Talcott Parsons in sociology is commonly credited with instigating this largely abandoned body of work, it must be noted that what is commonly considered to be its antithetical perspective in sociology, Marxism, also instigated equally grand designs, even though the motivation was certainly not the same. The attention of many schools of neo-Marxism, of which dependency theory was perhaps the most notable, was focused on "unequal exchange" within an inescapable global economic network. Christopher Chase-Dunn argued that under unequal exchange the "periphery" can develop only in relation to itself, since the economic differences between it and the "core" tend not to diminish thereby.[33] This implies that the notion of development refers not to an objectively definable economic condition of a society but, rather, to the effort to erase any *distinctions* between it and other "core" societies with regards to well-being. "Development," in this sense, denotes the abolition of global inequalities rather than an abstraction like "prosperity" per se. Thus what matters in a globally interactive economy is not objective wealth and well-being but wealth and well-being vis-à-vis other players, specifically those players who are highly visible in such an economy.

Dependency theory suggested that any enhanced condition of "well-being" in the peripheries was liable to be stripped of significance or value because while the peripheries were improving their circumstances, the core, the model for development, would have enhanced its own conditions of material well-being, thus keeping its distance and distinction from the periphery on that score. The first logic of well-being in a transnational economy, therefore, is that well-being is defined not in terms of local cultural standards but with respect to knowable others. In this particular type of economy the idea of well-being is driven by *emulation* pressures, usually most operative among the urban middle and upper classes. Thus Third World industrialization, far from being uniformly successful, was nonetheless uniformly informed by exterior models, even though the locus of such models may have shifted over time.

For example, in many Southeast Asian countries, such as Malaysia or Indonesia, development strategies were until recently premised on such slogans as "Look east," referring to a preference for the Japanese model over the U.S. model of economic growth. Yet the peripheral world sometimes offers us less audible examples of people who say the equivalent of "Look inside," when they wish to do what has already been done elsewhere. In an interesting anthropological study, Gudrun Dahl and Gemetchu Megerssa ask a local chief to describe to them the meaning of the term used by some of the Oromo in Ethiopia to signify "development." The term, *fidnaa*, paradoxically combines ideas of "growth" and "stability." It carries an insistence that development must be tied to rather than divergent from ancient and customary laws. The fact that this is not always done gives rise to an apparently new distinction between good and evil *fidnaa:* The difference between the two is not in the material bounty that may result but, rather, in whether the Oromo are the agents or mere receivers of that development. It is not lost on the Oromo chief who expounds this local interpretation of development that all schemes of development that do not adhere to the dictates of the good *fidnaa* ultimately result much more in enhancing governmental power than in actually helping anybody who is supposed to be helped by them.[34]

Historically, the sovereign ethics expounded in the *fidnaa* concept furnished grounds for largely voluntaristic evolution of global commonalities in the interpretation of the logic of economic life. Because the norm governing purely economic action has more to do with *interests* than with *identity*, we can discern instances and periods of transnational dispersion of economic ideas over broad spaces and different epochs. But in order to see those instances with clear eyes, one must first dispel the hermetic Weberian emphasis on elements of *uniqueness* (for example, "*Western* capitalism"), and begin hunting for transregional concordances. The world system perspective has contributed much to this line of study. One of its founders, Immanuel Wallerstein, views capitalism as the basic logic of a globally interactive system dating back to the sixteenth century. Another world system historian, Janet Abu-Lughod, goes even further back in history, detecting a global economic system consisting of eight interactive subsystems between A.D. 1250 and 1350, preceding European domination. Abu-Lughod stresses the similarities among "Asian, Arab, *and* Western forms of capitalism" rather than dissimilarities. Among the significant and often overlooked similarities, she lists the invention of money and credit, the availability of mechanisms for pooling capital and distributing profit, and the independent control exercised by merchants over their wealth.[35]

These similarities among various types of historical capitalism spell out a number of basic orientations that underlie economic action at a translocal level. First, pooling capital allows the economy to operate at a significantly larger scale than would be possible if the range of economic actions were confined to the limits of personal capital. Second, distributing risk makes adventurous, far-away, and otherwise difficult undertakings more appealing. The very willingness to expand into the realm of the unknown and take risks—even distributed ones—attests to a recurrent realization in the history of capitalism that the knowable, reachable, or local territory within which a market had hitherto restricted itself has become saturated. Third, expansion into new markets requires or presupposes universally acceptable or exchangeable media of exchange, as translocal exchange is obviously inconceivable without translocal—that is, abstract—standards of value.[36] Finally, the invention of credit testifies to the economic imperative of belonging to the market and to the prevalence of common expectations attendant to that belonging, even when individual participants did not have the resources to venture into the market on their own.

The four elements of economic outlook just mentioned, oriented by their nature toward others' ways of conducting business, expand the horizons of individual participants, create new channels for the expression and discovery of "interests," and place in motion a network of relations characterized by interdependence, trustworthiness, and predictability. The field of interests created by such engagements and by their rules is part of the world of the market. And those interests are articulated in terms of the relations—the trade partners, the overall context of conducting business, credit associations, insurance possibilities, media of exchange, rules of trade, and so on—that regulate the concomitant belonging to a certain market and one's status and potentialities within it. But there is another orientation toward economic life that is more involved in an idealized conception of life, outside the market and beyond its vagaries. As an expanded communicative web rather than simply as an expanded market, a transnational economy carries along in its cargo visions of well-being, clustered around images of the worthy, meaningful, or otherwise aspired-to lifestyles, across stormy seas, rugged mountains, and endless steppes.

Of course, none of this need imply that visions of well-being or interests emerge uniformly across the world, straightforwardly following the expansion of an economic net. The history of capitalism teems with examples of difficult cultural transitions in which new values became established only through substantial coercion. In her study of the evolution of a kingship system in the Tongan islands, Christine Gailey shows how the replacement of kinship-based hierarchical structures with state-based ones was intimately tied to the gradual incorporation of the islands into a broader Pacific economy. The process began imperceptibly in the work of a few European missionaries and traders but ultimately led to the introduction of new ideas of hierarchy and "proper" gender roles. The transition was sealed through the dynamics of European colonial rivalries, which caused a reshuffling of clannish patterns of authority and led to state formation. At the economic level the transition was accompanied by a shift from a gift-based to a cash-based system of economic exchange. One of the most difficult accomplishments was the introduction of the idea of wage-labor, which required a conscious policy of creating scarcities. The policy was first advocated by Wesleyan missionaries and involved changing the basis of the right of access to farmland from kin obligation to cash rent.[37] A closely related and equally difficult transformation was the replacement of gift giving with cash exchanges; in the case of some items, such as food, it took almost a century of prodding to make cash exchange the market norm.[38]

In *Cities of Salt* Munif captures a twentieth-century transformation of an even more epic proportion: He describes how an oil company essentially *founds* a state, whose task is to police a yet to be fully crystallized array of new values, including concentrated wage-labor. The magnitude of the transformation can best be appreciated if one keeps in mind that in cultures that are largely insulated from world economic cycles—such as Munif's seminomadic culture—values tend to circulate across generations in a remarkably consistent manner. At the time oil was discovered, the worthy life for the Bedouins was still defined along the lines observed by the historian Mas'udi nearly a thousand years before. Then, categories defining the quality of life included service to the tribe, generosity, austerity, health, and lack of residential confinement or pollution.[39] Mas'udi's list of qualities clearly indicate that neither an abstraction like "money" nor nonmonetary measures of wealth (such as cattle) were counted by the nomads as sources of good life. In fact, his report indicates that nomads who were aware of the conditions of life in the more well-to-do towns considered themselves to have the superior lifestyle nonetheless, on the basis of their own indicators of well-being.

That different motives are involved in economic action is not a novel idea in the social sciences. Max Weber's classic *The Protestant Ethic and the Spirit of Capitalism* was specifically designed to challenge the priority of economic motives (and in a way as a rebuttal to Marx's historical materialism). While Weber's work has been widely contested ever since it appeared, it did at least register—even if it did not satisfactorily diagnose—the observation that very often, economic undertakings are set in motion by motives other than the pursuit of a standard notion of well-being. Weber's approach pinned the profit motive to specific belief systems rather than positing it as a universal norm. Without a cultural support system, the profit motive fails. Thus one of the counterexamples to the Calvinist entrepreneur was the peasant who responded to an increase in the rate for piece work—an initiative designed to increase production—by actually producing less.[40] That phenomenon was studied more systematically around the same time by Aleksandr Chayanov, who sought to explain the failure of Russian peasantry to display the expected responses to economic incentives. Chayanov concluded that for the peasant a category like "profit" was meaningless. The peasant understood satisfaction of the needs of a confined social universe, usually the family, as being the sole reason to endure manual labor. As soon as that need was met, additional work lost its remunerative appeal—even when there was the potential for making profit—and the peasant ceased working.[41]

Chayanov's work seems to suggest, almost predictably, that this profoundly noncapitalist frame of mind is most rooted in sectors of the population furthest removed from exposure to the bourgeois experience. The experience of anticolonial common fronts shows how profit-based and non-profit-based paradigms, both future-oriented, vied against each other. In the mid-1940s the Congress Party in India spent a good deal of time discussing Gandhi's defense of the *khadi* philosophy of production, which instructed rural laborers to spin clothes for self-consumption rather than for sale or profit. Gandhi gave both moral and economic justifications for the idea, arguing that the proposed alternative—capitalism and heavy industrialization—invariably led to exploitation and that production for self-sufficiency was the best way to employ the millions of idle laborers in the Indian countryside.[42] In the long run Gandhi lost the argument. His proposal represented a peasant-based worldview within the peasant-bourgeois alliance that won India's independence, an alliance that ultimately led Jawaharlal Nehru and the Indian bourgeoisie to political power.

In contrast to Gandhi's vision, the rest of the leadership of the party—and eventually the country—put forth programs that were attentive to "successful" economic models, far away from the historical reality of the Indian village. Nehru spelled out the kind of thinking that was to stand for that orientation:

> The modern mind, that is to say the better type of the modern mind . . . is governed by a practical idealism for social betterment. It has discarded to a large extent the philosophical approach of the ancients, their search for ultimate reality, as well as the devotionalism and mysticism of the medieval period. . . . India, as well as China, must learn from the West, for the modern West has much to teach, and the spirit of the age is represented by the West.[43]

These words, which were uttered amid the struggle for independence from Britain, indicated that "independence" was not understood to signify dissociation from the models of economic organization that had been learned throughout the colonial period. To the contrary: They indicated that the lesson had been learned so well that the only remaining impediment for its actualization was colonial domination itself.

As much as it motivates *innovation*, the competitive logic of capitalism also requires a willingness to *assimilate* models of success in business or in life. This is why one must discard the influential dichotomy that Karl Polanyi suggested existed between "traditional" and "modern" society, whereby the "traditional" was supposed to be driven by emulation of behaviors and the "modern" by competition.[44] One of the important aspects of economic globalization, insofar as it informs value systems or models of social organization, is that the "traditional" periphery always follows the example and the model of the modern core. Only environmental limitations have ever caused the modern to salute the wisdom of the traditional. Competition is a global game, in which the core powers enjoy the advantages of technology, finance, and integrated markets and the peripheral countries have the "competitive advantage" of cheap and abundant labor, fewer taxes and regulation, and raw materials. From the perspective of ruling national elites—which is not necessarily that of transnational capitalists—one goal of competition for the core is to remain in the core and thus to remain an emulable model; in the periphery, the *national* goal, by contrast, is to beat the core at its own game, a possibility demonstrated first by the Japanese experience and then by that of the other "Asian tigers."

The Emergence of the Economic

These remarks take us back to the old debate regarding the degree of confluence between the economic and the social, or the extent to which economic imperatives can restructure cultural patterns. Polanyi's distinction between the modern and the traditional was premised on a more basic distinction between market and nonmarket logics. He argued that the "market" as we know it came into being only in the nineteenth century. For Polanyi, practices such as "reciprocity" and "redistribution," which defined traditional arrangements of economic life, as well as ports of trade with controlled access, were all "nonmarket" situations.[45] Braudel dismissed this distinction between market and nonmarket categories as meaningless, especially since it presumed a historically untenable distinction between "economic" versus "social" types of exchange,[46] which for him could not be understood separately.

This perspective was already developed in Marcel Mauss's seminal study of the gift, which proposed an anthropologically grounded model for a total confluence between economic and social exchange. For Mauss, *prestations,* as exemplified in the gift, could not be apprehended in terms of modern categories of economic action. The gift economy not only entailed no distinction between transactions such as buying and selling or borrowing and lending, but it also organically connected the economic and the emotive.[47] More recently, in a useful adoption of Mauss's study, Lewis Hyde proposed a distinction between "logos-trade" and "eros-trade." The former denotes forms of rationality presuming individual autonomy, which upholds modern capitalism and modern articulations of interests. The latter, by contrast, denotes the array of gift-like transactions whose aim is to integrate the individual into community.[48] Hyde argues that capitalism is possible only when individuals break away from an eros-trade paradigm, since the claims of the community formed by eros-trade usually compel individuals to dispense away as "gifts" resources that could otherwise be used for capital accumulation.[49]

If capitalist rationality can be summed up in terms of logos-trade, then all we have within its scope are the free play of individual interests. If this should entail the loss of all sense of communion, then one would expect there to be no disincentive (save for coercion) for the "losers" to rise up and *force* a redistribution of wealth. Indeed, many supporters of the welfare state, such as John Kenneth Galbraith, argue that capitalism was saved not by the market's innately free logic but by the sociopolitical regulations of the market and by the state's effort to guarantee a minimal standard of well-being. However, if one takes the long-range view of history, forms of political tutelage over capitalism, such as the welfare state, appear as brief reversals of the hierarchy of the economic over the political. The mechanism of this hierarchy is identified by Braudel in the natural drive of capitalism, which consists of its tendency to assimilate existing structures and institutions. An example of this trend today would be the recent efforts of deindustrializing cities and regions in the United States to maintain economic life through massive subsidies to attract new businesses. Braudel argued that in its historical evolution— that is, before its regulation in modern times—capitalism tended to *use rather than invent* political and social structures, and that it succeeded best when it reduced the state to a "shadow of itself."[50] Thus, one of the most important features of economic globalization today is its association with a rejuvenation of capitalism in its older, pre–welfare state form, where sociopolitical structures, to the extent that they are economically involved at all, merely facilitate the global expansion of capitalism.

As a globally expansive phenomenon, capitalism is perhaps best apprehended as a process rather than a system. The notion of a system describes best relatively stable structures, such as delimited boundaries presided over by more or less permanent institutions. The idea of a "system" may also describe a relatively confined market economy, which Braudel distinguishes from capitalism.[51] Capitalism can be apprehended as a process rather than a system in the sense that its built-in driving force is *perpetual* expansion and reconfiguration. Unlike systems, processes do not propose by necessity an integrative grid organically connecting the economic, political, and cultural aspects of life. Thus as a process, transnational capitalism today does indeed reshuffle the cards, since economic integration does not presume political or cultural integration. If anything, integration of political systems today (as in the EU) can be seen as a method for diffusing political authority rather than as an attempt to reinvent it at a higher level. And cultural integration of the world, if it is happening, possesses no structural or systemic prerequisites. The point is that *systemic structures,* while they still furnish support for global *processes,* no longer safeguard a logic of interaction, complementarity, reciprocity, and mutual reinforcement among the different spheres of social life.

Thus all we have are processes—economic, political, and cultural— taking place in distinct logical spheres. But they are clearly not insulated from each other, since each responds in various ways to the impact of the others. No economic involvement is independent, after all, of considerations of lifestyle, spheres of belonging, proper relations, and ways of evaluating one's worth in comparison to others. In the feudal economy, for instance, one of the crucial elements of hierarchy was blood lineage, a category forced into second place after capital with the rise of the bourgeoisie. This development occasioned a reevaluation of the economic value of the nobility, from which point onward it began to be seen as "useless," especially in comparison to the "active class"—the bourgeoisie in the towns.[52] The concept of "usefulness" emerged not only as an economic category but also as a criterion by which an opposition to the dominant paradigm of economic valuation could take root. The concept of "usefulness" was introduced primarily in reference to a style of life and business conduct with which the bourgeoisie was most comfortable. It referred neither to specific possessions nor to abstract concepts such as honor or blood, all of which could have been claimed by the nobility. Rather, it referred simply to a style of life that promised potential accessibility to broader social classes, since it only required the activation of universal human potentials (prudence, saving, reasoning, assessing, planning, and so on). It was to be the landmark ethic of a market enlarged enough to incorporate hitherto untapped resources and enlist yet-to-be-involved recruits. To be "useful" was to belong to the "active class," and to belong to the "active class" was to join a market that put little restriction on its domain, a market that was poised to enlist entire regions and eventually the world.

In one form or another, the image of the "active class" expressed the same attributes that were highlighted in Weber's portrayal of the Protestant ethic. Yet the notion spells out no religious, ethnic, territorial, or other kind of inherent distinction. The only distinction that is made here is between universal human properties: action versus idleness. The bourgeois rhetoric of useful action highlights one of the features of the spirit of modernity. Against the exclusiveness of the aristocracy, it sought to establish pragmatic universal categories for status. Far from being purely rhetorical, the universalizing properties of modernity also possessed structural support mechanisms. Those are summarized by Anthony Giddens, who traces to modernity a number of expansive rationalities, such as the separation of time and space, "disembedding mechanisms" employed through abstract systems, reflexivity, and regularized use of knowledge.[53] In contrast to the premodern confluence of time and place in everyday life, the separation of time and space in modernity is brought forth gradually by networks of interdependence that become so expansive that the consequences of widely dispersed transactions and relations are felt in localities that may have little input into their formulation and processes. Thus the experience of the "here," which is inherently local, becomes to a great extent determined by the "now," which has all kinds of global reference points.

The second major operation at the heart of modernity as outlined by Giddens, namely, the growth of abstract systems, involves not only standardizations of media of exchange but also the vesting of power in institutions that must be "trusted" in an abstract rather than personal or experiential fashion. Finally, the reflexive quality of modernity inheres in its abandonment of stagnant and inflexible truths for the sake of a continually evolving process of knowledge reevaluation, a process possible only when "new" knowledge becomes a regular expectation. According to Giddens, all three operations "presume universalizing properties that explain the expansionist" nature of modern life and the "globalization of social activity."[54]

The transformations just outlined describe the general structural elements of a path of cultural globalization embarked upon—at least in industrial societies—since the inception of modernity. As these elements guide us into the present, they make it possible for new conceptions of well-being to manifest themselves. In contemporary societies, Giddens detects as a significant cultural event the rise of "life politics" at the expense of the old "emancipatory politics."[55] While emancipatory politics are essentially oriented toward "others"—or at least presuppose them—life politics concern issues of freedom of decision regarding how an individual life should be lived. Life politics, according to Giddens, presuppose in themselves a certain degree of emancipation. But the essential point is that life politics, by focusing on the individual, release one from the burdens of association with, considering the outlook of, and responsibilities toward others.

This point may be contested on the ground that not all "others" are sacrificed at the altar of life politics; rather, it is specifically those communities whose integration was highlighted in the political logic of modernity, notably "nations" and "classes," that are bypassed. Feminist and gay movements, for example, are arguably about life politics and a new kind of individualism, but they do create new kinds of communities. These communities, furthermore, easily and frequently transgress national boundaries. But as far as transnational culture is concerned, by prioritizing quality of life and individual freedom above issues of belonging, life politics inadvertently contribute to the emergence of new genres of global culture. In the sphere of life politics, the stress is no longer on the active transformation of the world but, rather, on reducing the ability of the "world" (one's country included) to interfere with one's conduct of an already emancipated life. In fact, life politics capitalize on the modernist disunity of time and place and the permanent critique of received knowledge. These become sources for the introduction of a sense of individual autonomy that national cultures, themselves long infused with those universalizing ethos, can no longer suppress.

Commentators such as Daniel Bell, on the other hand, place little value on the potential of life politics to furnish the ground for a potential global culture oriented toward individual freedom and quality of life. Bell regards life politics as a major threat to the very culture that gave rise to capitalism. In his classic *The Cultural Contradictions of Capitalism* Bell notes that the prerequisites for capitalist economy, such as rationality, sobriety, and discipline—ostensibly provided by the Protestant ethic— were collapsing in the face of the "revolution of rising entitlements," as is most clearly evident in the aspiration to limitless material self-fulfillment attendant on consumer capitalism. For Bell, the hedonism and exhibitionism that are at the heart of life politics are fundamentally irreconcilable with the forces that brought forth capitalism, even though the pursuit of hedonism is inseparable from the entrenchment of capitalism itself. The ethical move in the history of capitalism from delayed to immediate gratification, coupled with modernism's self-referential proclivity to dramatize each moment, destroys a rational cosmos of time sequence and measures of value, leaving no standard for coherent judgment. For Bell, this erosion anticipates the irrationality expressed in postmodern thought,[56] which here is seen as a natural product of highly developed capitalist culture.

Apart from an unenthusiastic nod toward religion as a connective communitarian tissue, Bell offers no solution to the dilemma he introduces. In fact, he acknowledges that the only thing that would truly destroy capitalism today would be a return to the vaunted Puritan ethic of prudent consumption and delayed gratification.[57] And in general Bell never seems confident that moral calls today could by themselves facilitate a return to a romanticized fusion between the early capitalist ethos, communitarian ethics, and a transtemporal rational cosmos. But his thesis underscores the increased significance of issues of individual welfare with the spread and entrenchment of capitalism. For our purposes, however, it is important to disentangle the two kinds of "entitlements" that Bell mixes together, namely, those attached to hedonistic pursuits and those that consist of guarantees and protections demanded from a national government by its constituency. T. H. Marshall argued in his aforementioned thesis that the latter was an indispensable twentieth-century extension of the idea of citizenship whereby social welfare guarantees were appended to the civil and political meanings of citizenship that had emerged in the eighteenth and nineteenth centuries. This meant that the legitimacy of national structures of power hinged on their capacity to fulfill or live up to what had become expected obligations of governance.

In contrast to Daniel Bell, Marshall did not condemn those "entitlements" or their seekers. The difference in attitudes may be traced in part to the different sociocultural contexts, European versus U.S., within which these perspectives were introduced.[58] In Europe the feasibility of the welfare state was premised on contingent conditions—a small number of users, continuous economic growth, and fiscal solvency of the state—all of which ceased to be the case by the 1970s. Wolfgang Streeck suggests that Western European national governments' activation of what eventually became the EU after 1985 was underpinned in part by their growing inability to disavow increasingly expensive obligations toward their national labor forces within national territories. Thus far— and apart from Britain, where the Thatcherite war on the welfare state has scored significant material and psychological victories—the dismantling of the welfare state has met far greater resistance in Europe than it has on the other side of the Atlantic, where the idea of state-sponsored welfare has always had much weaker cultural and political support. In Europe the older history of welfare is tied to the earlier consolidation of interventionist governmental systems, and furthermore, the long internal peace within Western Europe after World War II was consciously related to these methods of taming the masses by economic guarantees, alleviating existential anxieties, and displaying capitalism's ability to offer bounties left and right at a point when its ideological contestant had all its teeth and a not-insignificant appeal.[59]

While originally broadening the idea of citizenship within national borders, the welfare state was reproduced in various Western countries and was ultimately stripped of national uniqueness. Thus, rather than focusing on their own welfare state as a unique source of social citizenship, citizens of a given set of countries with roughly comparable levels of or commitments to the idea of social welfare (for example, the EU) come to redefine the normative level of well-being within a more transnational than national framework. The sociologist Victor Scardigli, for instance, applied to Western Europe a model for measuring commonalities in lifestyle, consisting of three elements: types of productive activities, life conditions, and attitudes of the population.[60] On all three scores he detected a cross-national convergence toward a single lifestyle, a lifestyle for which mass consumption was a crucial defining element.[61] In itself this finding is not surprising. The interesting point is that the Western European case illustrates a *consequential* convergence in "lifestyles," since that convergence itself removes many cultural impediments that may otherwise face political, institutional, and economic integration. The point is not that integration then becomes inevitable but, rather, that the economic unification of any territory would be expected to be least problematic when the different parts of the territory in question exhibit comparable lifestyles and definitions of well-being. But by itself this accomplishment is not enough to substantiate a union, and as many recent examples testify, its lack does not in itself make the union impossible.[62]

Thus the historically emergent confluence between culture and political economy has less to do with any essentially "national" culture than with the efforts of various national jurisdictions to arbitrate the fragmentations, dislocations, and conflicts of interest generated regularly by large-scale business cycles. National culture's capacity to maintain a sense of parochialism is not unrelated to a relatively short-lived confluence between the social and civil meanings of citizenship, a confluence that served to shield the population from adverse effects of global capitalism. In its heyday, U.S. capitalism's nonchalant attitude toward nationalism[63] came in part from the fact of an economic domination so extensive that within the United States itself there was little need for protection against the global economic machinery.

The most widespread feeling associated with global capitalism is a mixed one: the allure of adventures, combined with the fear of being humbled in such a shifty marketplace. The latter is most evident in any attempt to withdraw from the global processes of capitalism through isolation or to limit a nation's exposure to them through fortified borders. These recurrent responses frequently occasion discourses that highlight government's role as the economic protector of first resort. More insidiously, they may also accentuate a collective cultural "character" in such a way that those classified as foreigners, immigrants, or otherwise non-nationals can be excluded on moral and political (as well as the usual economic) grounds. One can argue that a history or sociology of transnational economy can be written as a history or sociology of such withdrawals or exclusions, inasmuch as it can be written in terms of the growth of an expansive sense of communion.

As is well known, the classical Marxist analysis of capital emphasized a particular angle of exclusionary practice. The fact that capitalism is sustained by an appropriation of the surplus value means that capitalism sets limits on the *replicability* of life expectations. For example, theorists of unequal exchange who posit a core/periphery duality in the global economy emphasize that while both core and periphery are part of the same entangled web of interdependencies, the system itself is premised on structural inequalities, which prevent peripheral countries from catching up with core countries. Chase-Dunn and Hall stress that "*it is world-systems that develop,* not societies."[64] This grandiosely abstract formulation, so frequently encountered in world system research, must be pinned down more concretely, however, so that one can see the trees in the forest. For there are certain agencies in the world economy that "develop" more than others, and their "development" is what is most dialectically ingrained in the development of the system at large. The agency that "develops" most in the world system is naturally the transnational corporation, which knows that its world is one consisting of similar corporations, not of countries and societies. In his study of the auto industry, for example, Jordan Lewis compiled a great deal of evidence to show that though Ford and Mazda, for instance, are competitors, Mazda regards its *main* competitors to be Honda, Nissan, and Toyota, while those of Ford are Chrysler, General Motors, and Toyota.[65] This picture shows that lines of competition among big concerns do not follow national or political divisions. In spite of this different map of the world that the corporations keep for themselves, the existence of boundaries at the levels of politics and popular culture continues to make possible the occasional resort to exclusionary discourse based on foreignness, when one of the big firms loses shares in the marketplace.

But there are no foreigners at the level of global capitalism. As a process structured by globally operative economic rules, capitalism has no intrinsic connection to any particular parochial culture. In modern times the example of Japan is frequently cited in order to show how capitalism could be successfully integrated into a cultural context completely different from that of the West.[66] As for earlier times, Weber's assertion of the uniqueness of Western capitalism has been effectively contested. The universal reach of merchant capitalism, as Abu-Lughod shows in her study of the medieval world system, was coterminous with a plurality of cultural paradigms in various world regions that were heavy participants. An economic world system does not necessarily result in phasing out differences in value orientations or belief systems. In modern times, however, one can isolate a number of specific global forces that have become foundational for the reception of ideas about lifestyles and for reorienting the meaning of happiness in different contexts: the emulative impulse, the context of power relations, the transformations of modernity, the welfare standards, and the individualist premise of life politics. These are sites of contention, conflict, and fragmentation, but not because they summarize the essence of conflict between global modernity and "traditional" society; we are all moderns now. What the global forces summed up in the preceding discussion point to are sites of contention as they are *interpreted in relation to rather than in opposition to* local paradigms, "cultural" or otherwise. What role such ideas will actually play in the growth of transnational culture depends not so much on what they essentially mean as on how they are transmitted, interpreted, and understood in diverse cultural systems. I would like now to turn to the structure and dynamics of those channels through which ideas, images, discourses, and knowledge systems are carried across these distances.

Communication and the Circulation of Icons

The *substance* of any transnational culture is inherently less knowable than the simple *communicative fact* that it entails systematic interactions with manifest others, who appear as distinct cultural categories. Of course, there is no reason to presume that the communicative dynamic involves equality of any sort, since "communication" could very well be a translation of already existent political and economic imbalances between communicating parties. But the point is that if the notion of "culture" means anything when it comes to "cross-cultural" communication, then it would be a process for the digestion or translation of logics of relations into images. In this sense, the notion of culture refers to the method of assessment of the boundary between the self and the Other. The communicative aspect of culture consists of how it defines for the ego a space and a place to occupy in the world. To that end, knowledge of difference does not need to be accurate, complete, or certain. A fraction of a sentence, a totalizing term, a TV image may suffice to create this knowledge or reinforce already existent hints thereof.

Therefore, transnational "culture" is prefigured first in the *mechanisms* that allow the transnational flow of information, before it can be seen in the dissemination of relatively common beliefs, standards, norms, and habits. What is this information? How are its signals transmitted? Who transmits them? How are they interpreted? Who demands what types of information? These are the essential questions of contemporary global culture. Premodern transnational cultures were fed by different inputs, such as common spiritual ideas and expectations supplied by the great world religions. "Information," as a referent of knowledge to be supplied, was essential for global transactions only for Europeans, such as Marco

Polo, who were for the most part strangers to the old world system. Ibn Battuta, the Muslim contemporary of Marco Polo, frequently mentioned cross-cultural trade, which flourished despite the lack of linguistic commonality among trading communities.[67] His reports digress, for example, on markets in the wilderness of central Asia in which traders were never certain whether their exchange partners were humans or ghosts.[68] That the mysterious identity of trade partners does little to hinder trade itself is a well-established trope in economic history. The fabled "silent trade," of which there are reports from the time of Herodotus until the late seventeenth century, was conducted near the southern edge of the Sahara. Northern traders left sacks of salt on the ground to be picked up by sub-Saharan traders in exchange for gold dust or groundnuts at an appointed time each year, without the traders ever seeing each other.[69] As such reports illustrate, historical trade did not always presuppose extensive knowledge of the nature of "difference"; in fact, it frequently seemed to require obliviousness to both the concept and the reality of difference.

With the coming into being of the modern world system, the nature of trade partners, and all Others, could no longer be left to the integrity of anonymity. The first Chinese envoy to Europe, Hsieh Fuching (1890–1894), mentions in his diary that he was requested by officials at the Foreign Office in London to finally inspect the contents of a box, still wrapped in its original yellow silk, that had arrived from China more than seventy years earlier. Hsieh found in the box various gifts intended for King George III, which had been sent by the Jiaqing emperor (1796–1820). The box also contained a letter to the king written in Chinese, Manchurian, and Latin.[70] One of the most puzzling aspects illuminated by the story, of course, is the magnitude of disinterest in the possibilities offered by a rare contact with a legendary power such as China, so that a box destined from one royal personage to another could remain unopened until the nature of the contact between Europe and China had changed (but it is also noteworthy that the box had not been disposed of either).

The story is more than one of an aborted contact. The emperor's letter was essentially an apology for a diplomatic faux pas, in which a British envoy was dismissed for refusing to prostrate himself before the emperor as was customary. In discussing the incident, Hsieh Fuching mentions earlier episodes in which European envoys had been excused from the prostration because their arrival, unlike that of the envoy in question, had been preceded by an elaborate arrangement for a different kind of reception ceremony. In Jiaqing's case, the emperor was not content to simply dismiss the recalcitrant British envoy. Rather, he remained curious about the origins of the Englishman's unusual behavior and was finally told about cultural differences in manners and etiquette by governors of two maritime provinces that had more regular dealings with foreigners. Like many emperors preceding him, Jiaqing was willing to tolerate prearranged mannerist diversities. And hence the trilingual apology and the origin of the box of gifts wrapped in yellow silk, destined to remain uninspected amid the growing list of exotica in a London government office.

Could the box have been opened when it was received? Would that simple act of reciprocating a communicative gesture have changed history? Of course, we do not know the answers to hypothetical questions. But one can only wonder why, in an age of remarkable Western curiosity and discoveries, such a rare delivery was examined only when it was no longer capable of effecting any geopolitical shifts in the balance of power. It is difficult not to assume that had the box been opened and had its contents been appreciated as they were intended to be by the sender, there would have been some disruption of then-emergent notions regarding the West's self-assured distinction from "Oriental despotism." In his account of the incident, Hsieh Fuching mentions that the habit of prostrating oneself before the Chinese emperor was widely discussed at the time in the English press, which was unanimous in asserting that Englishmen *in particular* should not be subject to that kind of humiliation. The European indignation at the practice of Oriental prostration itself cannot be taken seriously. For in 1896, in an ostensibly far more enlightened age, just a few years after the box had been opened by Hsieh and nearly three-quarters of a century after the Oriental incident, the English press printed one of the most famous drawings of the colonial age, depicting Ashanti chiefs prostrating before upright, proud English officers, following the latter's conquest of the former.

At a basic level, therefore, one may distinguish between two kinds of information characterizing two general structures of global contact. When the contact is administered by political powers, as in the case just discussed, it tends to involve dynamics intended for the establishment of relative hierarchies. These dynamics are not necessarily all that such contacts consist of, but it especially tends to be the case when the relative standing or comparability of the "civilizations" in question is yet to be determined. The Chinese and the Ashanti, worlds apart from each other, were equally mysterious political qualities. From a governmental point of view, such mysteries can only sensitize its hierarchical imagination. The other general structure of contact is that characterized by more salient movements, such as those of trade, pilgrimage, adventure, and so on. While the incentives for trade, pilgrimage, or adventure point to different world outlooks, they are not always easy to separate apart in history. Pilgrimage and trade routes frequently overlapped in Arabia, Bengal, China, and elsewhere. For explorers like Ibn Battuta or Ibn Jubayr, pilgrimage and adventure were synonymous. But at the most basic level, when the power to impose hierarchies of the political sort is absent, the common dynamic regulating information in such venues involves a negotiated settlement with a world that *speaks back* to the explorer.

The problems of this latter dynamic are richly illustrated in Jonathan Spence's re-creation of the story of Hu, which portrays the traumatic encounter between Foucquet, a French Jesuit, and Hu, a lowly Chinese literatus who accompanied him to France in 1722. Hu eventually lapsed into madness and was confined to an insane asylum for most of his stay in France, which ended in 1726.[71] The complicated story is a remarkable illustration of the problem of communication attendant to the rise of modern, quasi-anthropological methods of exploration. As he left Canton Hu left behind as well his world of communicability; thereafter, he could talk only to those who spoke his language, who were certainly not in abundant supply in Europe then. Moreover, his madness, which is never fully accounted for in the sources, seems clearly implicated in two pivotal conflicts. The first concerns his own interpretation of Christianity, which he had adopted back in Canton—complete with flavors and accents of the local ethos of humility and duty. The second pertains to the delimited task of copying Chinese classics, a task for which he had been imported into Europe and which he reportedly tried to refrain from doing in his new world.

Hu's unexpected outbursts, which were taken as signs of mental illness—preaching in Chinese to curious Parisian crowds about the separation of the sexes; refusing luxury items such as blankets, fine clothing, or even carriage rides; frequently expressing a desire to *walk* back to China and write his own book of discoveries along the way—baffled his European companions, who expected him to be not the articulate discoverer but the mute discovered. In the story of Hu there was little in the way of dialogic expectations; Hu was never expected to be fit to discover Europe as Foucquet and the Jesuits were fit to discover China, and in any case Europe itself was not the issue for them, at least not directly. Foucquet's lifework in China centered on trying to prove the theological affinity between Confucian classics and the Gospel and thus to argue the case for a historically established communion with a massive chunk of world population and a formidable empire. In light of such a magnificent project, the overwhelming delight of discovering the unexpected rootedness of the far-removed Christianity in China decided the parameters of the communicative dynamic. According to Foucquet's theory, the Chinese classics had always spoken to Western Christianity, not to a self-referential cosmos.

Foucquet's project and Hu's madness, thus, are inversely related. For Hu, all previous reference points were stripped from him as he boarded a European ship peopled with total strangers. In fact, his departure was a last-minute, unscheduled interruption of the routine of his life. Having no theoretical project of his own, the world became for him a blank page again, for the first time since childhood. Thus the insane desire to walk rather than sail back to China and to register in detail a thoroughly novel world. For Foucquet, on the other hand, the knowledge needed to digest his discovery had already been supplied in his theological training *before* he landed in China. In some way, his tale illustrates the trials of the age of induction as a means for universal knowledge.

In this light, Foucquet's now little-known theory is not fundamentally different from later and more memorable projects. The popularity in Europe of such philosophical-literary movements as Romanticism was based in part on its harmonious communication with the spirit of the unknown and distant. Edward Said argued that the massive *Description l'Egypte,* the main intellectual product of Napoleon's ill-fated expedition into Egypt, could be apprehended as a project of inserting Egypt into a pregiven tableau of world civilizational history rather than as a value-free project of discovery.[72] For Said, it was noteworthy how little space, relatively, was devoted to contemporaneous Egypt in the *Description,* in a way not so dissimilar to Foucquet's earlier lack of interest in contemporaneous Chinese reality (or Chinese individuals, for that matter).

These episodes exemplify the emergence of a modernist exploratory trend whose primary technique was to catalogue comparative civilizational information following specified methods. In an interesting study of little-known early-modern European travels, Justin Stagl showed that the history of European travel began to exhibit formal "methodizing" tendencies around the 1600s and after. Those tendencies are evidenced in the growth of a genre of advice manuals to travelers regarding how to learn "properly" from their adventures.[73] While many of the manuals studied by Stagl stress what might be called "scientific" or "morally neutral" methods of observation, they regulate travel in the service of a larger process of *comparative* cultural inquiry. In the age of advice manuals, travel was no longer inwardly directed or intended primarily for the enrichment of the soul, as it had been molded in the declining practice of European pilgrimage. Travel was becoming a social activity, in the sense that its narrative was intended to be communicated beyond the soul.

The Role of the Medium

Today the emphasis has shifted away from the *content*-driven idea of providing a comparative encyclopedic "catalogue" of cultures toward a *form*-driven idea of communication prefigured by the medium itself.[74] In the global age, the structure, venues, and very possibilities of information transmission are inseparable from questions of control of and access to technological forms: telecommunications, mass media networks, air waves, satellites, systems for the storage, organization, and retrieval of information, and so on. One of the most important and basic considerations regarding all such information technologies concerns the degree of universal accessibility. This concern is in the nature of the form, which because of inherent issues of price, location, licensing, property, profitability, use-right, and so on, give rise to the specter of information monopoly.

The question of control and access to sophisticated information gathering technologies rises again with every invention in information technology, only to disappear again as that technology is irreversibly put into use. That dynamic is exemplified in the now-dormant debate over satellite telediction in the 1970s. The issue then concerned the deployment of U.S. satellites that could gather information on the subsoil of all continents, thereby providing the government in control of such satellites with the potential for possessing more information about deposits of raw materials and other unexplored natural riches than governments having sovereignty over the territories containing such resources.[75] Who has the right to know, share, or control this type of information? What is the status of national sovereignty in this regard? Does the existence of a technological capacity to accumulate information on a global scale call for transnational mechanism for the operation and control of that technology?

These questions, which were at the heart of the debate over telediction, could be formulated in a broader sense. The capacity of an outside force to know more about a society than that society could potentially know about itself has two prerequisites. In the first place, anyone having this capacity is usually in control of more than just satellites, computers, and other means for cataloguing encyclopedic systems in retrievable formats. When it comes to comparative cultural communication, modern communication technologies ought not to be considered apart from an inquisitive heritage evident in the history of libraries, translations, civilizational compendia, and the professionalization of the practices of transborder knowledge through such academic disciplines as anthropology, regional studies, or some branches of political science. In this context, the introduction of something like telediction added no new *substance* to transborder knowledge. It only magnified an old-fashioned method of noncommunicative gathering of information from a distance. The distance was spatial and technological rather than spiritual or anthropological.

Second, from the point of view of any power—whether governmental or corporate—that possesses a unique capacity for gathering, storing, and retrieving information, the problem is less one of access than of manageability. The existence of diverse fields and capacities for knowledge (satellites, communication technologies, academic disciplines, translations, and so on), inasmuch as it indicates varying levels and sources of interest in those that are manifestly Other, tends to create an information multifariousness, as well as information overload. This calls for an effort to *organize* this knowledge. Of course, we do not have just one way to organize available information. The "meaning" of information depends, in the ultimate analysis, on such factors as the interests, institutional context, sociopolitical reality, and ideology of the particular group set out to organize information (such as industries, governments, cultural analysts, missionaries, aid agencies).

As just addressed, the question of the availability and organization of transnational knowledge concerns noncommunicative episodes, in the sense that the one who gathers information and the one about whom information is gathered could be treated as distinct entities. More historically ubiquitous are those models for collecting and organizing knowledge that presuppose a communicative process. The contribution of this type of communication to the growth of collective identities was first highlighted in Karl Deutsch's seminal study of nationalism, *Nationalism and Social Communication*. In each society, Deutsch suggested, there existed essential units or channels of communication that enhanced feelings of togetherness. Those include transportation networks, cultural communities, markets, speech communities, and so on. Deutsch cited many historical cases to support the thesis that such communication channels make societies. The range of communicative conditions conducive to the growth of social solidarity through communication depended on technology; from the availability of material for advanced ship building in medieval Norway, which gave rise to the Viking way of life, to the role of Dutch dikes and polders in creating a cultural distinction between the Netherlands and Germany, to the use of a particular bridge-building technology in the Swiss Alps in the thirteenth century, which "furnished the economic basis for an independent 'pass state.'"[76]

The communicative model suggests that with the technical improvement of the means of communication, communities that were isolated from each other come to exchange those elements within the reservoir of the cultural symbols that tend to be most common between them. Ultimately, those larger symbols of commonality become the foundations of a unifying national culture. Ernest Gellner has criticized this model for its underlying presumption that certain ideas—for example, nationalism—exist in a latent state, waiting for the evolution of a system of communication to carry them around. For Gellner, the main concern is more with the *structure* of the medium of communication itself than with what is transmitted through it. It is the existence of abstract, one-to-many communication systems that engenders acceptance of new forms of interpersonal links. Thus, in this case, only those who accept the medium and understand it see themselves as belonging to the community of the nation.[77]

Despite different points of emphasis, the various models just summarized posit a view of social communication that presumes openness and universal accessibility rather than monopoly or restricted access. A further presumption in such perspectives flows from the Eurocentric limits of the thesis regarding the role of mass communication in the formation and maintenance of collective identities. Many historical and contemporary cases testify that *by itself* the introduction of mass communication channels creates no centripetal forces within claimed national borders. Many postcolonial societies, from continental India to tiny Rwanda, have experienced violent intergroup fissures in spite of decades of increasing saturation with means of mass communication. Fissures of varying intensity were also responsible for fragmenting former Eastern

Bloc countries that were organized around transnational principles, notably the Soviet Union, Yugoslavia, and Czechoslovakia. Of course, one ought not surmise that such a state of affairs could only have played itself out in a Third World organized by the trials of postcoloniality or in a Second World organized by internationalist principles. Fissures of the same nature in such Western locales as Belgium, Canada, and Northern Ireland have also withstood mass communication's onslaught upon society. Even in a country as saturated with means of mass communication as the United States, many suggest that race defines, as it has always done, distinct national categories.[78]

The frequent failure of centripetal forces to materialize as theories of mass communication propose seems to suggest that just as they could contribute to broadening the conceptions of belonging, solidarity, and identity, channels of communication could also serve merely to consolidate preexistent patterns, habits, values, and methods of reasoning. Mattelart, Delcourt, and Mattelart point out that mass media often simply trail behind a preexistent mode of evaluating information: "[In Africa], the journalist has very little credibility among the rural population: a piece of news must be supported, discussed and evaluated in terms of what is known about the informer."[79] In such a case, mass communication channels simply meet a parochial culture on its own terms. Rather than effecting any essential cultural change, mass communication here simply activates or reinforces preexistent patterns, values, and frames of solidarity. This suggests that for a channel or unit of communication to transform ordinary social relations, it is not enough that it is simply made available. It must operate in the context of ongoing social transformations, as these themselves provide *demand* for new means and styles of communication.

Karl Deutsch assumes that in connection to the formation of collective identities, mass communication operates mostly in the latter fashion. Concretely, he stresses the rate of population enlisted in a system of communication ("mobilized population") as a crucial indicator of the possibility of shifts in patterns of solidarity as a response to new communication technologies. The yardsticks he proposes for measuring the rate of "mobilized population" include the ratio of town to rural population; the percentage of people involved in occupations others than agriculture, forestry, or fishing; the preponderance of large employment units; newspaper readership; the number of people paying direct taxes to a central government, subject to military service, attending school, or participating

in large markets; the volume of mail; and rates of literacy, film atten-
dance, exposure to mass media, registered voters, social security registra-
tion, and so on.[80] This list of potential measurements of a population's
mobilization is clearly structured according to the notion of accessibility.
In other words, it involves a mass of people who are either in a position
to make use of or are exposed to channels that regularly connect them to
a larger social whole.

As pointed out earlier, one of the major problems of this perspective
is that it has little to say about how accessibility in itself creates a sense of
solidarity among those who use or are exposed to channels of communication. We know, for instance, that it is common for mass media programs
directed toward a hypostatized "common denominator" to be watched
with little attention, for voters to vote without enthusiasm, for school
students or military conscripts to feel constricted by discipline and to
want to leave, for city dwellers to feel alienated from the impersonality
and mass nature of their surroundings or to idealize or long for a vaca-
tion in the isolated country. In this sense, Deutsch's "mobilized population" serves only as a numerical indicator of the rate of accessibility of
channels of communication. It is not a useful indicator of spiritual energy
or investment, nor does it preclude the possibility that communication
channels can be used strictly for utilitarian, everyday purposes rather
than as sources for spiritual energies and abstract systems of bonds.

National as well as transnational solidarities, therefore, cannot be
premised solely on the mere existence of communication channels or
practices that have wide reach or are otherwise accessible. The question
of connective culture is clearly broader than questions of communication
or information. On the other hand, it would seem obvious that the
growth of expansive fields of cultural commonalities and patterns of solidarity could be hampered if there were no or only inferior channels and
practices of communication and information. But at this point, it is precisely those communicative and informational aspects of "culture" that
are most ubiquitous at the transnational level. One cannot argue that *in
itself* the existence of transnational systems of information dissemination
forms a basis for the evolution of a transnational culture. Rather, one
needs to evaluate the confluence of venues of communication and information with the emergence of historic forces in the economy, politics,
and social life. And since these interactions have yet to crystallize into
recognizably stable patterns, their probable ramifications for the prospects of a transnational culture cannot be fully expounded from our van-

tage point. What can be suggested, however, are the dynamics of hope and use that occasion the coming into existence of a system of communication or information on a large scale, as we are witnessing today.

Exchange of Factuality and Imagination

Inseparable from the nation-state's self-awareness, one trajectory involved in the process of creating a channel, unit, or trope of mass communication corresponds to efforts by governments to preserve or enhance a national *distinction*. This is usually done when it is feared that the imagined national-rootedness of certain tropes needs special preservationist effort as they compete against supranational themes driven by supranational media. Addressing the status of the European film industry as early as 1982, a French official put it succinctly:

> The lesson of the last 20 years in Europe is clear: there can be no national cinema without a policy of aid to the national cinema. This is true for France, for Italy, for Germany. . . . The example of Great Britain (which made the opposite choice) is very instructive in this respect: a film industry survives, but *British* cinema has practically disappeared.[81]

The demonstrated survival of a film industry in Britain (precisely because it either dropped or universalized local themes) seems to clearly indicate a purely *economic* rather than *cultural* survival because it came at the price of losing national distinction. The theory that the French (or German or Italian or Dutch) cinema will fail if not subsidized assumes that local themes need subsidy because they are more difficult to market internationally and are thus less profitable to produce. Moreover, such productions face stiff international competition *within* their own home territory. That is, their natural audience is proving itself hospitable to transnational cultural invasions.[82]

In part, the incentive for a national government to preserve a sense of national cultural distinction has much to do with its understanding of the ground of its own legitimacy. In much of the 1970s and 1980s, different Western European countries committed massive resources to the creation of information structures (satellites, cable systems, telecommunication, and the like) despite public indifference. From a regional economic perspective such expenditures were clearly wasteful, since they duplicated each other along economically fading national lines. That such grand projects were grand manifestations of supply without any realistic assessment of demand spells out a principle that is at the heart of the political culture of nationalism: In the absence of regional integration, information systems in a region tend to develop more in order to keep national governments from falling behind their neighbors in terms of cultural capacity than in order to meet public demand for such systems.[83]

Whereas national governments focus on instrumental cultural capacity vis-à-vis other governments, national commentators are generally obsessed with the more philosophical question of the danger posed to national essence by the flood of generic transnational cultural and entertainment imports. Thousands of examples of this concern can be readily cited today. To pick one typical example, some local commentators in Malaysia expressed the need to respond to Western producers' predilection to pay attention only to exotic or long-abandoned practices (for example, topless tribal women) at the expense of the contemporary, mundane everyday life in the country.[84] Those commentators found themselves ultimately defending government controls over mass media programming. They rejected the claim that such controls lead to a prevalence of non-market-driven "dull" programs, arguing that only the Western eye perceived them as such. According to this view, by freeing media from the bonds of the market, benevolent media controls would create a noncommercial space for productions that are grounded in the ordinary realities of local life.[85]

Though driven by different motivations, the two outlined approaches (subsidy and control) tend to take the national market as a natural market for a given culture. Both perspectives entail an awareness that the world outside is encroaching upon one's own territory. But it is also observed that in some cases, the domination of a national information market by local enterprises is connected to the ability of these enterprises to develop a working symbiosis with and an orientation toward the world outside. This is because the consumer base of a "national" entertainment industry is determined not in terms of the size of a population bounded by political borders but, rather, in terms of audiences that have an analogous linguistic-cultural universe. Thus a film or a program produced in Mexico or Argentina could be marketed throughout Latin America and in Spain; those produced in Egypt or Lebanon circulate just as readily throughout the entire Arab Middle East and North Africa.

In every world region, in fact, one finds at least one vigorous center of visual media production, whose products are intended for the region as a whole as well as for "domestic" audiences. In the Middle East and North Africa it is Egypt; in Spanish-speaking America, there are Mexico and Argentina; in central Asia and the Persian Gulf it is India; in Southeast Asia it is Hong Kong. In addition to such regional centers, in every region of the world statistics show a disproportionate predominance of U.S.-produced commercial films in the entertainment market—so much so, in fact, that in some circles the wide reach of the U.S. entertainment industry is frequently cited as evidence for the emergence of a global culture, and some readily refer to "Americanization" when they wish to summarily describe contemporary cultural globalization.

This view of cultural globalization is justified only if one pays attention to nothing more than the surface. The predominance of U.S.-produced films over imported films in almost every region of the world is evident, although there are regional differences (for example, weaker penetration in Asian countries). This has been the case in spite of a significant effort on the part of various national governments to sustain a viable national film industry, an effort that is now in general decline. France is the country in Europe that most consciously resisted the "Americanization" of its culture. Yet 22 percent of the commercial films shown in France in 1993 were cross-national coproductions; another 60 percent were imports, and of the latter well over half were U.S. films. This was one of the lowest rates of film imports from the United States in Western Europe. France also displayed some of the highest rates of exchange in Europe with non-Western sources of commercial entertainment. Overall, however, the numbers clearly show an entertainment context that is greatly governed by Western sources (a state of affairs that contributes to the idea that there is such a unified or relatively distinct set of values that can be termed "Western culture"). In other words, in addition to the preponderance of films imported from the United States, many of whose tropes, styles, genres, and characters are quite familiar to European audiences, much of what remains of the film market in Europe consists of exchanges that take place within the EU bloc itself, including a rising number of inter-EU coproductions.[86]

The experience of other countries offers a useful comparative perspective on how the globalization of culture operates in different regions. For example, with the exception of the Philippines—which has a unique historical connection to the United States—Southeast Asian countries are markedly less interested than are Western Europeans in U.S. commercial entertainment productions, even though the rate of importation continues to be significant. By contrast, films from other major production sites in Asia (namely, Hong Kong, Japan, and to some extent India) are strongly competitive in the region, while they do not fare nearly as well in Europe. Similarly, the rate of exchange with Western Europe is pretty much as dismal, in relative terms, as that represented in Western Europe for commercial films originating in Asia. This contrast seems to suggest one trend that is found in many regions: While many of the commercial entertainment productions from the United States have enough transnational character to carry them across borders in significant numbers, they tend to compete almost exclusively with productions done within those regions. The relative dearth of the kind of cultural exchange represented in film between, say, Europe and Asia illustrates the point. Thus what we seem to be witnessing is a *variety* of local cultural frames competing directly with a *single* transnational source of cultural supply.

But there is a larger picture to be gleaned. The remarkable global presence of the U.S. film industry may not be related to any factor more strongly than to that industry's financial resourcefulness, which in an age of global capitalism has the capacity to open markets already exposed to other features of a globally organized marketplace. Almost everywhere, the rate of importation is greater than the rate of local production. For most countries in the world, in fact, it is dozens of times greater. Countries with large local markets and a historically established film industry, such as India, France, Germany, Italy, or Egypt, tend to display relatively smaller ratios of film imports to locally produced films, mainly because the size of their national audience and natural export markets allow more local films to be produced profitably. But even here, it is not unusual for imports to be several times local production. In some places, a thriving film-production industry resulted not so much from market conditions as from conscious official efforts to subsidize cinema as an aid in the building of a national culture (in Indonesia, for example). In other cases, a healthy rate of film production seems to be correlated with unique historical conditions of cultural independence, as in Thailand, one of the few countries in the world never to have succumbed to colonial rule. Thailand today is also one of the few countries in the world that still manages to watch (barely) more local than imported films. The only others who demonstrably accomplish such a feat are the United States and India.[87]

The data marshaled here seem to suggest that at least as far as the area of film is concerned, there is a clear transnational market. But this does not necessarily mean that there are standard global watching habits. Contemporary poststructuralist philosophy has questioned the appearance of totality by highlighting the heterogeneity of interpretations. Reception theory argues that what matters is not that diverse audiences are watching the same show but, rather, that such audiences are infusing the same show with their own ways of seeing. When two culturally distinct audiences watch *Dynasty*, for instance, do they pay attention to the same plot, events, characters, or twists? Earlier comparative research has already indicated that they do not. In Australia, Germany, Spain, or France, locally produced domestic dramas easily beat the once-popular *Dallas* or *Dynasty* whenever they were in direct competition.[88] In Germany and Austria it was only a matter of time before locally produced incarnations of the highly popular *Columbo* were offered. In Egypt the entire modern history of the country was recently serialized in a production closely modeled after American domestic dramas. This shows that it is not "American" culture that is universal but, rather, certain tropes that could be translated anywhere, and in such a way as to make them appear unmistakably "local."[89]

"Americanization" can be so unthreatening precisely because it is not so much a representation of a specific national culture as a set of universally adaptable tropes. Forms of cultural expression that have already been transnationalized after having emanated from a Western center of dissemination are no longer thought of as "imports." The earlier spread of the novel as a form of literary expression illustrates this dynamic. In her study of that process of transmission, Mary Layoun argues that, very much like what we witness today in terms of commercial film, the novel in places like Egypt or Japan first found its audience among urbanites who were most likely to be impacted by transnational culture. Eventually it was reproduced within local contexts, partially replacing previous forms of literary expression, such as poetry and folktales.[90]

Thus the issue concerns not "Americanization" as such, a term that survives either because of its rhetorical value for opponents who regard it as cultural imperialism or because of the propensity of U.S. patriots for lazy self-inflation. More precisely, the issue concerns the limits and nature of universal *adaptation* to which any cultural trope lends itself. In the context of transnational culture, "adaptation" refers to the possibility that imported themes and tropes inform productions that appear locally flavored and locally relevant nonetheless. The more this possibility is acted upon, the more we detect the major shift in receiving habits attendant to the transnational era. While the essential cultural distinction between groups in modernity has been seen at the level of *both form and content,* transnational trends today are breaking up this perspectivist unity. In the light of cultural exchange today, the more enduring cultural distinctions (national or otherwise) are visible to the audience not in the form but mostly in the content of cultural production. The form is the manner of presentation and the pure structure of the story; the content is the topical specificity and uniqueness of its events. *It is the form that embodies transnational culture.* Very often, it is the ability of one form to accommodate several contents that transnationalizes it. This is especially the case with commercial entertainment, which, as Mattelart, Delcourt, and Mattelart suggest, is necessarily transnational in character:

> Commerce knows no frontiers. Markets have no limits. But states recognize the limits of other states and public services subscribe to this recognition. Commercial norms are necessarily more international than those of public service.... [In its quest for broad reach, a commercial market is free to reject] the cultural needs of *specialised* audiences.[91]

This does not necessarily imply that "specialized" audiences are unprofitable. If all audiences in the world are in some way "specialized" audiences, then the only programs that can be shown profitably across them are those that allow each such audience to consider itself addressed in some fashion and to enjoy the nonexclusive reverie of its image, interests, or worldview paraded within the same episode.[92] In the United States an example of this phenomenon would be the enormously successful *Cosby Show.* It has a clear multiracial following, but research demonstrates that it is watched very differently by blacks and whites.[93] The form of the show, its characters, and their stories, daily situations, and aspirations are transracial—even universal—in their playfulness. Furthermore, the fact that the program generally refrains from contentious pedagogical postures allows different audiences to "fill in the blanks" with desired and distinct meanings.

It may therefore well be the case that transnational culture essentially clusters around efforts to fill various voids. To appreciate the complex dynamics of this structure, one must ask whether the imaginary character of transnational culture is operative largely in the field of entertainment. Michèle Legros noted that in Belgium, after the airwaves were opened up to foreign senders, national television lost ground in entertainment programs but retained its audience in "informational" programs. That fact raised the possibility that as fictional imagination comes under the control of "foreigners," factual discourse remains directed toward the local, more intimate domain.[94] Does this mean that in the end, local reality comes to be felt through an internationalized imagination? In other words, does the gradual spread of internationalized imaginary equipment infuse the orientation toward local reality with "exterior" rather than "indigenous" models? How does the spread of transnational culture influence factual discourse at a local level?

Tables 1 and 2 provide one useful indicator for this dynamic, namely, the rate of translation of books in a few significant categories (Table 2) compared to rates of local production in the same categories (Table 1) in selected countries.[95] While this comparison may be marred by differences in literacy rates and book readership and by a lack of meaningful ways to measure the competing oral culture in some places, the trend among the book audiences is unmistakable. In countries from different regions and with widely divergent socioeconomic profiles, the rate of arts and literature among translations far exceeds what it is within locally produced books. Nearly everywhere, titles in arts and literature—usually the biggest category of titles—are less than 40 percent of the total. But within translations, such titles do not fall below 40 percent of the total, and frequently their rate is much higher. In half of the selected countries, arts and literature were represented two to three times more among translations than among locally produced books. The actual level of exposure to this category is certainly even higher, given that works of fiction are usually brought to the market in significantly higher runs than more serious nonfiction works, a category that includes academic and scientific books. Furthermore, a relatively low rate of local production of literary works does not seem to entail less interest in the literary and artistic imagination of the world.

A similar pattern can be detected in two other categories, namely, philosophy and religion, even though the rates are generally lower. If we think that these, combined with literature and the arts, represent the realm of the imaginary and the ideal, then it may be fruitful to compare how they fare with respect to genres representing the "factual" realm. As the tables indicate, the categories representing factual discourse, those grouped under social and natural sciences, are generally not encountered among translations as frequently as they are among local books. In fact,

Table 1. Percentage of Titles Published in Selected Countries

	Philosophy	Religion	Social Science	Natural Science	Arts and Literature
Egypt	1.9	10.6	12.7	15.1	16.0
India	3.6	7.4	28.3	15.4	40.5
Thailand	2.5	4.0	36.2	37.1	11.8
Japan	4.3	1.8	29.3	20.9	39.6
France	4.5	3.1	31.7	18.5	37.7
Germany	5.1	5.4	36.2	17.8	26.6
Italy	5.4	6.2	30.8	14.8	38.0
Brazil	10.6	13.1	32.4	14.4	15.8

Source: UNESCO. *Statistical Yearbook.* Paris: UNESCO, 1996.
Note: Data for Japan and Thailand are for 1992; for Egypt, 1993; for all others, 1994. For statistical purposes social sciences include geography and history, and natural science includes both pure and applied.

for the social sciences in particular, the percentage of titles is usually several times lower among translations than it is among local books. This observation seems to confirm the universality of what Legros suggested on the basis of the Belgian experience regarding the comparative vulnerability to transnationalism of the imaginary as opposed to the factual realms. While there is still no evidence suggesting the inevitable growth of horizontal solidarity across—and sometimes even within—national borders, there is a great deal of evidence from communication practices (films, mass media broadcasts, translations, and so on) to suggest that there is at least one dimension of human intellectual engagement that is more heavily invested in crossborder transactions than others: the fictional, literary, entertainment-oriented, or otherwise imaginary and ideational domains. Factual or informational discourse matters less and less the farther it is from one's house. While the factual-informational nexus continues to be referenced by local, national, or regional yardsticks, the imaginary-ideational one seems to be well equipped, or even more naturally expected, to escape such a prison. The ground for this capacity has already been offered by the globalization of modernity and, furthermore, by the loss of control over globalization by institutional actors, who are most associated with the declining factual and informational realm. As Kant once suggested, the "world" can only be imagined.

This does not mean, however, that the informational aspect of trans-

Table 2. Percentage of Translated Titles

	Philosophy	Religion	Social Science	Natural Science	Arts and Literature
Egypt	6.2	22.5	21.7	8.5	40.3
India	6.1	17.4	21.5	4.8	49.3
Thailand	19.4	1.0	2.8	12.0	64.8
Japan	5.9	4.0	20.9	21.6	47.0
France	5.9	8.5	15.2	15.1	54.5
West Germany	8.0	7.7	11.5	11.7	60.7
Italy	7.5	11.8	16.6	17.3	46.2
Brazil	9.3	13.1	13.9	14.6	48.5

Source: UNESCO. *Statistical Yearbook.* Paris: UNESCO, 1993.
Note: Data for Thailand are for 1985; for all others, 1994. For statistical purposes social sciences include geography and history, and natural science includes both pure and applied.

national communication is any less consequential. Information and news, transmitted across borders at a vast rate and creating worldviews and reactions to them nearly everywhere, tend to be generated by a small number of sources. Today there is only a handful of truly international news agencies, all based in the West. The recent wars in the Persian Gulf and the former Yugoslavia offered a not too vigorously contested prelude to how the dissemination of information on a world scale could be so effectively controlled by a single source—or at least by a number of sources sharing the same goal. This degree of information control is *repeatable,* since all the structures that brought it about are still in place, their logic and manner of control having been largely accepted, or at least left unchallenged. On the other hand, it could be said that this is neither new nor without foundations in the political economy of imperialism. Transnational channels of information do not operate outside of the ideational limits of the politico-economic determinants of the world system.[96] Our only consolation is that the transnational channels of the imaginary have the capacity to transcend such determinants, and at a more profuse pace. Yet in order for those alternative channels of the imaginary to work effectively upon the world and upon global life, they will need more and more the aid of the autonomous habits and liberated energies of alternative civil societies everywhere.

Control, Rationality, and Solidarity
in the Global Age

Now I would like to draw what I think are the most pertinent and practical implications of the range of arguments presented in this volume. It is useful to revisit the analytical distinction among the three spheres of economy, politics, and culture that is common in studies of globalization. In particular, what is of interest here are those elements that reveal new patterns of dialogue and disjunction among such spheres.

Economy and the Question of Control

Research on patterns of economic life in the modern global era lends general support to three main observations.

1. The obvious schemes of economic deregulation that one sees in most countries and across borders suggest a reemergence of a pre-Depression (or even late-nineteenth-century) model of economic life, long suppressed by statist regulations and Keynesian paradigms. However, there is an important novelty to be taken into account here; namely, that capital now operates at a higher degree of global coordination, centralization, and systematization than during the pre-Depression era and is therefore less anarchic in operation, though certainly more prone to quick movement. The reign of global financial capital, which changes hands now at eight times the rate of its circulation just five decades ago, is one of the clearest manifestations of this mobility. Put differently, one of the fundamental economic features of globalization is that capital has managed to reacquire the sense of autonomy from politically inspired regulation that it lost several decades ago. Yet its new autonomy possesses new features, notably that the institutions facilitating the movement and flow of transnational capital are more sophisticated. Along with this we find a largely successful effort by coordinated capital to provoke just enough of political

147

coordination to ensure that the world becomes as open as it is possible for it to be, so that the autonomy and prosperity of global capital may be sustained.

2. Along with this, we are witnessing the reemergence of even older features of capital, namely, from the precolonial, chartered companies era, although here as well there are some important modifications. As is well known, one of the main problems with the chartered companies was their need for new types of control over new types of markets. Control was then a novel obsession, especially in light of the decentralized and diffuse voluntarism that had characterized earlier patterns of global trade. That predicament mandated that the chartered company would assume state-like functions, most notoriously coercive and bureaucratic ones. It is unlikely that this pattern will be reenacted as it was.[1] What is more likely, however, is the enactment of a modern variation of the cooperative, voluntary rules that governed the medieval world system as described by Janet Abu-Lughod, translated into a set of new institutions of transnational corporate governance and adjudication of claims, some of which are described by Saskia Sassen. That is, the kinds of controls that regulate claims and rights attendant to the free flow of globally operative capital are now likely to be of an institutionalized but not politically accountable type. This leads to types of control that are both diffuse and shared. What this means, essentially, is that terms of control exercised on behalf of economic interests on a global scale come more and more to possess less-transparent features than either those terms of control that characterized the chartered companies era or those terms that characterized the subsequent era of political tutelage over such companies and over the economy at large.

3. These points raise the question that has been addressed many times in the course of this volume, namely, that of the possibility of politically regulating economic life in the global age. The likely instrument of governance on a global scale is the World Trade Organization or, in a braver world, something modeled after the European Commission. Such an institution would confine itself to ensuring coherence of economic governance and policies. Though these institutions are not accountable to voters, they are not exactly "totalitarian" because they are not expected to operate at the global level exactly as governments have operated at the national level. These new technocracies are unlikely to model themselves after the *corpus mysticum* as national governments have, since they rep-

resent nobody in particular and are simply administrative structures enforcing treaties. But if the idea of "regulation" entails enshrining on a global scale the same capacities that until the recent past were possible only within national boundaries, then we are obviously talking about the semblance of a "world state." The term has already been suggested by many who cannot imagine modes of regulation other than those paralleling what has become customary through long habit and exposure. But novelties require original thinking. One cannot afford to remain weighed down by the sheer force of the customary when its application in one context may be fruitful and in another disastrous.

A "world state" is only likely to be the most totalitarian institution that humanity has ever come to know. One may argue that if it somewhat mitigates conditions of exploitation, then it can be accepted as an updated version of the Social Contract, a version fit for a global age where economic concerns have become paramount; in this case, some freedom would be removed from the world in exchange for a semblance of "economic justice."

There are four basic problems with this proposal. The first concerns the question as to the source of the criteria according to which some values can be ranked above others. In this instance, the question is whether totalitarian control with unlimited reach and power is preferable to conditions that may be conducive to exploitation, or, put differently, whether the danger to freedom inherent in totalitarian proposals is less menacing than the danger of exploitation inherent in relatively free economic life. Proposals in one direction or another frequently miss this starting point, which requires that one should defend and make clear the criteria according to which one danger is worse than another, especially since no one has thus far been able to propose any total scheme lacking in any danger.[2]

The second basic problem with the proposal for global governance that would operate after the model of a "world state" flows from the first. That is, some would contest my assertion that such a state must by necessity be totalitarian. They would argue that with proper safeguards the world state can be democratized and thus made to operate with sufficient legitimacy and on behalf of large, huddled constituencies rather than small but resourceful interest groups. This is possible only in some fantasy land. In the first place, the character of any political institution is most likely to be determined by its creators, who can be counted upon not to make any conscious mistakes in constructing it so that it fulfills expected functions. Who is likely to be the creator? An institution of global governance is certainly not going to be brought into being by "global society" as such, as this is an abstraction that exists nowhere at the operational level. Rather, it is likely to be created by existing governments and existing bureaucracies, which have demonstrated time and again that when they seek the help of global institutions, they do so precisely because their democracies have become too burdensome and restrictive to their action. The global level, in other words, has always been used by national governments as a foil to the undesirable facets of internal politics, and there is no reason to expect that global governance would be used for any other purpose. In the third place, any enlargement of the scale of political institutions, as observed in a rich tradition running from Aristotle to Rousseau, entails a direct threat to democracy, since totalitarianism can be curtailed best at the tangible level of tangible communities. Most malfunctions of contemporary democracies—for example, in the United States, the thoroughly corrupt system of legalized bribery, panoptical control, mass indoctrination, and popular conformity—can be traced directly to the scale of those democracies. It is highly unlikely that extending this model into an even greater global level would lead to happier results, for at the global level not just individuals but even large political organizations become totally invisible to governance and thus easier than ever before to dismiss or ignore.

The fourth major problem with a proposal that would model global governance after statist governance has to do with what it hides from our sight, namely, that questions of control do not necessarily invite visions of *total* control. We may, for example, want to consider models of partial control, or even models that can be described as variants on "organized anarchy." The global age indeed invites us to imagine not how the world can be controlled better but, rather, how we can unlearn the modernist heritage and fantasy of total, panoptical, and instrumental mastery over society. What the world requires most is not more-total governability but the introduction of spaces of ungovernability. These spaces, in turn, would be more in tune with the requisites of cultivating the less institutionalizable aspects of human life, thus making it possible for autonomous action upon the world to flourish everywhere.

That is to say, if it is accepted that any great transformation involves by its nature major social dislocations, the combat strategy would require a level of originality, innovation, and adjustment commensurate with the magnitude of these realities but also attentive to the *opportunities* that each new threat in the world provides us. In this case, the decline of the customary, statist custodians of societies finally leaves adequate space for the reactivation of dormant energies, notably, those of civil society, but now on a global scale. In other words, by weakening the nation-state globalization offers us the opportunity to activate sources of social life long suppressed by nationalism and to imagine new types of global connections between them. The social world created by such connections would by its nature be more prosaic and less bureaucratic than statist polities, less prone to diplomatic games, and perhaps even more attuned to the face value and constancy of principles. Its action, unlike that of the totalitarian "world state," would therefore be charted along a path characterized by a multiplicity of centers of action, a diversity of causes, and a wide range of possible tactics and alliances rather than emanating from a strong and unchallengeable center. Its structure, in other words, will not always guarantee its success in its undertakings, but it will make it possible for life in the world to free itself once more from the tutelage of morose institutionalities.

Politics and the Question of Rationality

These remarks suggest that the forms of politics most appropriate for the global era would possess altogether different formats and venues than has hitherto been imaginable. However, and as outlined earlier in this volume, once existing political institutions find the rug pulled from under their feet by economic or cultural forces—as these depart from the modernist symbiosis among the three spheres—they may resist extinction and give us, therefore, thoroughly irrational politics. That is, when institutions built for the requirements of one era are no longer fit for a new era, they frequently seek to survive by imagining new purposes. These new purposes, however, are appropriate for the new era only to the extent that they conform to its integral rationality; otherwise the institution's new purpose becomes a recipe for irrational behavior, as discussed in chapter 2.

How do we know the difference between systemic rationality and irrationality? What needs to be specified here is what the term "rationality" signifies in different epochs. As outlined in the Introduction, a rational outlook does not correspond to "reason" as such, nor should it be understood as a venue from which one arrives at "truth." Rather, a rational outlook is primarily an *integrated* outlook, in which the various spheres of life are brought together into systemic complementarity and in which this complementarity cultivates a sense of wholeness. In the context of the three spheres discussed here, a rational outlook would be the kind of outlook that connects at the deepest level the logics of economy, politics, and culture and advises action in the world on the basis of this connection and harmony of vision. Irrational behavior, which we see mostly today in the field of new imperial politics but which also has some cultural and even economic expressions, stems precisely from the disintegration of this sense of wholeness.

In this scheme it is possible to imagine and outline different grades of rationality. Not all rationalities are equal. The superiority of one form of rationality over another, however, is not to be outlined in terms of the lazy (and hopefully outmoded) generalizations about levels of "civilizational" attainment of a culture or society. For example, if it is accepted that rationality means meaningfully and organically integrated (rather than superficially, tenuously, haphazardly, or temporarily integrated) world outlooks, then we may actually expect to see it exhibited more in stable, "traditional" societies than in postindustrial societies experiencing constant dislocations or in rapidly industrializing societies experiencing frequent alterations of erstwhile predictable patterns of life. If one is to express it as a physical law, one can say that irrationality introduces itself at a rate inverse to the synchronicity of the wheels of the various spheres of social life.

Irrationalities of that sort are thus to be expected to some extent in every society and every epoch. The dilemma concerns how to confine irrationality to the corners of social life where it is least dangerous. The problem of our epoch, as outlined before, consists in that precisely the opposite seems to be happening; that is, irrationality now exists and operates at the *summit* of society rather than at its margins. It is exhibited in a political life devoid of the capacity or the willingness to act upon the economic and cultural forces of the global period, and within institutions that maintain an inherited capacity for great levels of destruction and coercion. Irrational politics are to be expected in this type of world, but our fateful problem is how to remove as much of the coercive and destructive armory of the state as is commensurate with making its expected irrationality safe enough to live with—both for the world at large and for individual societies.

The other main problem for political life brought forth by globalization has to do with the future of nationalism. On the surface, it may be possible to assert that globalization finally offers the world an opportunity to bury the hideous face of nationalism once and for all (including not only bombastic and nervous expressions of nationalism but also deep-seated and unconscious nationalisms, notably, that of the United States).[3] However, the arrival of irrationalities to which any new era delivers profuse invitations quickly complicates this happy expectation. Various types of nationalism, ethnonationalism, and religious nationalism have begun to emerge in the recent past all over the world, at a time when it was thought that nationalism was on its way out as a frame of solidarity. It is easy but mistaken to see these movements as expressing similar global patterns or to take the surface for the essence. For these expressions of collective sentiments and new forms of solidarity, on which I will say more in the following section, conform in the global era to the effort to belong to rather than to isolate oneself from the world.

Despite all the noise it seems to be making today, the nation is dead. Though it was once one of the most successful modernist frames of solidarity—expressing an attempt at a symbiosis with institutional structures of the state and economic sensitivity to collective welfare—the national project, precisely in that form, has now expired. What is left of it now are the irrational, disconnected residues from an earlier aura of harmony, which had been buttressed by a modicum of integration of abstract solidarity into political and economic outlines.

There are parts of the world, of course, that are exceptions, notably, the Balkans, Israel/Palestine, and Turkey. In each of these cases one can detect not a global pattern but, rather, an exception to the logic of the times, born out of exceptional circumstances. Those circumstances are usually expressed in terms of a weighty heritage, which is maintained as incendiary material at the disposal of political actors and which, especially on the part of the stronger players in each case, has been used as the raison d'être of the polity itself. But even in such cases, one can detect the irrationality of insulated political logics in their divorce from the larger logic of the times. This is no more evident than in such visions of settlement for national conflicts as one finds in the Middle East. These visions anticipate that any solution to the conflicts that plague the region would, while claiming to rectify horrible past injustices and satisfy national aspirations, *at the same time* require more regional integration, diffuse statehoods and sovereignties, and advice to all inhabitants to pursue common goals of prosperity rather than "ideology."

Culture and the Question of Solidarity

Such a vision would only be in tune with the new types of solidarity that seem to be emanating in various permutations across the globe and that point to different formats than the ones we have hitherto experienced. At one level, we can detect the rebirth of subnational solidarities in various countries—regional, tribal, ethnic, or the like. In Europe, the ones that have so far succeeded best in institutionalizing themselves are those of Scotland and Wales. We can expect this pattern to spread further, as it is one of the natural outcomes of the weakening of the sovereignty of the nation-state, its relinquishing of social responsibilities, and sometimes its voluntary devolution of power to local centers.

At a different level, that is, above the nation-state, we find various schemes of global solidarity also taking shape, on the heels of the exhaustion of the energies that had sustained it.[4] We can isolate at least four such types of global solidarity.

1. *Spiritual movements.* The global growth of religious solidarities, especially, and the effort to recruit new converts seems to recall an older pattern of solidarity than that of nation-state. This trend, which began to gather momentum in various world regions from the late 1970s onward, is characterized by a different level of religious fervor than the one that had typified traditional societies, both in the peripheries and in the centers. The new fervor is not just characterized by seemingly deeper and more communalistic sentiments than had been the case with adherents from older generations. Significantly, it is also coupled with a more vigorous sense of global mission.

There are two immediately discernible versions of these spiritual solidarities. A "weak" version is manifested, for example, in versions of Eastern spirituality being adopted in the West or in Gaia-like ideologies; the emphasis is on personal growth and connecting the individual, through personal, voluntaristic, and meditative effort, to larger cosmic potentials that are nonetheless seen to inhere in the individual. The second, or "strong" version, typifies what has come to be called "fundamentalism," both in the East and the West. Unlike the weak version of spiritual solidarity, the strong version involves more emphatic commitments to communalistic ventures whereby the spiritual effort is coupled with the building of social institutions—schools, hospitals, charities, banks, mutual aid societies, and the like—that solidify the ranks of such movements at the same time that they fulfill roles within the context of the everyday life of the faithful.

Both of these versions are in many respects in tune with rather than opposed to the spirit of their times, as discussed in chapter 3. Their main targets are not such programs as "development," "progress," or "modernization"—terms that they themselves frequently use. Rather, they seek to counter the global conditions of vagueness that are associated with cultural globalization (discussed in chapter 3) in order to replace it with *deep meaning*. This deep meaning, in turn, emanates not so much from pure logical requisites as from social standpoints: a desire to show the resourcefulness of the spirit in providing vigor and autonomy in an otherwise thoroughly governed world and to demonstrate this autonomy in a direct challenge to imperialism and political authorities. These attitudes do not reject globalization. If anything, they are themselves among the products of cultural globalization. Like all other such products, they link an individual psyche into global spirits, but here through an aura of authenticity rather than of passivity and surrender.

2. *Class solidarities*. The gradual decline of organized class solidarities, and the concomitant decline in the power of organized labor in many countries over the past few years, frequently obscure the growth and entrenchment of such solidarities at the global level. It is easy to overlook this fact because the nature of the global class solidarities are not thus far taking the forms expected in Marxist theory, which has become the habitual prism through which we seek to discern such manifestations. There are two important qualifications that are warranted in this regard (neither of which necessarily contradict Marx).

First, the term "class" is useful because it presupposes an orientation toward "interests." That is, what the term describes here is the primacy of the *transnational* connectivity of those classes that have shared interests, above *transclass* connectivity in each society presupposed in outlines of national solidarity. In other words, with its orientation toward material conditions, class solidarity can just as well be described, and perhaps more accurately, as "interests-oriented solidarity."

Second, transnational class connectivities so far appear to be more developed at the less visible, upper echelons of each society. Robert Reich, among others, shows how the global classes that are most aware of their connection to each other tend to be concentrated among the professionals in society, especially among those active in financial sectors, computer programming, and other types of "symbolic analysis." According to him, these classes tend therefore to be most secluded from and least attentive to downtrodden classes that may be living just a neighborhood away from them. They tend to seek to insulate themselves as much as possible, even at the level of charity, from those who are geographically close but distant in economics and skills, while they cultivate their connections, marketabilities, common interests, and income potentials among their peers at the global level.

This picture gives us an image of a national household that is contained only by geography, when geography is less of a prison for the interests than it has ever been. This of course remains more true for some classes than others, and it is a late-coming perspective to those who have not been at the forefront of the effort to further the logic of globalization, namely, indigenous industrial working classes. Only now do we find a nascent realization among labor organizers in various countries that the enhanced global capacities of capital require the enhancement of the coordinated global capacities of labor. But just as is the case within individual countries, this type of interest-oriented solidarity faces competition at the global level from frames of solidarity oriented toward aspects of life other than those of material interests.

3. *Global causes.* The idea of "interests" as a basis for solidarity can be generalized, whereby in some sectors it comes to be captured in terms of interests that are indeed identified as "material" yet that are *shared* beyond various kinds of lines, including class lines. Adherents of these types of solidarity assert that there are global causes precisely because large sectors of humanity have shared interests, interests that can be articulated in broader terms than economic interest to the self and beyond national borders. Movements that exhibit such an outlook include variants of environmentalism, pacifism, feminism, and so on. In spite of the variety of causes, such movements generally follow a different line of emphasis than either spiritual movements, which concentrate on combating conditions of vagueness in the culture, or movements based on class affinities, which narrow down the definition of interests to those defined by class locations. By contrast, movements oriented toward global causes in any genre tend to articulate interests on the basis of passions for causes that are seen to be fundamentally human and irreducibly global. These causes emanate from orientations toward a broad definition of the social range of their causes, and fur-

thermore, they rely on a belief in the imperative of voluntary action on a global scale.

4. *Life-emancipatory movements.* In addition, global life further unleashes the potentials of those movements oriented toward propensities of liberation or expression that are restricted within each society on its own. More precisely, these would be the movements oriented toward individual freedom to pursue particular lifestyles that contradict or are at odds with mainstream cultural patterns in every society. Examples of these movements would be those oriented toward gay liberation, the emancipation of sexual practices, youth movements, those oriented toward fetishes of all kinds, those clustered around musical styles, and so on. In many ways such movements derive energy from their status as statements against normal patterns of behavior. Indeed, their very possibility within each society requires some of the sociological features that globalization only accentuates, namely, they have to thank for their possibility environments characterized by anonymity or autonomy. Such environments throve in the context of cosmopolitan urbanity, which in turn is experienced here as an antidote to the relative immutability of lifestyles fostered by the parochialism of town life. Globalization only deepens and furthers the possibilities hinted at in the possibilities offered by cosmopolitan urbanity, offering a wider net of world association and cross-learning regarding the question of how to conduct one's life, insofar as that conduct requires the supply of globally derived energies.

This summary of the main cultural and political features of the global era shows us a scene of enormous dislocations, which can be experienced either as possibilities or as new nightmares. My argument, of course, is neither that globalization will be an ineluctable panacea nor that it will ruin what is good about received habits and traditions. Alongside every great transformation the world offers both novel dangers and new opportunities to remake it. There is never a guarantee, other than broad knowledge informed by an integrated rational perspective and coupled with the possibility of action in the world, that the dangers will be averted or that the opportunities will be acted upon. As I argued elsewhere in this volume, the most dramatic possibility and the most pressing task concern the reduction of the weight of governmentality upon societies and the cultivation of the possibilities of freedom in the world; in sum, the great task now is to clip the wings of those large systems that can no longer be expected to act according to the precepts of integrative rationality.

The task, therefore, is first and foremost to develop the perspectives and knowledge bases that make it possible for us to use these possibilities of freedom, and to counter the danger of particularly those irrationalities that are armed to the teeth. There is no longer a point in impotently lamenting, as many do, the passing of customary securities or in doggedly adhering to old habits of seeing the world. Life in the global era requires a particular kind of action: integrally informed rather than fragmented, intelligent and effective in its application, and daring in its proclivity toward what is original rather than what is presupplied. Of course, globalization can proceed otherwise and produce new nightmares of totalitarianism, monoliths, global conformities, sedate sensations, or global Disneylands. But then that would be only because we will have refused to acknowledge and act upon the possibilities it once offered and instead continued to seek to save an old world that could not be saved.

Notes

Preface

1. Bamyeh, "Transnationalism."

1. Governmentality and the New Global "Order"

1. Roland Robertson traces this congruity back to the logic of the Enlightenment; see in particular 78.

2. Sassen, "The State and the Global City," 33–35. See also her *Globalization and Its Discontents*.

3. Marx, 2: 477.

4. See Rosenberg, 142–58.

5. Some may be inclined to contest this point on the ground that when no uniform and strategic logic is apparent, it must be sought in hidden intentionalities. However, the presence or lack of a hidden logic must be adjudicated not on the basis of metaphysical faith in the existence of what we cannot see but, rather, on our ability to discover a solidly connective logic among various spheres of life, which advise the behavior of political actors in regular and strategic fashion. And it is precisely this connectivity that contemporary globalization has done away with. This point will be explored further in chapter 2.

6. See Hoffmann.

7. For some of the more systematic critiques, see Falk; Rosenberg.

8. Foucault, "Governmentality," 89–90.

9. Gordon, 9.

10. Ardener, 22.

11. In contrast to this relational constraint on governance, the arenas of markets and cultures point to more fluid concepts of social life. It is not as though these latter fields do not have their own rules as well but, rather, that their rules are less likely to be confined by formal character, particular national borders, or such notions as exclusive "sovereignty."

12. Anderson, 36.

13. See, for instance, Hobsbawm and Ranger, eds.; Mosse; and Eugene Weber, *Peasants into Frenchmen,* among many others.

14. For a description of the ideational systems involved, see Bloch, 2: 375–420.

15. Reynolds, 250–339.

16. The former Soviet Union had at least formally recognized such a multiplicity (including a theoretical right of secession) but practically annulled it by central planning.

17. See Lall, 6–7. It can also be argued that orthodoxy can be considered a symptom of decline rather than a cause. Either way, the argument remains the same: State decline in this case is correlated with its abrogation of the kind of openness to congregational multiplicity that had defined it earlier.

18. Aquinas, 322.

19. In recent times, and without any benefit of historical knowledge, ideas of non-state-centered systems of governance seem to be gaining new ground. For a brief summary, see Sassen, "The State and the Global City," 33.

20. Aristotle, *Risalat Aristotalis ila al-Iskander fi Siyasat al-Mudun,* 46.

21. Chikafusa, 57–58.

22. Aristotle, *Politics,* lix. The editor, Ernest Barker, extrapolates this point from Aristotle's lost treatise *On Colonies.* The roots of the distinction are evident in the *Politics* itself, as well as in *Risalat Aristotalis.*

23. The term "enclave" was coined by Michael Brown, who defined it in terms of development and underdevelopment; see Brown.

24. See Olwig, esp. 159–208. The same can be said about all parochial cultures once their isolation is broken and once they become invariably other enclaves in a global system. Stephen Hugh-Jones argues, for instance, that the degree of voluntarism that occasioned the exposure of native tribes in Amazonia to a cash economy, technological trinkets, imported clothing, and so on shows that after exposure it makes little sense to speak of native culture and global culture as essentially countermodels. To argue the essentiality of nativism after contact— and especially in light of the voluntary aspects of the contact—is in a sense to deny local populations agency in making their own history; see Hugh-Jones, 69–70.

25. Hobsbawm, 131–62. The attempt continues to be made in the Balkans today, where it is cynically opposed by the same powers who had done their own share of ethnic cleansing and who had never bothered to rectify the material and spiritual damage that they themselves had inflicted upon others in the process.

26. The most important recent works remain Hobsbawm; Gellner; Anderson; and Tilly, *Coercion, Capital, and European State, A.D. 990–1990* and *The Formation of National States in Western Europe;* among many others.

27. Hobsbawm, 136.

28. Cabral, 147. Emphasis added.

29. Ibid., 151.

30. For a summary of the many criticisms, see Latouche.

31. Schmitt.

32. Kojève.

33. Maurer, 151–52.

34. Hegel, *The Phenomenology of Spirit*, 119.

35. Honneth, 148–211. Honneth bases this model partially on George Herbert Mead's symbolic interactionism.

36. The case of the Americas may be exceptional in this regard, since in many respects the very novelty of the New World (and its growing accommodation of outcasts) itself invited future orientation and a conscious distance from the organizational paradigms of the Old World.

37. See al-Jabarti, 22–23.

38. Ibid., 36.

39. In this respect, al-Jabarti's chronicle recognizes the structural interchangeability of faith and politics, since faith came to the fore again after the defeat of Egypt's rulers by Napoleon: When governments collapsed or when centers of political authority became uncertain, the only source of control that continued to operate emanated from the moral authority of the religious elite.

40. In fact, the first French proclamation in Egypt began by justifying the expedition on the basis of the old regime's cavalier disrespect for the sanctity of merchants' private property. Here Napoleon justified his invasion on the basis of the collapse of juridical certainty in Egypt. Yet al-Jabarti's chronicle dwells at length on the occupation regime's inconsistencies on this same question and its frequent disregard for the sanctity of private properties in general.

41. Emmanuel.

42. Thus it is not coincidental that smaller territories, enclaves, and islands were in general given up much later, if at all, than larger dominions.

43. A number of recent, influential publications show this attentiveness very clearly. See, for instance, Paul Kennedy's, *Preparing for the Twenty-First Century*, Lester Thurow's *Head to Head: The Coming Economic Battle among Japan, Europe, and America*, Samuel Huntington, *The Clash of Civilizations and the Remaking of World Order*. The theses presented in such works are not difficult to challenge, since nearly all of them are premised on presumptions of stagnant cultural and sociopolitical forms. They are significant, however, in at least two respects: (1) They invariably take their analytical units to be larger than nation-states (for example, trading blocs or global cultural patterns). (2) They seem to be influential among policy-making circles; in other words, they seem to have the ears of governance.

44. See Barber.

45. See, for instance, Tilly, *Coercion, Capital, and European State* and *Formation of National States;* Kennedy, *The Rise and Fall of the Great Powers;* Hart; and Schumpeter.

46. See esp. Snyder, 305–22.

47. Braudel, *Civilization and Capitalism, 15th–18th Century.*

48. Abu-Lughod, 362.

49. See Bovill, 145. For a full account of European state-sponsored expeditions of discovery into that region, see 187–219.

50. For histories, see Glamann; Chaudhury.

51. Steinberg, 90.

52. The first volume of *Cities of Salt* concentrates on such dynamics.

53. See Zubaida, 121–82.

54. Many nineteenth-century travelogues of trips to Europe, from Rifa'ah Rafi' Tahtawi's to Hsieh Fuching's, clearly show their authors becoming increasingly aware of the necessity of transformation in their own societies; at the same time they ponder how such a transformation could take place without upsetting ancient mores and norms.

55. See Kapteijns, 117–46. Compare this small tale to another of epic proportions, as rendered by Tzvetan Todorov in his *Conquest of America.*

56. Albeit with much international assistance, especially in Congo's case.

57. Comte, 197.

58. Ibid., 317–18.

59. Schäffle, 2: 442.

60. Comte, 306.

61. See esp. book 1, chs. 13–14. The reference to Zeus is in *Risalat Aristotalis.*

62. Mothe La Vayer, cited in Foucault, "Governmentality," 91. Emphasis added.

63. Cited in Yu-lan, 1: 313.

64. Tai, 97–145.

65. Foucault, "Governmentality," 98–100.

66. See Durkheim, 50–59.

67. In his recent *Seeing Like a State,* James Scott uses the term "legibility" to describe the various schemes employed by states in contemporary times to catalogue and make decisions regarding subject populations who would otherwise remain unknown to it.

68. Elias argues that various terms for a collective ethical control imposed on the individual, such as Freud's "super-ego" and Hegel's "spirit," are but different descriptions of the same phenomenon.

69. For a similar analysis cast in Freudian terms, see Kaye, esp. 99.

70. For an extended discussion, see Bamyeh, "The City and the Country: Notes on Belonging and Self-Sufficiency."

71. Hegel repeatedly noted in his time the everyday nature of abstraction, a process which for him was inseparable from the impossibility of unmediated uniqueness; see Hegel, *Enzyklopädie der philosophischen Wissenschaften im Grundrisse,* para. 479, p. 350.

72. The basic elements for this thesis can be found in ibid., para. 132, p. 121, and para. 506, p. 361.

73. While Hegel spells this out in terms of conceptual definitions rather than uniqueness, the point can be easily deduced from that digression. See esp. ibid., para. 472, pp. 345–46.

74. For an extended discussion of this theme, see Min, 39–61, esp. 47, 51.

75. For a discussion of the long-term ramifications for collective identity resulting from the *Verlagssystem*, see Bamyeh, "The City and the Country." The point is not to explain the nation-state exclusively in terms of the putting-out system but to suggest one of the bases for what it imagines to be its tasks. It is no accident that the notion of "national economy," as an expression of this enlarged conception of the domain of self-sufficiency, was one of the most popular currents of early economic thought in the nineteenth century.

76. See Schumpeter.

77. For Nietzsche, the Social Contract had always been a sentimental myth. He makes clear that by "state" he means "some pack of blond beasts of prey *(Raubtiere)*, a conquerer and master race which, organized for war and with the ability to organize, unhesitatingly lays its terrible claws upon a populace perhaps tremendously superior in numbers but still formless and nomad. . . . he who is violent in act and bearing—what has he to do with contracts!" See Nietzsche, Second Essay, sec. 17.

78. For an excellent and still unsurpassed review, see Coker. The idea itself is much older than the nineteenth century. In the *Muqaddimah,* Ibn Khaldun (d. 1406) had already noted that civilizations (not states per se) display a process of maturation and decay following the model of human growth (not static physiological condition). The Neoplatonic political philosophy of al-Farabi (d. 950) was far more metaphysical than that of Ibn Khaldun, but the organismic model was nonetheless an important feature of it.

79. Lilienfeld, 1: 64–68.

80. Ibid., 186–87.

81. Needless to say, the orientations toward efficiency, morality, and power (as the attributes of enclaves, realms, and empires, respectively) are not mutually exclusive. The point concerns rather the detrimental nature for each type of polity of emphasis on the dimension most essential for its survival.

82. Moore, 414.

83. Ibn Battuta, who hardly sympathized with the Mongols, nonetheless made that point and faulted those rulers who eventually lost to the Mongols for having more or less invited the invasion by their harassment of long-distance merchants. See Ibn Battuta, 3: 23–24.

84. Hegel, *Grundlinien der Philosophie des Rechts,* 7: 345–47.

85. The dimension of power was not absent from the calculations and self-understanding of realm and enclave. But the point is that the outward orientation

of empire dictates more attention to questions of relational power than to other dimensions along which governance may think of itself.

86. See, for instance, Canetti or Arendt.

87. For a historical overview of the emergence of this form of consciousness, see Khalidi. The history of this identity shows that it developed to a great extent in reaction to external threat. The other side of this equation, prefigured in Zionist ideology, is clearly part of the general history of nationalism; Zionist ideology was also the product of a reaction to European anti-Semitism in an age of national discourse. But for geopolitical reasons it was also bolstered by European imperialism.

88. Hobsbawm, 46–79.

89. See Pflanze, 99.

90. See Marshall.

91. See Streeck. Streeck, however, does not address the question of totalitarianism.

92. Habermas, "The New Obscurity: The Crisis of the Welfare State and the Exhaustion of Utopian Energies," 1–18, esp. 10.

93. Habermas, *Strukturwandel der Öffentlichkeit*, 74.

94. Eisenstadt, 243.

95. Cowgill, 244–76. Cowgill mentions a third trouble, namely, the question of the accountability of and trust in officeholders. The outline of this problem, however, is less clear than that of the other two.

96. Abu-Lughod, 367.

97. See Havell, xi–xii.

98. Though showing distinct patterns of local self-reference, the classic sociological study by Arthur Vidich, *Small Town in Mass Society* was one of the first to debunk the myth that small towns are insulated from mass culture and to show their intricate dependence on links to the national economy and federal programs.

2. The New Imperialism

1. Foucault, "Governmentality," 92.

2. See Hirschman.

3. See, for example, Kant's arguments in *Perpetual Peace*, which offer an important version of this line of thought stressing the role of economy and trade in taming the rapacious nature of unanchored political life.

4. This point would follow Braudel's important yet frequently overlooked distinction between "capitalism" and "market economy." For Braudel market economy is an ancient form characterized by a vast multitude of participants whose conditions do not allow them to experience the prospect of exceptionally vast accumulation. Capitalism, by contrast, is the economy of the few great predators at the top level of the market economy. It becomes a proper name for the sys-

tem as a whole only when the actions of such predators begin to shape the market everywhere. See Braudel, *Afterthoughts on Material Civilization and Capitalism.*

5. For a summary of this line of thought, see Moore, 111–55.

6. In 1775, for example, the value of exports from the small colonial possessions in the Caribbean to the colonial mother countries was several times the value of exports from all of the Americas. In real terms their value must have been even more, since the cost of control was much lower on the islands than it was on the continent, as subsequent events were to prove.

7. The case of the large Portuguese colonies in Africa, which were not surrendered until the 1970s, may seem to contradict this genealogy. But it must be kept in mind that such colonies had long ceased to be particularly remunerative to the political order in the mother country. In fact, in Portugal holding on to them was a significant factor in dragging the old regime under.

8. Charles Lipson notes that the emergence of capital markets since the nineteenth century has been most pronounced in countries that had asserted themselves as international powers. Eventually the dynamics of a significantly enlarged capital market forces these governments to also assume responsibility for large-scale financial failures, a point amply demonstrated in recent history. On this score, however, Lipson seems to contradict his own conclusion, by arguing for the continuity of the basic principles of private responsibility for commercial debt, when his observations show clearly that no internationally assertive governments can fail to assume responsibility for the failures of large capital markets—especially since those capital markets had been one of the important sources of the comparative global power of states; see Lipson. For a discussion of the structure of the historical cycles of debt, see also Suter.

9. In the traditional theory of imperialism as advanced by Lenin, the foundations of imperialism were located in the dynamics of capitalism. Such a theory precluded the possibility of a "Soviet imperialism," a less theoretically grounded term that was proposed later. But even if we accept the American and the Soviet as equivalent imperialisms, it must be kept in mind that the basis of their claims to legitimacy consisted of opposing *economic* ideologies, each of which understood itself as being global in potential.

10. See, for example, the critiques of Latouche and of Sahlins, among many others.

11. Until recently macroeconomic measures correlated, if not with actual feelings of well-being or lack thereof, then at least with future orientations, which were based on a vision that linked together macro and micro levels of existence in society. And that link, in turn, was supported in the era of "modernization" by a forward-looking conception underlining the emergence of large, commonly governed communities.

12. For an elaboration of this argument, see Abu-Lughod, 362.

13. For some details of this incident, see Bovill, 145.

14. For an exposition of the emergence of one such route in west Asia under conditions of minimal—and occasionally total lack of—political control, see my *Social Origins of Islam*, ch. 2. For a more general argument along these lines, see my "The City and the Country."

15. See Sassen, "The State and the Global City," 33–35.

16. The *World Investment Report* makes two observations that seem to bolster this view: (1) Financial capital is more important in developed than in developing countries; and (2) transnational corporations offer their affiliates the advantage of privileged access to internally (that is, *globally*, albeit internal to the corporation) generated financial capital; see 140–48.

17. In the United States the product of such financial capital activities as finance, real estate, and insurance finally surpassed that of manufacturing in 1991, concluding the uninterrupted ascendance of financial capital in the economy. One of the advantages of financial capital in an advanced capitalist society consists of its higher productivity per worker, which is nearly three times that of the productivity of a worker in manufacturing. See U.S. Bureau of Labor Statistics.

18. Braudel, *Civilization and Capitalism*, 2:318.

19. Of course, there is no real devolution of power here, as the federal government did not even bring up the logical correlate to any true devolution: namely, that the federal center would have to forfeit as much in taxes as would have to be paid directly to states or even to local governments (that is, to whomever the power has been "devolved" onto), so that they could actually undertake their novel responsibilities. There have been those with sufficient foresight to protest this farce, decrying it as "unfunded mandates." Yet even in this case, there has been a curious paucity of voices protesting the farce by actually calling for a real transfer of power, with all the financial and tax consequences that such a notion would entail.

20. See Sassen, *Losing Control? Sovereignty in an Age of Globalization*, 1–30, who goes as far as referring to the proliferating arbitration centers as a new global system of justice and to the global bond-rating agencies as a new global system of gatekeeping. See also Cutler, Haufler, and Porter, eds. On the role of the city in the global economy, see Sassen, *The Global City: New York, London, Tokyo*, and King among many others. It is perhaps symptomatic of the trend toward networks formed by sites other than nation-states that the literature on the "city in the global economy" is already rapidly burgeoning.

21. The index of transnationality, which is one of the measurements used to rate a corporation's foreign involvement (assets, sales, employment) compared to that in its home base, shows that the variables that have the most impact on the degree of corporate transnationality are the type of industry and the relative size of the domestic market rather than any specific local policies; see *World Investment Report*.

22. Altvater calls these "clubby communities"; see esp. 59.

23. Hegel, *Grundlinien der Philosophie des Rechts,* sec. 278, 315–16. For a more elaborate discussion, see Min, esp. 47, 51.

24. The debate concerning what to do with the expected budget surplus in the United States seems to confirm this point. The parameters of the mainstream debate make it clear that the surplus will *not* be spent on enhancing social citizenship. Rather, the most widely circulating ideas suggest that it should be spent on cutting taxes, enhancing military capabilities (thus the power of the new imperialism), paying off old debts, or propping up those social systems—such as social security—that are viewed as indispensable (although even in this area there is much talk about privatizing the whole social security system—i.e., finally removing government from responsibility for providing one of the last vestiges of social citizenship).

25. See Guéhenno, 19–34.

26. The sociological debate regarding this point has centered on whether the state represents a class or an elite, on the one hand, or whether it is pluralistic, in the sense that it is open to the representation of a variety of interests, on the other. I am not presuming here that the state has a "nature" along one of these lines. Rather, I tend to think that it is a question of the resources available to the state. Pluralism can indeed be a passing or recurrent phenomenon, depending to an important extent on whether the state has in the first place sufficient resources allowing it to exhibit this luxurious and shiny mantle.

27. For a vociferous articulation of this view, see Zakaria.

28. A reviewer of an earlier draft of this essay complained that these were the "only" examples, aside from the Gulf War adversaries, that I provide of the targets of this imperialism. But it is hard to overestimate the resort to such unfettered categories, not to mention that we are talking about vast "types" represented in whole nations and even, as we see in the case of Samuel Huntington, entire civilizations!

29. The support by archconservative forces for the Contras in Nicaragua in the 1980s is arguably not entirely part of the logic of the old imperialism, as the Sandanistas themselves were willing to make sufficient accommodation to capital given the chance, a stance that was not lost on important sectors of the world's financial community. Their opinion, however, was disregarded by the Reagan administration.

30. In a study of the curriculum vitae of 502 high-ranking government officials between 1945 and 1972, Laurence H. Shoup and William Minter found that more than half had also been members of the Council on Foreign Relations; see Grose, 48–49.

31. See Lovelace, whose analysis is conducted within the parameters of the Joint Chiefs of Staff's *Joint Vision 2010.* Some proposals in that manual, such as expanding the role of the military into such domestic areas as disaster relief and combating terrorism, were announced by the U.S. secretary of defense on October 10, 1999.

32. On the embeddedness of symbolic politics in the dynamics of globalization, see Streeck.

33. There are those, like a reviewer of an earlier draft of this essay, who will complain that I am ignoring some "hidden rationalities." It seems to me, however, that it is only sheer faith in the system's intelligence that can support this kind of assumption that there is an integrative rationality hiding so deep from view that only exceptional sagacity can discover it. Assuming the existence of light when the evidence points only to darkness is an exercise of faith. And, similarly, there is little point in refuting arguments that the earth is flat when the burden of proof has shifted to those who assert the notion. My point is not that the system has absolutely no plan, only that it has no *integrative rationality* that would impose strategic and multidimensional coherence on the plan. All evidence points to this, and the point is freely acknowledged even by system apologists, such as Fareed Zakaria and Ira Cohen, among others.

34. Hobsbawm, 177.

35. In his review of Barber's book, Mark Juergensmeyer rightly argues that movements classified as "jihads"—Khomeini's included—can be seen as more opposed to Western imperialism than to transnationalism as such; see 588–89.

36. For an eloquent portrayal of both the actual distance of the Saudi royal house from traditional mores of governance that had predated it and the inscription of the regime's very introduction in the dialectics of old imperialism, read Munif's magisterial *Cities of Salt*.

37. Thus it is no accident that in Europe the country that remains closest to U.S. global policies is Britain, which also happens to be the one force within the camp of the old imperialism that has resisted the most consequential facets of European integration.

38. There are exceptions, of course, but only when the stakes are just too high, such as in the case of the large loans extended to Russia to ensure the reelection of Boris Yeltsin. But even in that case, it was made clear to all protagonists that in the long run there would be no deviation from the uniform global blueprint and that Russia will have to play the same game, as it is being prodded to do now, under the pain of no more forthcoming loans.

39. The editors of *Foreign Affairs,* where Huntington's thesis was first published, themselves compared Huntington's potential legacy to the actual legacy of George Kennan (whose thesis was also first published in that journal).

40. For an excellent overview and contextual analysis, see Michael.

41. Huntington, 304–8.

42. Machiavelli, 61.

3. The Cultural Landscape of Globalization

1. The different uses of the term, which were already outlined in Kroeber and Kluckhohn and in Williams, are of interest here only to the extent that they

reflect on the expansive properties of habits, identities, belief systems, lifestyles, or the like.

2. Foucault, "The Discourse on Language," 216.

3. Max Weber, *Economy and Society*, 1: 342.

4. McNeill, esp. 34–35.

5. Fabian, 144.

6. For an interesting discussion of the transformation of the *imagines mundi*, see Justin Stagl's analysis of selected pictographs from European travel narratives in the 1600s and 1700s. Stagl traces a move from an episteme of the "closed cosmos" to one of undefined space; see 155–70.

7. See Kalb, 166–67.

8. Habermas, *The Theory of Communicative Action*, 1: 55.

9. Kant, *Fundamental Principles of the Metaphysics of Morals*, 5–6.

10. Mill, 24–25.

11. A symptom of that shift was the devaluation of the lifestyle of the noble but *idle* aristocracy in light of a new cultural ethos, advanced by the ascending bourgeoisie, regarding the economic use of time.

12. For a few examples, see Jameson; Lash; Derrida.

13. See my "Frames of Belonging."

14. For a rich range of discussions regarding the capacities and limits of cosmopolitanism, see the recent volume on the subject edited by Cheah and Robbins.

15. Dunn, 11.

16. In *Nations before Nationalism* John Armstrong proposes a premodern model of collective identity that seems particularly pertinent to the European city-states. The model highlights the *inverse* relation between the strength of civic consciousness on the one hand and the magnitude of territorial expansion of the city into the countryside on the other.

17. Abu-Lughod, 33.

18. The investment in the fabled Roman roads can be seen as symptomatic of this emphasis on reliable transportation as a raison d'être of the empire.

19. Ibn Battuta, 3: 23–24.

20. Armstrong argues that before nationalism, civic consciousness and territorial expansion of European city-states were inversely related; see 108–29.

21. Goodin, 13.

22. Ibid.

23. Anderson, 40.

24. The most succinct rendition of this position in recent scholarship is perhaps Giddens.

25. Geertz.

26. Pandey.

27. Todorov, 53–123.

28. There are obviously many structural limitations to the exercise of such

democracy. But in relative terms, the much higher degrees of participation and political freedom are undeniable.

29. This fact seems more discernible to researchers closer to the area of Islamic studies than to global political commentators lacking specialized knowledge. For a good example of the former, see Mirsepassi.

30. Saitoti, 110.

31. Ibid., 128.

32. Ibid., 129.

33. See Chase-Dunn.

34. See Dahl and Megerssa. Ferguson makes a similar point regarding a development project in Lesotho, which only succeeded in augmenting the power of the government and its bureaucracy over rural populations.

35. Abu-Lughod, 15–18.

36. That novelty was by no means unappreciated. Montesquieu, for example, asserted that apart from its usefulness for global trade, new means of exchange enhanced the autonomy of the markets from politics and thus curtailed the specter of despotism in the world: "Foreign exchange operations *(le change)* have taught bankers to compare coins from all over the world and to assess them at their correct value. . . . These operations have done away with the great and sudden arbitrary actions of sovereigns *(les grands coups d'autorité)* or at least with their success"; cited in Hirschman, 74.

37. Gailey, 194–211.

38. Ibid., 218, 241. A frequent problem in the history of development was that "traditional" societies—for lack of a better term—usually set aside some resources outside of market exchange and refused to treat them as commodities. In the case mentioned in the text, the resource in question was food. In Ferguson's study of development in Lesotho, it was more specifically cattle, which, to the chagrin of development agencies, peasants were very reluctant to handle as another market item.

39. Mas'udi, 2: 96–97.

40. Max Weber, *The Protestant Ethic and the Spirit of Capitalism*, 58–60.

41. Chayanov.

42. Chatterjee, 117–25.

43. Cited in ibid., 138. Nehru adds, "But the West is obviously in need of learning much" from the East, although the spirit of the latter addition is far less committal and urgent than that of the first.

44. Polanyi, 46–47.

45. Ibid., 47–54.

46. Braudel, *Afterthoughts*, 226–28.

47. Mauss, 32–33.

48. Hyde, 61–68.

49. See in particular Hyde's story concerning the inability of a poor family in

a U.S. inner city to use an inheritance for upward mobility because the family felt obligated to use it to support a wide array of relatives and acquaintances; ibid., 75–76.

50. Braudel, *Afterthoughts*, 64, 75. In Munif's novel *Cities of Salt*, the company seems actually to *invent* the state. Yet even there the state had some roots in more-ephemeral forms of traditional governance. These forms, in turn, became far less ephemeral and more interventionist as the growth of the company dictated.

51. Braudel, *Afterthoughts*, 49–57. Braudel makes a useful distinction between "market economy" and "capitalism." For him, capitalism is an appendage to a more salient market economy. It denotes transactions taking place at the top level of the market, namely, the economy of the large predators.

52. Ibid., 504.

53. Giddens, 16–21.

54. Ibid., 21.

55. Ibid., 215.

56. Bell, 118–19.

57. Ibid., 74–78.

58. The origins of the welfare state show a diversity of understandings of the degree and meaning of citizenship. Stephan Leibfried, for instance, offers four basic models (Scandinavian, German, Anglo-Saxon, and Southern European), which he suggests may be converging in light of the current crisis; see 133–56.

59. National consolidation is another factor. The introduction of welfare in Bismarck's Germany and other European countries early in this century served to further legitimize a contested national governance. Combined with the unleashing of patriotic spirits in World War I, it gave more credence to the idea of *national* (especially as opposed to *class*) belonging.

60. Scardigli, 21.

61. Ibid., 23, 105, 115–16.

62. The example of the unification of East and West Germany may illustrate this point, especially given that the two societies were exhibiting different patterns of life and cultural outlook—as they discovered in the process of uniting—and were by and large coming to accept each other's independence just shortly before unification. But the unity here was premised on a conscious policy of bringing the East to the economic level of the West, rather than treating it as a colony—a practice that we see elsewhere in the world and that impedes the possibilities of convergence.

63. For example, Malik Mufti argues that in the 1950s there was a basic disagreement between Britain and the United States regarding the proper threat facing Western interests in the Middle East. Whereas Britain insisted that it was Arab nationalism, U.S. policymakers usually dismissed the significance of nationalism, and insisted that communism should be regarded as the main threat.

64. Chase-Dunn and Hall, eds., 6.

65. See Jordan Lewis, *Partnerships for Profit*.

66. For instance, see Lowenthal, 75.

67. Ibn Battuta, 2:265–66.

68. Ibid., 401.

69. For a discussion of the sources, see Bovill.

70. Fuching, 43–44, 65–66.

71. Spence.

72. Said, 81–88.

73. Stagl, 47–94.

74. It may be objected that comparative civilizational projects, such as Huntington's, or policy-oriented manuals illustrate a continuing investment in cataloguing total cultural systems in relation to each other. But it must be kept in mind that such manuals usually lack the detailed anthropological fullness of account and are possible only at the price of consciously ignoring a wide range of readily available information.

75. Mattelart, Delcourt, and Mattelart, 10–11.

76. Deutsch, 30.

77. Gellner, 126–27.

78. For example, see Hacker.

79. Mattelart, Delcourt, and Mattelart, 77.

80. Deutsch, 126.

81. Cited in Mattelart, Delcourt, and Mattelart, 67.

82. A good overview of the future of European film in this light is Halle.

83. The roots of this desire can be tied to the observed significant role that media played in the creation of new national identities in the postcolonial world. That role was prefigured in nineteenth-century patterns of consolidation of common educational systems in European nation-states. Karl Heider's study of the Indonesian film industry, for example, sketches the historical role played by that rather vibrant industry in giving form over the years to a sense of commonality among the inhabitants of a vast archipelago. It contributed to further standardizing the Indonesian language, and it employed discernible cultural symbols unique to Indonesia as a whole and common to its diverse inhabitants.

84. Lowe and Kamin, 14.

85. Ibid., 32. The unquestioned assumption here is that there is a demand for the portrayal of customary ordinariness. More clearly asserted is another assumption: that commercial control over local mass media will not in itself guarantee the production of "locally relevant" programming, even when it is in the interest of commercial media to reach a mass audience.

86. For an exploration of the connection between the economics of coproductions and shifts in types of genres, see Halle.

87. The trend in Thailand is toward more imports. Japan, which until very recently watched more local than imported films, finally succumbed to imports.

The other large country where this was the case until recently, Russia, is following suit.

88. Mattelart, Delcourt, and Mattelart, 102.

89. "Americanization," in fact, may have been possible precisely because of "America's" own distance from various localisms, so that any imperial threat the United States may pose anywhere can be seen apart from cultural threats. Arjun Appadurai reminds us that "for the people of Irian Jaya, Indonesianization may be more worrisome than Americanization, as Japanization may be for Koreans, Indianization for Sri Lankans, Vietnamization for the Cambodians, and Russianization for the people of Soviet Armenia and the Baltic republics. . . . for polities of smaller scale, there is always a fear of cultural absorption by polities of larger scale, especially those that are nearby"; Appadurai, 32.

90. This argument is fully explored in Layoun, which traces the globalization of the novel as a genre.

91. Mattelart, Delcourt, and Mattelart, 91. Emphasis added.

92. For a more elaborate set of studies of the multicultural aspects of the media, see Shohat and Stam, eds.

93. See Justin Lewis, *The Ideological Octopus*, 159–202.

94. Cited in Mattelart, Delcourt, and Mattelart, 29.

95. The latest data available for book production are from 1994, but no data are yet available for translation beyond 1987. Trends from previous years, however, are more or less consistent with the patterns shown here.

96. There is no Third World news agency that has more than a regional reach at best. If anything, most Third World inhabitants rely in one form or another on a significant input of international news—even about neighboring countries—from Western media sources. Johan Galtung once proposed a theory of information imperialism couched in terms of a world system characterized by the duality of a center and a periphery. According to Galtung, four basic patterns characterize information imperialism, especially as far as "information" refers to news flow: (1) News about the center tends to be dominant; (2) there is a great discrepancy in the ratio of center news to periphery news as compared to the ratio of center news to another center country's news; (3) news about the center is more present in the media of the periphery than the other way around; (4) there is a relatively low or nonexistent flow of news between peripheral countries (i.e., news not provided *by* the center), especially across regional borders; Galtung; see also Galtung and Vincent.

Conclusion

1. Such schemes as privatizing parts of the prison system in the United States and calls to likewise privatize as many governmental functions and services as is logical and feasible do not hark back to the logic of the chartered company. From the point of view of capital, these endeavors are desirable but not

necessary extensions of its domain, and capital's survival does not depend on such an extension. Rather, this type of extension into erstwhile governmental arenas is more connected to capital's general propensity to expand into every usable arena opened up by the withdrawal from it of a former custodian.

2. Furthermore, proponents of one solution or another frequently operate outside of history, where this volume, on the other hand, has tried to embed itself. History is relevant here because everything is both new and old. We are certainly approaching global conditions that in so many ways have never before been experienced. But in another respect, some features of these novelties have historical parallels, and more importantly, the values that we use to assess these novelties are themselves historically grounded, if not ancient; exploitation, totalitarianism, inequities, and democracies—all have existed before. The historical record of the complexities, variations, and interactions of such experiments must certainly be relevant here. The more obsessed with the future we are, the more we ought to read history, and furthermore, to read it not as a set of quick instrumental instructions but at the deepest level of meditation possible.

3. Unfortunately, Anderson's notion of "creole pioneers" remains the least-discussed idea in his book.

4. For a recent set of more philosophically oriented discussions of the forms of solidarity made possible by the advent of contemporary globalization, see Cheah and Robbins, eds. Kant looms large in this volume, where most contributors seek to reclaim cosmopolitanism for our age. The only exceptions are Benedict Anderson and Richard Rorty, who defend nationalism and contest the viability of alternatives to it, and Kwame Anthony Appiah, who defends statism in its current form.

Bibliography

Abu-Lughod, Janet. *Before European Hegemony: The World-System, A.D. 1250–1350.* Cambridge: Cambridge University Press, 1989.

Altvater, Elmar. "Financial Crises on the Threshold of the Twenty-First Century." In Leo Panitch, ed., *Ruthless Criticism of All That Exists.* London: Merlin Press, 1997.

Anderson, Benedict. *Imagined Communities: Reflections on the Origins and Spread of Nationalism* [1983]. London: Verso, 1991.

Appadurai, Arjun. *Modernity at Large: Cultural Dimensions of Globalization.* Minneapolis: University of Minnesota Press, 1996.

Aquinas, Thomas. *Selected Political Writings.* Translated by J. G. Dawson. Oxford: Blackwell, 1959.

Ardener, E. W. "The Construction of History: 'Vestiges of Creation.'" In E. Tonkin, M. McDonald, and M. Chapman, eds., *History and Ethnicity.* London: Routledge, 1989.

Arendt, Hannah. *The Origins of Totalitarianism.* New York: Harcourt Brace Jovanovic, 1973.

Aristotle. *Politics.* Edited and translated by Ernest Barker. Oxford: Clarendon, 1946.

———. *Risalat Aristotalis ila al-Iskander fi Siyasat al-Mudun.* Edited by Józef Bielawski. Warsaw: Polskiej Akademii Nank, 1970.

Armstrong, John. *Nations before Nationalism.* Chapel Hill: University of North Carolina Press, 1982.

Bamyeh, Mohammed A. "The City and the Country: Notes on Belonging and Self-Sufficiency." *Arena Journal,* no. 3 (1994): 246–61.

———. "Frames of Belonging: Four Contemporary European Travels." *Social Text* 12, no. 2 (1994): 35–56.

———. *The Social Origins of Islam: Mind, Economy, Discourse.* Minneapolis: University of Minnesota Press, 1999.

———. "Transnationalism." *Current Sociology* 41, no. 3 (1993).

Barber, Benjamin R. *Jihad vs. McWorld.* New York: Times Books, 1995.

Bell, Daniel. *The Cultural Contradictions of Capitalism* [1978]. New York: Basic Books, 1996.

Bloch, Marc. *Feudal Society.* 2 vols. Chicago: University of Chicago Press, 1961.

Bovill, E. W. *The Golden Trade of the Moors.* London: Oxford University Press, 1958.

Braudel, Fernand. *Afterthoughts on Material Civilization and Capitalism.* Translated by Patricia Ranum. Baltimore: Johns Hopkins University Press, 1977.

———. *Civilization and Capitalism, 15th–18th Century.* 3 vols. Translated by Siân Reynolds. New York: Harper and Row, 1982.

Brown, Michael. "Developing Societies as Part of an International Political Economy." In Hamza Alawi and Theodor Shanin, eds., *Introduction to the Sociology of "Developing Societies."* New York: Monthly Review Press, 1982.

Cabral, Amilcar. *Unity and Struggle: Speeches and Writings of Amilcar Cabral.* New York and London: Monthly Review Press, 1979.

Canetti, Elias. *Crowds and Power.* Translated by Carol Stewart. New York: Noonday, 1962.

Chase-Dunn, Christopher. *Global Formation: Structures of the World-Economy.* Oxford: Blackwell, 1989.

Chase-Dunn, Christopher, and Thomas Hall, eds. *Core/Periphery Relations in Precapitalist Worlds.* Boulder, Colo.: Westview, 1991.

Chatterjee, Partha. *Nationalist Thought and the Colonial World: A Derivative Discourse.* London: Zed, 1986.

Chaudhury, K. N. *The Trading World of Asia and the English East India Company, 1660–1760.* Cambridge: Cambridge University Press, 1978.

Chayanov, Aleksandr. *The Theory of Peasant Economy* [1925]. Edited by D. Thorner, R. E. Smith, and B. Kerblay. Homewood, Ill.: Irwin, 1966.

Cheah, Pheng, and Bruce Robbins, eds. *Cosmopolitics: Thinking and Feeling beyond the Nation.* Minneapolis: University of Minnesota Press, 1998.

Chikafusa, Kitabatake. *A Chronicle of Gods and Sovereigns.* Translated by Paul Varley. New York: Columbia University Press, 1980.

Coker, F. W. *Organismic Theories of the State: Nineteenth Century Interpretations of the State as Organism or as Person.* New York: Columbia University Press, 1910.

Comte, Auguste. *Auguste Comte and Positivism: The Essential Writings.* Edited by Gertrud Lenzer. Chicago: University of Chicago Press, 1975.

Cowgill, George L. "Onward and Upward with Collapse." In Norman Yoffe and George L. Cowgill, eds., *The Collapse of Ancient States and Civilizations.* Tucson: University of Arizona Press, 1988.

Cutler, A. Claire, Virginia Haufler, and Tony Porter, eds. *Private Authority and International Affairs.* Albany: State University of New York Press, 1999.

Dahl, Gudrun, and Gemetchu Megerssa. *Kam-Ap, or Take-off: Local Notions of Development.* Stockholm: Almqvist and Wiksell, 1992.

Derrida, Jacques. *L'autre cap.* Paris: Minuit, 1990.

Deutsch, Karl. *Nationalism and Social Communication.* Cambridge: MIT Press, 1966.

Dunn, Ross. *The Adventures of Ibn Battuta.* Berkeley and Los Angeles: University of California Press, 1986.

Durkheim, Émile. "What Is a Social Fact?" In *The Rules of Sociological Method.* Translated by W. D. Halls. New York: Free Press, 1982.

Eisenstadt, S. N. "Beyond Collapse." In Norman Yoffe and George L. Cowgill, eds., *The Collapse of Ancient States and Civilizations.* Tucson: University of Arizona Press, 1988.

Elias, Norbert. *Über den Prozess der Zivilisation.* 2 vols. Basel: Haus zum Falken, 1939.

Emmanuel, Arghiri. "White-Settler Colonialism and the Myth of Investment Capitalism." *New Left Review* 73 (1972): 35–57.

Fabian, Johannes. *Time and the Other.* New York: Columbia University Press, 1983.

Falk, Richard. *Explorations at the Edge of Time.* Philadelphia: Temple University Press, 1992.

al-Farabi. *Al-Farabi on the Perfect State.* Oxford: Clarendon, 1985.

Ferguson, James. *The Anti-Politics Machine: "Development," Depoliticization, and Bureaucratic Power in Lesotho.* Cambridge: Cambridge University Press, 1990.

Foucault, Michel. "The Discourse on Language." Translated by Rupert Swyer. In *The Archaelogy of Knowledge.* New York: Pantheon, 1972.

———. "Governmentality." In Colin Gordon, Graham Burchill and Peter Miller, eds., *The Foucault Effect: Studies in Governmentality.* London: Harvester Wheatsheaf, 1991.

Frank, Andre Gunder. *Reorient: Global Economy in the Asian Age.* Berkeley and Los Angeles: University of California Press, 1998.

Fuching, Hsieh. *The European Diary of Hsieh Fuching.* Translated by Hsieh Chien. New York: St. Martin's Press, 1993.

Gailey, Christine Ward. *Kinship to Kingship: Gender Hierarchy and State Formation in the Tongan Islands.* Austin: University of Texas Press, 1987.

Galtung, Johan. "A Structural Theory of Imperialism." *Journal of Peace Research* 8, no. 2 (1971): 81–117.

Galtung, Johan, and Richard Vincent. *Global Glasnost: Toward a New World Information and Communication Order?* Cresskill, N.J.: Hampton, 1992.

Geertz, Clifford. *The Social History of an Indonesian Town.* Westport, Conn.: Greenwood, 1965.

Gellner, Ernest. *Nations and Nationalism.* Ithaca, N.Y.: Cornell University Press, 1983.

Giddens, Anthony. *Modernity and Self-Identity: Self and Society in the Late Modern Age.* Stanford, Calif.: Stanford University Press, 1991.

Glamann, Kristoff. *Dutch-Asiatic Trade, 1620–1740.* Copenhagen: Danish Science Press, 1958.

Goodin, Robert. "If People Were Money . . ." In Brian Barry and Robert Goodin, eds., *Free Movement.* University Park: Pennsylvania State University Press, 1992.

Gordon, Colin. "Governmental Rationality: An Introduction." In Colin Gordon et al., eds., *The Foucault Effect: Studies in Governmentality.* London: Harvester Wheatsheaf, 1991.

Gran, Peter. *Beyond Eurocentrism: A New View of Modern World History.* Syracuse, N.Y.: Syracuse University Press, 1996.

Grose, Peter. *Continuing the Inquiry: The Council on Foreign Relations from 1921 to 1996.* New York: Council on Foreign Relations, 1996.

Guéhenno, Jean-Marie. *The End of the Nation-State.* Translated by Victoria Elliott. Minneapolis: University of Minnesota Press, 1995.

Habermas, Jürgen. "The New Obscurity: The Crisis of the Welfare State and the Exhaustion of Utopian Energies," translated by Phillip Jacobs. *Philosophy and Social Criticism* 2, no. 2 (1986): 1–18.

———. *Strukturwandel der Öffentlichkeit.* Darmstadt, Germany: Luchterhand, 1962.

———. *The Theory of Communicative Action.* 2 vols. Translated by Thomas McCarthy. Boston: Beacon, 1984 and 1988.

Hacker, Andrew. *Two Nations: Black and White, Separate, Hostile, Unequal.* New York: Scribners, 1992.

Halle, Randall. "Frames of Belonging: The Effects of Transnational Developments on German National Cinema." Paper read at Modern Language Association of North America Conference, Toronto, December 1997.

Hart, Marjolein t'. "Staatsvorming, sociale relaties en oorlogsfinanciering in de Nederlandse republik." *Tijdschrift voor sociale Geschiedenis* 16 (1990): 61–85

Havell, E. B. *The History of Aryan Rule in India.* London: Havrap, 1918.

Hegel, G. W. F. *Enzyklopädie der philosophischen Wissenschaften im Grundrisse* [1827]. In *Gesammelte Werke,* vol. 19. Edited by Wolfgang Bonsiepen and Hans-Christian Lucas. Düsseldorf: Rheinisch-Westfälische Akademie der Wissenschaften, 1989.

———. *Grundlinien der Philosophie des Rechts* [1821]. In *Gesammelte Werke,* vol. 7. Edited by Wolfgang Bonsiepen and Hans-Christian Lucas. Düsseldorf: Rheinisch-Westfäliche Akademie der Wissenschaften, 1989.

———. *The Phenomenology of Spirit* [1807]. Translated by A. V. Miller. Oxford: Oxford University Press, 1977.

Heider, Karl. *Indonesian Cinema: National Culture on Screen.* Honolulu: University of Hawaii Press, 1991.

Hirschman, Albert O. *The Passions and the Interests: Political Arguments for Capitalism before Its Triumph.* Princeton: Princeton University Press, 1977.

Hobsbawm, Eric. *Nations and Nationalism since 1780.* Cambridge: Cambridge University Press, 1990.

Hobsbawm, Eric, and Terence Ranger, eds. *The Invention of Traditions.* Cambridge: Cambridge University Press, 1983.

Hoffmann, Stanley. "An American Social Science: International Relations." *Daedalus,* Summer (1977): 41–60.

Honneth, Axel. *Kampf um Anerkennung: Zur moralischen Grammatik sozialer Konflikte.* Frankfurt am Main: Suhrkamp, 1992.

Hugh-Jones, Stephen. "Yesterday's Luxuries, Tomorrow's Necessities: Business and Barter in Northwest Amazonia." In Caroline Humphrey and Stephen Hugh-Jones, eds., *Barter, Exchange, and Value: An Anthropological Approach.* Cambridge: Cambridge University Press, 1992.

Huntington, Samuel. *The Clash of Civilizations and the Remaking of World Order.* New York: Simon and Schuster, 1996.

Hyde, Lewis. *The Gift: Imagination and the Erotic Life of Property.* New York: Vintage, 1983.

Ibn Battuta. *Voyages d'ibn Battuta (Rihlat Ibn Battuta).* Paris: Editions Anthropos, 1969.

Ibn Khaldun. *The Muqaddimah: An Introduction to History.* Translated by Franz Rosenthal. Princeton: Princeton University Press, 1967.

al-Jabarti. *Napoleon in Egypt: Al-Jabarti's Chronicle of the French Occupation, 1798.* Translated by Shmuel Moreh. Princeton: Markus Wiener, 1993.

Jameson, Fredric. *Postmodernism, or the Cultural Logic of Late Capitalism.* Durham, N.C.: Duke University Press, 1991.

Juergensmeyer, Mark. Review of Benjamin Barber, *Jihad vs. McWorld. Contemporary Sociology* 25, no. 5 (1996): 588–89.

Kalb, Gertrud. *Bildungsreise und literarischer Reisebericht: Studien zur englischen Reiseliteratur (1700–1850).* Nürnberg: Verlag Hans Karl, 1981.

Kant, Immanuel. *Fundamental Principles of the Metaphysics of Morals* [1979]. Translated by Thomas Abbott. New York: Liberal Arts Press, 1949.

———. *Perpetual Peace* [1795]. New York: Liberal Arts Press, 1957.

Kapteijns, Lidwien. "Dar Sila, the Sultanate in Precolonial Times, 1870–1916." In Said S. Samatar, ed., *In the Shadow of Conquest: Islam in Colonial Northeast Africa.* Trenton, N.J.: Red Sea Press, 1992.

Kaye, Howard L. "A False Convergence: Freud and the Hobbesian Problem of Order." *Sociological Theory* 9, no. 1 (1991): 87–105.

Kennedy, Paul M. *Preparing for the Twenty-First Century.* New York: Random House, 1993.

———. *The Rise and Fall of the Great Powers: Economic Change and Military Conflict from 1500 to 2000*. New York: Random House, 1987.

Khalidi, Rashid. *Palestinian Indentity: The Construction of Modern National Consciousness*. New York: Columbia University Press, 1997.

King, Anthony D., *Re-Presenting the City: Ethnicity, Capital, and Culture in the 21st-Century Metropolis*. New York: New York University Press, 1996.

Kojève, Alexandre. *Introduction to the Reading of Hegel*. Translated by James H. Nichols Jr. Ithaca, N.Y.: Cornell University Press, 1969.

Kroeber, Alfred, and Clyde Kluckhohn. *Culture: A Critical Review of Concepts and Definitions*. New York: Vintage, 1960.

Lall, Arthur. *The Emergence of Modern India*. New York: Columbia University Press, 1981.

Lash, Scott. *Sociology of Postmodernism*. London: Routledge, 1990.

Lash, Scott, and John Urry. *The End of Organized Capitalism*. Madison: University of Wisconsin Press, 1987.

Latouche, Serge. *La mégamachine: Raison technoscientifique, raison économique, et mythe du progrès: Essais à la mémoire de Jacques Ellul*. Paris: La Découverte, 1995.

Layoun, Mary. *Travels of a Genre: The Modern Novel and Ideology*. Princeton: Princeton University Press, 1990.

Leibfried, Stephan. "Towards a European Welfare State?" In Catherine Jones, ed., *New Perspectives on the Welfare State in Europe*. New York: Routledge, 1993.

Lewis, Jordan. *Partnerships for Profit: Structuring and Managing Strategic Alliances*. New York: Free Press, 1990.

Lewis, Justin. *The Ideological Octopus: An Exploration of Television and Its Audience*. New York: Routledge, 1991.

Lilienfeld, Paul von. *Gedanken über die Sozialwissenschaft der Zukunft*. Berlin: Mitau, 1873–1881.

Lipson, Charles. "International Debt and National Security: Comparing Victorian Britain and Postwar America." In Barry Eichengreen and Peter H. Lindert, eds., *The International Debt Crisis in Historical Perspective*. Cambridge: MIT Press, 1989.

Lovelace, Douglas C., Jr. *The Evolution in Military Affairs: Shaping the Future U.S. Armed Forces*. Carlisle Barracks, Pa.: Strategic Studies Institute, 1997.

Lowe, Vincent, and Jaafar Kamin. "TV Programme Management in a Rural Society: Decision-Making Process in Radio and Television Malaysia." Occasional Papers no. 14. Singapore: AMIC, 1982.

Lowenthal, Richard. *Social Change and Cultural Crisis*. New York: Columbia University Press, 1984.

Machiavelli, Niccolo. *The Prince* [1513]. Translated by Robert M. Adams. New York: Norton, 1992.

Marshall, T. H. *Class, Citizenship, and Social Development.* Garden City, N.Y.: Doubleday, 1964.

Marx, Karl. *Capital* [1867]. Harmondsworth, England: Penguin, 1976.

Mas'udi. *Muruj ad-dhahab wa Ma'aden aj-Jawhar.* Edited by Charles Pellat. Beirut: Université Libanaise, 1966.

Mattelart, Armand, Xavier Delcourt, and Michele Mattelart. *International Image Makers: In Search of an Alternative Perspective.* Translated by David Buxton. London: Comedia, 1984.

Maurer, Reinhart. *Hegel und das Ende der Geschichte.* Stuttgart: Kohlhammer, 1965.

Mauss, Marcel. *The Gift: The Form and Reason for Exchange in Archaic Societies* [1950]. Translated by W. D. Halls. New York and London: Norton, 1990.

McNeill, William H. *Polyethnicity and National Unity in World History.* Toronto: University of Toronto Press, 1985.

Michael, John. *Anxious Intellects: Academic Professionals, Public Intellectuals, and Enlightenment Values.* Durham, N.C.: Duke University Press, forthcoming.

Mill, John Stuart. *Utilitarianism* [1861]. Edited by Samuel Gorovitz. Indianapolis, Ind.: Bobbs-Merrill, 1971.

Min, Anselm. "Hegel on Capitalism and the Common Good." *Philosophy and Social Criticism* 2, no. 2 (1986): 39–61.

Mirsepassi, Ali. "The Crisis of Secular Politics and the Rise of Political Islam in Iran." *Social Text* 12, no. 1 (1994): 51–84.

Moore, Barrington. *The Social Origins of Dictatorship and Democracy.* Boston: Beacon, 1966.

Mosse, George. *The Nationalization of the Masses: Political Symbolism and Mass Movements in Germany from the Napoleonic Wars through the Third Reich.* New York: Fertig, 1975.

Mufti, Malik. *Sovereign Creations: Pan-Arabism and Political Order in Syria and Iraq.* Ithaca, N.Y.: Cornell University Press, 1996.

Munif, Abdelrahman. *Cities of Salt* [1984]. Translated by Peter Theroux. New York: Vintage, 1989.

Nietzsche, Friedrich. *The Genealogy of Morals* [1887]. Translated by Walter Kaufmann. New York: Vintage, 1989.

Olwig, Karen Fog. *Global Culture, Island Identity: Continuity and Change in the Afro-Caribbean Community of Nevis.* Chur, Switzerland: Harwood, 1993.

Pandey, Gyanendra. "Encounter and Calamities." In Ranajit Guha and Gayatri Spivak, eds., *Selected Subaltern Studies.* New York: Oxford University Press, 1988.

Pflanze, Otto. *Bismarck and the Development of Germany: The Period of Unification, 1815–1871.* Princeton: Princeton University Press, 1971.

Polanyi, Karl. *The Great Transformation: The Political and Economic Origins of Our Times* [1944]. Boston: Beacon, 1957.

Reich, Robert. *The Work of Nations: Preparing Ourselves for the 21st Century.*
   New York: Knopf, 1991.
Renan, Ernest. "What Is a Nation?" Translated by Martin Thom. In Homi K.
   Bhabha, ed., *Nation and Narration.* London: Routledge, 1990.
Reynolds, Susan. *Kingdoms and Communities in Western Europe, 900–1300.*
   Oxford: Clarendon, 1984.
Robertson, Roland. "Social Theory, Cultural Relativity, and the Problem of
   Globality." In Anthony D. King, ed., *Culture, Globalization, and the World-
   System.* Minneapolis: University of Minnesota Press, 1997.
Rosenberg, Justin. *The Empire of Civil Society: A Critique of the Realist Theory of
   International Relations.* London and New York: Verso, 1994.
Sahlins, Marshall. *Stone Age Economics.* Chicago: Aldine-Atherton, 1972.
Said, Edward. *Orientalism.* New York: Vintage, 1978.
Saitoti, Tepilit Ole. *The Worlds of a Maasai Warrior.* Berkeley and Los Angeles:
   University of California Press, 1986.
Sassen, Saskia. *The Global City: New York, London, Tokyo.* Princeton: Princeton
   University Press, 1991.
———. *Globalization and Its Discontents.* New York: New Press, 1998.
———. *Losing Control? Sovereignty in an Age of Globalization.* New York:
   Columbia University Press, 1995.
———. "The State and the Global City: Notes towards a Conception of
   Place-Centered Governance." *Competition and Change* 1, no. 1 (1995):
   31–50.
Scardigli, Victor. *L'Europe des modes de vie.* Paris: CNRS, 1987.
Schäffle, Albert. *Bau und Leben des sozialen Körpers.* Tübingen: H. Laupp, 1896.
Schmitt, Carl. *Der Begriff des Politischen* [1932]. Berlin: Duncker and Humblot,
   1963.
Schumpeter, Joseph. "The Crisis of the Tax State." In *The Economics and
   Sociology of Capitalism* [1918]. Princeton: Princeton University Press, 1991.
Scott, James C. *Seeing Like a State: How Certain Schemes to Improve the Human
   Condition Have Failed.* New Haven, Conn.: Yale University Press, 1998.
Shohat, Ella, and Robert Stam, eds. *Unthinking Eurocentrism: Multiculturalism
   and the Media.* London and New York: Routledge, 1994.
Snyder, Jack. *Myths of Empire: Domestic Politics and International Ambition.* Ithaca,
   N.Y.: Cornell University Press, 1991.
Spence, Jonathan D. *The Question of Hu.* New York: Vintage, 1989.
Stagl, Justin. *A History of Curiosity: The Theory of Travel, 1550–1800.* Chur,
   Switzerland: Harwood Academic Publishers, 1995.
Steinberg, David, ed. *In Search of Southeast Asia.* Honolulu: University of
   Hawaii Press, 1987.
Streeck, Wolfgang. "Public Power beyond the Nation-State? The Case of
   the European Community." In Robert Boyer and Daniel Drache, eds.,

States against Markets: The Limits of Globalization. London and New York: Routledge, 1996.

Suter, Christian. *Debt Cycles in the World-Economy: Foreign Loans, Financial Crisis, and Debt Settlements, 1820–1990.* Boulder, Colo.: Westview, 1992.

Tahtawi, Rifa'ah Rafi'. *Takhlis al-Ibriz fi Talkhis Bariz.* Cairo: Al-Hay'ah al-Misriyah al-'Ammah Lil-Kitab, 1993.

Tai, Ta Van. "The Status of Women in Traditional Vietnam: A Comparison of the Code of the Le Dynasty with the Chinese Codes." *Journal of Asian History* 15, no. 2 (1981): 97–145.

Thurow, Lester. *Head to Head: The Coming Economic Battle among Japan, Europe, and America.* New York: William Morrow, 1992.

Tilly, Charles. *Coercion, Capital, and European State, A.D. 990–1990.* Cambridge, Mass.: Blackwell, 1990.

Tilly, Charles, ed. *The Formation of National States in Western Europe.* Princeton: Princeton University Press, 1975.

Todorov, Tzvetan. *The Conquest of America.* Translated by Richard Howard. New York: HarperCollins, 1985.

U.S. Bureau of Labor Statistics. *Employment and Earnings.* Washington: GPO, January, 1993.

Vidich, Arthur. *Small Town in Mass Society.* Princeton: Princeton University Press, 1968.

Wallerstein, Immanuel. *The Modern World-System.* New York: Academic Press, 1974.

Weber, Eugene. *Peasants into Frenchmen.* London: Chatto and Windus, 1979.

Weber, Max. *Economy and Society* [1956]. 2 vols. Edited by Guenther Roth and Claus Wittich. Translated by Ephraim Fischoff et al. Berkeley and Los Angeles: University of California Press, 1978.

———. *The Protestant Ethic and the Spirit of Capitalism* [1904]. Translated by Talcott Parsons. London and New York: Routledge, 1992.

Williams, Raymond. *The Sociology of Culture.* New York: Schocken, 1982.

World Investment Report. New York and Geneva: United Nations, 1998.

Yu-lan, Fung. *A History of Chinese Philosophy* [1937]. Translated by Derk Bodde. Princeton: Princeton University Press, 1952.

Zakaria, Fareed. "Our Hollow Hegemony." *New York Times Magazine,* November 22, 1998.

Zubaida, Sami. *Islam, the People, and the State: Essays on Political Ideas and Movements in the Middle East.* London and New York: Routledge, 1989.

Index

Mohammed A. Bamyeh teaches transcultural processes, political theory, and historical sociology at New York University. He edits the journal *Passages: Journal of Transnational and Transcultural Studies* and is the author of *The Social Origins of Islam: Mind, Economy, Discourse* (Minnesota, 1999), which was recognized with an Albert Hourani Book Award from the Middle East Studies Association.